UNDERSTANDING LANGUAGE

UNDERSTANDING LANGUAGE

Doris T. Myers
University of Northern Colorado

BOYNTON/COOK PUBLISHERS, INC.
UPPER MONTCLAIR, NEW JERSEY 07043

Library of Congress Cataloging in Publication Data
Myers, Doris T.
　Understanding language.

　1. Linguistics.　2. Language and languages.
I. Title
P121.M97　1983　　410　　83-15536
ISBN 0-86709-083-9

Copyright © 1984 by Boynton/Cook Publishers, Inc. All rights reserved.
No part of this book may be used or reproduced in any manner without written permission except in the case of brief quotations embodied in critical articles and reviews.

For information address Boynton/Cook Publishers, Inc.
52 Upper Montclair Plaza, P.O. Box 860, Upper Montclair, N.J. 07043

84 85 86 87 88 5 4 3 2 1

Preface

This book began, as I suspect many others do, with mimeographed handouts, first supplementing and then replacing the course text. The course for which the book was developed is a freshman-level introduction to language. It is required of English majors and minors and elected by various other students as a general education course. In the process of writing the book I discovered, for reasons to be explained later, that it is suitable as a text for elementary composition courses as well as introductory English linguistics.

My first concern was to make the book easy to read. For freshmen or sophomores with only hazy memories of the traditional parts of speech, the most elementary "straight linguistics" texts are too difficult. To leap into transformational syntax from a shaky footing in junior high language arts is an almost impossible feat. While using the texts then available to me, I found myself devoting all the lecture-discussion time to a line-by-line explanation of the reading assignment, an eminently unsatisfactory procedure: every course, no matter how difficult the subject, should include some opportunity for experiencing the joy of mastery through independent study. Linguistic concepts are difficult. I have tried to simplify without adulterating them by stating them in English, scrupulously avoiding all dialects of Linguish and Anguish.

My second concern was to cover a broad range of linguistic knowledge. Many of the books directed toward introduction to language or language-based composition courses consist of reprints of Orwell's "Politics and the English Language" along with the graceful fulminations of the usage mavens. Such books simply confirm the students' pre-existing misconception that language study is nothing more than making fussy distinctions between words. This book surveys the classical descriptions of phonology, syntax, and word-level semantics; then it goes on to introduce more modern concepts such as presupposition, speech acts, and discourse cohesion. Furthermore, each topic of linguistics is related both to other academic disciplines and the practical concerns of English composition and literature. Thus the presentation of phonology is related to English spelling and poetry; language variety is related to sociology and local-color literature; and discourse cohesion is related to anthropology, mass communications, and the folktale.

Writing the book made me realize more vividly than ever before how much an idea is clarified by the effort to express it on paper. Instead of remaining passively neutral toward some of the controversies in language study, I had to take a stand. And in the process of submitting my conclusions to students for their reactions, I learned some of the weaknesses and limitations of my stand. On the theory that what is sauce for the goose is sauce for the goslings, I began to ask my students to respond in writing to the linguistic topics. Thus the book developed as one which would be useful in a composition course.

As everyone who has ever been involved with composition knows, too many classes degenerate into an exercise of gamesmanship between teacher and student. The teacher says, in effect, "Produce some writing so I can mark the errors," and the student replies, "You can correct my commas, but keep your grubby red pencil off my mind." The composition class thus becomes a meaningless interlude of punishment irrelevant to other academic pursuits. Currently there is a spate of composition textbooks designed to detour the meaninglessness game by an emphasis on "writing across the curriculum." But why should the composition instructor toil to become conversant in biology, political science, and management, instead of teaching from an already existent professional strength—language? I know that many English teachers, nurtured within the gentle confines of literary criticism, tremble and fall silent at the prospect of dealing with linguistics. Still, even the newest teaching assistant has more professional knowledge about language than about quasars or thanatology. He or she is experienced in the structure of expository writing, the history of English, and the analysis of literature—all professional strengths in language. And this book is user-friendly for the instructor as well as the student.

Used as the reader for a composition course, this book leads to a more educationally sound "writing across the curriculum" because the focus on linguistics is really a focus on the world at large. Linguistics is, or at least can be, a truly interdisciplinary subject. The edges of it overlap a roll-call of academic disciplines, from anthropology to philosophy to zoology (or at least the ethology part of it). As the bulk of available knowledge has mushroomed, the percentage of time that can be devoted to the study of language has diminished. And we squander the little time we have by teaching composition through analyzing essays on economics! Surely it makes more sense to leave the dismal science to others, to teach writing through attention to language.

In short, this book can be used in two ways: either as a basis for teaching Introduction to Language through writing, or as a basis for teaching Composition through introduction to language. In either case, students can be asked to read the text on their own and then respond to it in writing. In a language class, the instructional periods would be devoted to lectures building on the elementary presentation of the textbook, discussion of problematic areas in linguistics, and demonstrations. At least one day a week should be allowed for students to exchange results of their written homework. In a composition class, lectures would focus on how the linguists' observations about language behavior show up in writing, both student and professional. More attention would be given to a rhetorical analysis of the homework assignments—their implications with respect to writer, subject, and audience. Students could use their new knowledge about how language works to decide which niceties of English usage are important and to design individual techniques for learning them. In either case, this approach encourages students to become *amateurs* of language (in the original sense of that word) and to take charge of their own education.

Each chapter after the first one is self-sufficient, so that the topics of linguistics may be presented in any order. I have experimented with many different arrangements over the years. The advantage of beginning with Chapter 2 on words or Chapter 8 on dialect is that students usually have some previous knowledge of and interest in these topics. The advantage of beginning with Chapter 3 on phonology is that experimenting with sounds makes everyone look ridiculous, so that students lose their inhibitions and develop class spirit right away. And so forth. The repetition involved in making the chapters self-sufficient is a pedagogical advantage, because it helps to break down the student habit of unloading the memory banks after each exam.

Because the emphasis of this book is on the relationship of linguistics to composition, literature, and the human condition, I have glossed over the serious differences among the professionals concerning what it means to do linguistics these days. My general approach comes from classic structuralism, but I have not hesitated to incorporate the most central findings of the transformationalists when helpful. I have made no effort to reconcile opposing views of language, preferring simply to state the findings of the six blind men about their linguistic elephant.

Thanks are due first to Prof. Paul A. Olson of the University of Nebraska, who taught me that a Chaucer scholar need not be a narrow specialist, and to Prof. Robert E. Longacre of the University of Texas at Arlington, who first made me see linguistics as an exciting journey into the humanness of humanity. The linguistic problems using exotic languages have been simplified from the instructional materials of the Summer Institute of Linguistics? I am grateful for the permission to use them. I would also like to thank those directly involved in the book: Robert Boynton for his knowledgeable approach to editing; Natalie Collins and Dorothy Stein for typing; and most of all, my students, for putting up with confusing first drafts and forcing me to clarify. Finally, my deepest gratitude is to my husband Tom, who proofread, discussed, encouraged, nagged me to finish, and did a lot of cooking.

---

* From *Laboratory Manual for Morphology and Syntax*. Exercises 1, 99, 100, 110, and 130. Copyright © Academic Publications Department of the Summer Institute of Linguistics.

Contents

1. Three Approaches to Language — 1
2. Where Words Come From — 14
3. Language Study on a Sound Basis — 37
4. What Petey Forgot — 64
5. Those Red-Pencil Blues — 95
6. I Mean . . . You Know — 122
7. Taking Bigger Bites — 143
8. It Takes All Kinds — 170
9. The Trouble with English — 189

1

Three Approaches to Language

In 1976, a young man named John Vihtelic was driving a country road in Washington. He blacked out momentarily and missed a narrow bridge. When he came to, he found himself at the bottom of a ravine, pinned inside the wreckage of the car. It had overturned, and his left foot was caught between it and a large tree root. For a long time he expected someone to come along and rescue him, but finally he realized that the car couldn't be seen from the road and the noisy stream blotted out his cries for help. For fifteen days he survived alone. Then he figured out how to free his foot, crawled up to the roadside, and caught a ride with a truck driver.

Vihtelic's tools for survival were few. His only food was one apple. His drink was water from the stream, which he obtained by soaking a T-shirt attached to a bit of fish line. He fastened the car mirror to a tennis racket to make a signaling device, but no one ever saw it. He used a suitcase to draw a rock within reach to make a hammer, and then he used the tire iron as a chisel to cut away the root which pinned him in the car. And he had one other tool for survival: language.

The importance of language to Vihtelic's survival is not at first evident, since he was utterly alone and unable to shout louder than the water. But he was better prepared for disaster than most people would have been, because he had been trained as a medic in the Green Berets. How did he acquire this training? Through language. Because it enables us to profit from the combined experience of many people, language is one of humanity's top survival skills.

But language isn't just useful for communicating with other people. Vihtelic talked to himself, speaking encouragements aloud to prevent panic. He used language to think about his situation and devise a way to escape. He found a piece of wrapping paper in the glove compartment and wrote letters to his girl friend expressing his love for her. He prayed. He used a little chant to help him throw accurately in the essential task of drawing water from the stream without breaking his only line:

    Seven wraps of the string,
    Throw as hard as you can,
    Lots of loft and
    Over the log![1]

Language was as important to him as his tools, for it kept him in touch with himself.

Vihtelic's feat was amazing, but our ordinary, everyday use of language is just about as startling. We use it constantly, from sleep to sleep—listening to the weather report, talking with friends, writing memos, watching a movie. Language accompanies, facilitates, and governs all our daily activities. And then to bed, to dream in words as well as pictures.

Our use of language is so natural that we don't notice it. It's the medium of our existence, like the air that carries its sound. Usually we become aware of it only when it breaks down: in hearing an unfamiliar word, in adjusting to an unusual pronunciation, in a momentary problem with "correct" grammar.

But breakdowns are rare. Normally a person chatters away, thinking about the content of what he's saying and how the other person is reacting, but completely unaware of the highly coordinated movements of the one hundred muscles involved in speech. The speaker must not only get the sounds right, but also coordinate them with his breathing. A person who is not speaking, just breathing quietly, takes about four seconds to inhale and exhale. When speaking he must modify the rhythm, inhaling quickly at a normal break in the sentence and then exhaling slowly for ten, fifteen, or even twenty seconds until he reaches the next sentence break.[2]

As if all this weren't complex enough already, we have to adjust our speaking to the other person, timing responses properly so as to avoid rude interruptions or speaking out of turn. We adjust the loudness of our speech to the hearer and the environment, speaking one way at a cocktail party and another way in a library. We adjust our tone of voice, body movements, and word choices according to the social roles of ourselves and the other speaker(s), expressing respect to an employer, intimacy to a member of the family, and casual equality to associates.

To list all the items a person must know to participate in a simple conversation would take reams of paper. How do we juggle all these variables? Oddly enough, we can do it only because we don't think about it. Once learned, the language process is as automatic as riding a bicycle, as natural as breathing itself.

---

[1] Harold T. P. Hayes, *Three Levels of Time* (New York: E. P. Dutton, 1981), p. 39.
[2] See Dennis Fry, *Homo Loquens: Man as a Talking Animal* (Cambridge: Cambridge University Press, 1977), p. 23.

Misconceptions about Language

Because language is so natural, so all-pervasive, and so complex, most people, even well-educated ones, have many false notions about it.

One common error is to think of language more in terms of writing than speech, probably because learning to write is a much more conscious process than learning to speak. We don't remember learning to speak, but we do remember the "balls and sticks" of manuscript printing, the struggles to manage the pencil, and finally the first name in cursive, shaky but proud. Writing seems so important that occasionally someone will remark that a certain tribal group "had no language until the missionaries taught them to write." That's like saying that John had no bread until Mary taught him to make toast. Without bread, there's nothing to toast; without speech, there's nothing to write. Alphabetical writing, Egyptian hieroglyphics, drum talk—all are ways to symbolize the spoken language.

Another common error might be called linguistic chauvinism. People feel that their own language is somehow natural, while other languages are strange and awkward. You sometimes hear that a particular language has no way to say such-and-such, and slightly disparaging conclusions about the speakers of the language may be drawn. Sometimes the "fact" is simply misinformation, as in the case of a German I knew who thought that English had no equivalent of "ich liebe dich." "The English speakers," he said, "must say 'I am in love with you.' They are less direct than we Germans." Sometimes the supposed lack is simply a difference in culture. A tribe that lives by hunting and gathering is not likely to have ways to express "prime rate" and "systems coordinator." All languages are, however, flexible enough to allow the speakers to say anything they wish. And all languages must be equally natural, since babies throughout the world learn their own languages at about the same rate.

People also feel that the word somehow reflects the nature of the thing. Actually, words are arbitrary vocal symbols, just as road signs are. The U.S. Highway Department has decreed that a triangle shall mean "Yield" and an octagon "Stop," but there's no natural, inevitable relationship between sign and meaning. It would work just as well if the triangle meant "Stop." In the same way, language works just as well whether you call the place you live *house*, *casa*, or *dom*. Every language of the world has a few words, such as "buzz" and "moo," that sound like what they mean. But even these imitative vocal symbols are more arbitrary than they first appear. For example, the English imitation of a bell is "ding-dong," but the German one is *bim-bam* and the Japanese one *chirin-chirin*.[3] If the words were truly imitative, they would be about the same for all languages.

Another misconception is to think of a language as primarily a list of

---

[3]The Japanese example is cited in Dwight Bolinger, *Aspects of Language*, 2nd ed. (New York: Harcourt Brace Jovanovich, 1975), p. 232.

words. People often assume that learning a new language is mostly a matter of learning a new set of arbitrary vocal symbols. Actually, vocabulary is the easiest part of language learning. It's much more difficult to learn how to put the words together into sentences, and more difficult still to learn to "sing" the sentence with the proper rhythms and pitch levels. For this reason, even a person who is extremely fluent in the second language almost always retains a foreign accent.

Language Design

Nobody knows exactly how many languages there are in the world. Estimates range between four and six thousand. Each language has its own speech signs, as we have seen. Each also has its own arbitrary way of combining those signs. For example, English speakers feel that it's natural and logical for subjects to come before predicates. They would say you need to name what you're talking about before you say what it did. But many languages of the world place the predicate first. The ways that various languages have of singing the sentences are also pretty arbitrary. Indeed, sentence melody varies between dialects, as you can observe when you listen to a BBC announcer. Thus each language may be analyzed into three interacting systems: phonology (sounds), semantics (meanings), and syntax (arrangements).

For a long time students of language thought that these systems were completely peculiar to each language, so that there was no way to anticipate what they might find when they encountered a new language. More recently they have discovered some *linguistic universals*, principles of design that apply to all languages.

Phonology. We commonly think of each vocal symbol—each word—as a unit. But words can be analyzed into smaller vocal symbols—sounds, or "letters of the alphabet," as we, with our bias toward the written language, commonly call them. These sounds do not mean anything in themselves, but can be combined to produce an unlimited number of meanings. Each language has its own inventory of sounds. English has about 36 (depending on dialect), Hawaiian only thirteen, Circassian more than seventy. Other sounds which the human vocal apparatus could produce are outside the system; speakers of the language ignore them. Each language has specific methods of combining sounds into syllables. For example, if you know that the first sound of an English word is /b/, then it's a sure bet that the next sound is /r/, /l/, or some vowel. Why? Because that's the English system. Each language also has its own ways of combining syllables into larger speech groups, as will be discussed in Chapter 3.

Semantics. Just as every language has its own inventory of sounds, every language has its own inventory of words and word-like units—its vocabulary, or *lexicon*. The word "lexicon" commonly means "dictionary," and we language users behave as if we had a mental dictionary of our language. Not everybody knows the same words, but we share a large enough vocabulary to communicate easily. Our mental dictionaries seem to be organized in several ways—by part of speech (noun, verb, etc.), by phrases that go together, such as "ham and eggs," and by sets of synonyms and antonyms.

The semantic system of a language also involves many other features of meaning besides the lexicon, but they're too complex to discuss here. Some of them are specific to a certain language. Others seem to be a facet of the way the human mind works and are therefore universal.

Syntax. This is the system of arrangements in a language, not just arrangements of words, but of units smaller and larger than words. In English word parts such as *un-*, *anti-*, and *pre-* are always prefixes, while *-ous*, *-ity*, and *-ize* are suffixes. This is a feature of English syntax. We put the adjective before the noun it modifies, but some languages put it after. This is also a feature of syntax. Because syntax is so important to the skillful use of the written language, it has been emphasized in schools much more than phonology and semantics. If you have studied language before, chances are you spent most of your time on syntax.

Items of phonology, semantics, and syntax exist within a carefully structured *hierarchy*. To prove to yourself the importance of hierarchical structure, consider the following two rows of x's:
Row I: xxxxxxxxxxxxxxxxxxxxxxxxxxxxxxxxxx
Row II: xxxxx xxxxx xxxxx xxxxx xxxxx xxxxx xxxxx x

It's much easier to count the x's in the second row because they're organized into patterns of five. Psychological research has suggested that human beings cannot handle more than seven bits of information at a time. But if *six* bits of information are organized into a pattern, then those six bits can be treated as only one unit, thus freeing the processing capacity to take on additional information.[4] In language there are many kinds of bits—sounds, words, sentence patterns, semantic relationships. There are groups of items, and groups of groups, and groups of groups of groups. All this complexity would be too much to handle, except that the patterning itself is done according to a fairly simple system of what we shall call *slots* and *fillers*. Let's look at an example.

In dealing with the syntax of English we are used to a pattern of this type:
The _____ hit the boy.

The kind of unit which should go in this blank is a word, and a special kind of word. We can fill the blank with *bully, parent, girl, bat, truck, wave,* or any number of other words, but we would never use *-ize, improve,* or *of* to fill it.

---

[4]George A. Miller, "Information and Memory" in *The Psychology of Communication: Seven Essays* (1967; rpt. Baltimore: Penguin Books, 1969), pp. 3–13.

The blank represents a point of choice, since we have to choose a word to put in it. There are at least five points of choice in the sentence, five places where you could substitute another word. The points of choice are not always words, of course. If you look at the pattern again, you see an invisible blank after the word *boy*, a point of choice which could be filled with *s* for plural.

The phonology of a language also has slots and fillers. Consider this syllable: p—t. We can fill the blank with any vowel sound, but not with a consonant.

A blank in a pattern—that is, a point of choice—is called a *slot*. The choice which fills the slot will be called a *filler* if we are thinking of an individual item, or a *filler-class* if we are thinking of the whole range of choices for that slot. Thus, all the vowels make up a filler-class, and *o* is a filler if the syllable is *pot*.

Both slot and filler contribute to the total meaning of the pattern. The syntactic pattern, "The _____ hit the boy," is so familiar that we strongly expect the filler to be the name of a person or a thing. When, unexpectedly, we find the slot filled with the word "unexpected," the strength of the patterns contributes to efficiency of communication, since we can often guess a missing part just by knowing what the pattern is and what kind of filler the slot ought to have. The ready-made patterns limit the speaker's freedom in a sense, but by reducing the number of decisions to be made, the patterns also free the speaker to concentrate on the message rather than the means of communicating it.

Such patterning is a basic design feature of human language, one which serves to distinguish it from animal communication. Animals express each meaning by one and only one noise, while human beings can express a particular meaning by a variety of noises. Instead of a fixed mating call, an English-speaking person can say any number of things, from "You here with anybody?" to "Haven't I met you before?" or even "Great weather we're having, isn't it?" Each one of these is a filler of the slot that might be labeled "Friendly greeting to member of opposite sex."

In contrast, the mallard duck uses one sound to call a mate and another to signal that he has found a body of water for the flock to land on. (This, incidentally, enables hunters to learn the noises and imitate them to call the ducks into shooting range.) Because there's a fixed relationship between sound and meaning, there can be no system of slots and fillers. Unless there is a choice, at least two fillers, there is no slot, for a slot is a point of choice. Thus, animals and birds have a limited repertory of messages they can send. Human beings are constantly making up new things to say and new ways to say old things.

Because animal communication is not innovative, it is basically the same all over the world. Sheep grazing on the slopes of the Pyrenees bleat just like the sheep on the wind-swept plains of Wyoming, but the Basque sheepherder who comes to Wyoming must learn a new language if he wishes to communicate with other people. For the same reason, animal communication doesn't change the way human language does. Cats still mew the way they did in ancient Egypt, but the language of the human beings who fed them has ceased to exist in spoken form.

Animal communication seems utterly different from human language. Psychologists have experimented with teaching human language to chimpanzees and, most recently, a gorilla. Impressive as it is, the achievement of these animals further illustrates the uniqueness of the human ability to use language. The first efforts, with a chimp named Viki, failed because the researchers were trying to teach her to speak. An animal can make noises to communicate different messages, but it can't make the precise sounds with which human beings construct words. It took heroic efforts from both man and primate to enable Viki to produce very faulty versions of "papa," "mama," and "cup." Human beings have a unique physical adaptation to speech: an especially large cavity just back of the mouth which allows the sound to resonate well, and lips and tongue which are much more mobile than those of any other animal. Lacking this, chimps can't have a slot-and-filler system by which individual sounds are combined into syllables and words because they can't differentiate enough sounds. The primates are, however, able to learn that arbitrary symbols stand for items in the real world, and later experiments designed to bypass phonology completely have achieved more success. One chimp, Lana, communicates by pushing buttons corresponding to words on a computer console. Another chimp, Sarah, manipulates plastic shapes. The best results have been attained by using American Sign Language, the communication system of the deaf. In one experiment Washoe, a chimp, learned 132 signs in the first four years; in another experiment Koko, a gorilla, has a present working vocabulary of about 375 signs and has used many more occasionally.[5]

Even with these accomplishments, the apes' language is simple compared to that used by all except the most profoundly retarded human beings. Most of the symbols used by the apes are unitary, indivisible rather than patterned. Although they have developed some syntax, their sentences are usually just two or three words long, five at most. Human sentences, in contrast, are seldom *less* than five words long, and written sentences are even longer. Finally, the apes have learned to use language from human beings by a tedious process of conditioning. Human children learn to talk just by being exposed to language, without any special instruction. Some observers feel that the researchers are interpreting the apes' performance as showing

---

[5]Francine Patterson, "Conversations with a Gorilla," *National Geographic*, Vol. 154, No. 4 (October, 1978), 438–465.

more language knowledge than they actually have; but even if the researchers' interpretation is correct, the gap between animal and human language ability remains wide.

Studying about Language

As we have seen, language is ordinary, yet mysterious; simple, yet incredibly complex. It's not surprising that language through the centuries has been a major object of study. In fact, before the 20th century, language in one form or another was the chief content of almost all education, both elementary and advanced.

There are three approaches to the study of language, resulting in three different but related academic disciplines: rhetoric, literary criticism, and linguistics. Rhetoric studies language as a tool for obtaining political or economic power. Literary criticism studies language as beauty, as an art form. And linguistics studies language scientifically, as a phenomenon.

Rhetoric deals with the effective use of language. It is sometimes defined as "the art or skill of persuasion," sometimes as "the rules of speaking or writing well." Although the term "rhetoric" may be unfamiliar to you, the study of it is not. If you have ever taken courses in composition, speech communication, debate, newswriting, or advertising, you have studied rhetoric. People who especially need to be skilled in rhetoric include lawyers, politicians, salesmen, and preachers. (Some would add teachers to the list, since they need to persuade students to learn.)

The academic discipline of rhetoric consists of analyzing the techniques of persuasion as used by the most skilled persuaders. Aristotle was one of the earliest persons to make such an analysis. Athens was a democracy, and decisions of city policy were made after much discussion in a large town meeting. This meant that the citizens (from our point of view a rather elite group, since it excluded women, slaves, and other menials) needed to have good communication skills. The man who could persuade others to adopt his ideas wielded much power. If Dale Carnegie had been born in ancient Athens, he would have felt right at home as a rhetoric teacher, although some Athenians criticized the teachers for accepting pay.

They still do, partly because the academic study of rhetoric is often disappointing. The student pays his money and follows the teacher's rules, but his speaking or writing doesn't seem to improve. Part of the problem is that academic study involves conscious analysis, while language works best when we are least conscious of it. Part of the problem stems from students' behaving like students. Trying to get through the course with minimal effort, they apply the principles in a mechanical, superficial fashion instead of striving for a deep understanding and then practicing the skills until they can use them without conscious effort. Because of such failures to produce practical results, rhetoric has come, through the centuries, to be a dirty word, a synonym for emptiness and insincerity. Nevertheless, it can be a useful term for a useful discipline.

Literary criticism is the academic study of poems, stories, and dramas. The knowledge of rhetoric overlaps with the knowledge of literary criticism, since the techniques of using language effectively also involve using language beautifully. When we study literature, we are interested in experiencing an art form and receiving pleasure from it. Language is the medium of literature, just as canvas and pigments are the medium of painting. Literary criticism, however, is concerned with more than just the beauty of the language in literature. It also studies schools and movements in literary art, how one author influences another in style, and recurring themes or plots in world literature.

Linguistics differs from rhetoric and literary criticism in its approach to language. It's the scientific study of language. Its purpose is simply to find out the facts: how sentences are constructed in a particular language, what determines the placement of accents, how words change form (if they do) to become plural. As a scientific study, linguistics naturally avoids the value judgments that are such an important part of rhetoric and literary criticism. Scientists of language, or linguists as they are called, use the scientific method. They form a hypothesis, gather evidence to confirm or deny it, and then form a new or revised hypothesis. Instead of studying language in order to use it for entertainment or to get one's own way, the linguist studies language for its own sake—because it adds to our understanding of ourselves and our world. This knowledge may have some practical application—almost all knowledge does—but usefulness is not the original motivation.

Because language is such an all-pervasive human activity, linguistics is one of the truly interdisciplinary studies. But its broad concerns grow out of its fundamental purpose, to describe the systems of individual languages. The effort to apply close, objective observation to a language presents subtle difficulties: first, what are you going to observe? People's behavior when they're talking or writing, of course, but that in itself presents difficulties. Suppose you set out to record the pronunciation of the word *greasy*. You find all sorts of differences in the way people say it. Some say *greazy*, some pronounce the *g* more like a *k*, and someone might even say *greedy* by mistake. How do you know that these are all the same word, despite their differences? How do you know that *greased* is a different word? You can ask people, but since so much of their language knowledge is unconscious, they may not be able to tell you. Thus, what the linguist is really trying to observe is the system behind the variant behaviors, the knowledge on which the behaviors depend. This knowledge of system is called *language competence*, and describing it is the central concern of linguistics.

Like rhetoric, linguistics has caught a lot of flack because people do not understand what its purpose is. Because the linguist as a scientist avoids value judgments, many people think that the study of linguistics leads you to prefer "incorrect" expressions. Part of the problem stems from the linguistic meaning of the word *grammar*. To a linguist, the grammar of a language is its structure—its components of phonology, syntax, and semantics. To nonlinguists, grammar refers to the rules for using language appropriately. Much of the "correct grammar" that we are taught in school is a matter of appropriateness, not of basic structure.

Thus, the composition teacher may give you this rule: Do not write "Can I come in for an interview?" You may have been told that using "can" in this situation causes a failure to communicate, but this isn't true. The composition teacher is viewing it as a rhetorical choice. He tells you to avoid it, not because the employer won't understand, but because it might offend him enough to refuse the interview. You haven't failed to communicate, but you have failed to be persuasive. Your language has been ineffective.

The linguist, focusing on an objective observation of how the language works, will report that some speakers use *can* and others use *may* in the slot. Then she'll be accused of advocating incorrect usage. Not so. The linguist doesn't advocate; she reports. In private life she may hate the use of *can* instead of *may* and correct the child who says it. Wearing the parent hat is quite different from wearing the scientist hat.

Linguistics can contribute to rhetoric by providing accurate observations of what various speakers and writers do in their social and situational roles. Language changes constantly, but because so much change is below the level of consciousness, people are unaware of it. Trained to focus on language as a phenomenon, the linguist is equipped to report what words and expressions people actually use, as opposed to what they think they ought to use. For lack of such information, a rule like the one forbidding *can* remains in the texts long after it has ceased to be relevant to correct, appropriate communication. It's hard to imagine that a modern employer would care, or even notice, whether an applicant used *can* or *may*. Because of the hyperconservatism in textbooks, much of what people learn about language puts them in a bind. They feel guilty because they use supposedly "incorrect" expressions; yet their intuitive sense of what is normal and current (that is, truly appropriate) prevents them from adopting the supposedly "correct" expressions they have learned in school.

Both the scientific and the nonscientific studies of language are useful. Neither one can replace the other. We've seen that rhetoric is applicable to the daily life of everyone who must use language persuasively. Linguistics is applicable to all the social sciences, but its most important contribution will probably be to education. Shinichi Suzuki developed his method of teaching music through his insight into language learning. When he went to Germany to study music, he was amazed to see how fluently the children spoke German. He decided that if babies could learn something as complex as the

German language, they could surely learn to play the violin.[6] Of course, it took contact with a foreign language to bring about his insight, for he had never realized what genius it takes to learn Japanese. The most amazing feat of learning anyone ever accomplishes is to master his native tongue, and the more that linguists find out about how it's done, the better our educational methods can be.

Branches of Linguistics

To the beginning student, struggling with the terminology of linguistics and trying to absorb abstract concepts illustrated with thousands of detailed observations, it may seem that everything knowable about language is already known. In actuality, practically nothing is known; and new research changes the picture so fast that linguistics books are often outdated before they ever see print. Here's a brief overview of the fields of linguistics and the kinds of problems each one tries to solve:

Descriptive linguistics is devoted to writing grammars (descriptions of phonology, syntax, and semantics). The descriptive linguists either work from data collected by someone else, or go to a language community to collect their own, in which case they are called *field linguists*.

Theoretical linguistics is concerned with philosophical questions about what is the essential nature of language and what sorts of formulas best describe a grammar. At present two important questions are these: "What kinds of linguistic universals are possible?" and "How is natural language related to mathematics and formal logic?"

Historical linguistics traces the changes in the phonology, syntax, and lexicon of a language. It is especially relevant to *lexicography*, or dictionary-making. It overlaps with *comparative linguistics*, which traces the relationships among languages, grouping them into various "language families." The best-known language family is Indo-European, to which English, French, German, Russian, Greek, and Hindi belong.

Psycholinguistics studies the relationship of language and the mind, especially trying to answer the questions "What is cognition?" and "What do we do when we understand language?" Research projects include the teaching of human language to primates, observing children as they learn their native tongue, and trying to define "understanding language" so specifically that a computer can be programmed to do it (a project which overlaps with another field called *computational linguistics*). The study of how speech and language are related to the brain is not psycholinguistics, as one might expect, but *neurolinguistics*.

Sociolinguistics studies varieties of language and the way social groups

---

[6]Shinichi Suzuki, "Children Can Develop Their Ability to the Highest Standard," in *The Suzuki Concept*, ed. Elizabeth Mills and Sr. Therese Cecile Murphy (Berkeley: Diable Press, 1973), pp. 10–11.

use language as one way to define themselves as a group. Sociolinguistics has contributed to education by making teachers aware of the differences between dialects of English, but what is even more important, the differences of language customs among communities. For example, a teacher might offer a treat or a privilege to a child, saying, "Do you want some candy?" The child replies, "I don't care." Within his language community this may be the polite, the proper reply, but the teacher, who belongs to a different social group, is disappointed by his lack of enthusiasm. Knowledge of such differences obviously makes classroom life easier.

All of these different fields of linguistics can be pursued as knowledge for the sake of knowledge; and all of them contribute eventually to *applied linguistics*. It includes a variety of activities, such as developing methods for foreign language instruction; developing methods and materials for bringing literacy to underdeveloped areas; and helping people surmount various language disabilities, such as deafness. Since English has become a medium of world trade and scientific communication, TEFOL, or Teaching English as a Foreign or Other Language, has become an important vocation in applied linguistics.

Stylistics is a field of study located halfway between linguistics and literary criticism. It focuses on different ways to say "the same thing" and the relationships of these choices to speaker, situation, and literary form. Since style is an important part of both literature and rhetoric, the study of stylistics can have broad applications to language usage.

In this book our primary concern will be linguistics, but from time to time we'll look at the application of linguistic principles to rhetoric and literary criticism. Chapter 2 deals with lexicon, Chapter 3 with phonology, Chapters 4 and 5 with syntax, and Chapter 6 with semantics. The last part of the book deals with larger issues. In Chapter 7 we'll consider discourse structure, the slots and fillers of language patterns larger than the sentence. Chapter 8 deals with dialectal variations in American English. Chapter 9 wrestles with a definition of "correct" English and tells how it came to be considered correct. I have tried to make the chapters self-sufficient, so that you can study them in any order.

Writing for Insight and Review

If you're like most people, you prefer the telephone call, the visit, or the interview to written communication. Such oral messages are easier and faster. Nevertheless, writing fulfills a unique function in our lives. We write, not just to communicate with others, but to become aware of our thoughts and feelings through expressing them in writing. Psychologists often suggest that their clients keep journals to help them become aware of their true feelings and to locate the source of their emotional problems. Writing is also useful in helping to fix information in the memory. Sometimes students try to avoid the chore of note-taking by taping professors' lectures, but they soon find that writing down important points and examples is in itself an efficient method of learning.

So, at the end of every chapter in this book you'll find discussion questions and writing assignments designed to review, reinforce, and expand on the information presented in the chapter. Even if the instructor doesn't ask you to hand them in, you'll want to do at least some of them. Writing out what you know will help you to gain knowledge that is deep and applicable. Facts memorized for a test fade rapidly. Facts organized in your own words into a paragraph or essay have more staying power.

Write a few paragraphs about each of the following:

1. In a sense, the language community you belong to is the group of people who speak the English language, all over the world. In another sense, you belong to the language community of American English rather than British English or Australian English. What other small language communities do you belong to? What are some of their special language habits? For example, if you're a Catholic, the word "father" has a special meaning shared by members of the Catholic speech community.

2. The principle of slots and fillers doesn't apply just to language, but to other structured human activities. Describe a meal, a game, a social event, a political campaign by listing the points of choice and the class of fillers for each one. For example, one of the slots in a baseball game is the pitch. The class of fillers includes fast ball, curve ball, etc.

3. Pets seem to understand language more than they really do. What do they do to give this impression? How could you set up a situation to determine how much they really understand?

4. What are some of the rules of "grammar" that you have been taught but do not follow? Why don't you follow them?

2

Where Words Come From

Most of the intricate structure of language is below the level of our consciousness, but we are aware of words. We mark the beginning of a child's language acquisition from the day he says his first recognizable word. We begin to learn a foreign language by learning to pronounce a few of its words. When we take up a new branch of knowledge, such as biology or music, we must learn a new set of words. And part of our being accepted into a new social group involves learning that group's words. For the ordinary person, language consists almost entirely of words.

The linguist's view of language is quite different. He or she is aware of many other units of language besides the word: phonological units such as phonemes and syllables; syntactic units such as phrases and sentences; and semantic units such as predications. For several reasons, linguists often regard words as the least important, least rewarding level of linguistic analysis. First, speech issues from the mouths of human beings in a continuous stream, and the way it's divided up into words differs from language to language. Latin uses one word, *amabimus*, to say the same thing that English says in three words: "We will love." Thus word division seems arbitrary. Second, it's almost impossible to define what a word is. Should we consider "love" and "loved" two different words, or two forms of the same word? What about "love" and "lovely"? The usual solution, to regard "love" and "loved" as the same word and "lovely" as a different word, also seems arbitrary. The usual definition of a word is this: a word is a form that stands alone—anything a native speaker of the language is willing to pronounce as a separate unit. This definition leads to additional problems. For example, when we say "not sane," "not" is a separate word, but when we say "insane," "in-" is only part of a word.

Despite these problems, the word is a good place to begin the scientific study of language because it's a recognizable unit in each of the three major components of language. It's a unit of phonology, because in most languages there are rules for pronouncing words which differ from the pronunciation of syllables or phrases. It's a unit of syntax, because words belong to part-of-speech classifications such as *noun* and *verb*. And, most obviously, the word belongs to the semantic component because it means something. There's much to learn about words: the smaller units which compose them, the rules for putting together these smaller units, how they originate, and how they change through history. This chapter will provide a brief introduction to all these topics.

Morphemes

Since the word is such an arbitrary, hard-to-define unit, linguists have found it helpful to add another unit of analysis, the *morpheme*. A morpheme is a *form* associated with a specific meaning. The form may be a single vowel or consonant, a syllable, or more than one syllable. The meaning may be primarily *lexical*, such as "phon-," which means "sound" in "phonology," "symphony," and "telephone"; or the meaning may be primarily *grammatical*, such as "-ed" (past tense) or "-ly" (adjective or adverb). The meaning of the form must be fairly stable. The "-ed," for example, means "past tense" whether it's found on "loved," "washed," or "played." Many English words consist of a single morpheme: cat, car, mother, person, friend. Other English words have more than one morpheme: catty (2), automobile (2), mothers (2), impersonally (4), unfriendliness (4). Look at these words carefully to see where the morpheme divisions occur.

Morphemes are classified in several ways. One classification divides them into *free* and *bound* morphemes. A free morpheme is one which can stand alone as a separate word, such as "good" or "mother." A bound morpheme is one which must be attached to other morphemes, such as the "-ness" in "goodness" or the "-ed" in "mothered."

Another classification divides morphemes into *bases* and *affixes*. A base is the main part of a word, such as the "low" in "lowly." An affix is a morpheme added on to the base. If the affix appears before the base it's called a *prefix;* if after the base, it's called a *suffix*. The word "unfriendly" has two affixes—one prefix and one suffix. Some languages have affixes within words, and these, logically enough, are called *infixes*. Words of more than one morpheme do not necessarily contain affixes. "Bedroom," for example, is made up of two bases that are also free morphemes. "Biology" is made up of two bases that are bound morphemes.

Analysis of morphemes would be easy if there was always a one-to-one correlation between form and meaning; but human languages, like human lives, are not that neat and tidy. Often the same morph (form) will have two or more meanings. The "-er" suffix, for example, means "more" in "sweeter," but it means "one who performs something" in "player." The "-en" suffix has three meanings: it makes a word into a verb in "brighten," into an adjective in "silken," and into a plural in "oxen." In such cases, we don't have one morpheme with three meanings, but rather three separate morphemes with the same *phonetic shape* (pronunciation). On the other hand, the past tense morpheme has several phonetic shapes. It's pronounced as a /d/ in words like "lived" and "squealed," but it's pronounced as a /t/ in words like "walked" and "sipped" and as a syllable /ɨd/ in "patted." (Notice that the three pronunciations all have the same spelling, "-ed." English spelling is often *morphemic* rather than *phonetic*.)

To make things even more complicated, sometimes a morpheme isn't pronounced at all. It has no phonetic realization. For example, the verb "hit" is the same whether it is present or past tense. "I *hit* another car yesterday" is past; "I *hit* that bump every time" is present. Some noun plurals have no phonetic realization: we say "a sheep" and also "six sheep." Sometimes a morpheme fails to be realized because of a process called *neutralization*. When a word ends with three or more consonants, some speakers simplify the pronunciation by leaving off the last one. If the final /t/ sound of "walked" is left off, the pronunciation of the word is exactly the same as that of "walk." Thus the inflectional contrast has been neutralized. It has no phonetic realization.

Another complication is the bits of language that look like morphemes but are not. Since we know that "worker" contains the "-er" morpheme, we are tempted to divide "mother" into two morphemes, but "mother" is a minimal unit of meaning which cannot be further divided. A worker is one who works, but a mother is not one who "moths." The "-er" in "mother" does not mean anything by itself, and therefore it's not a morpheme. We find the same situation when we compare "friendly" and "jolly." The "-ly" in "friendly" means "like"; a friendly person is one who acts like a friend. But a jolly person is not one who behaves like a jol. The resemblance between "mother" and "worker," or between "friendly" and "jolly," is merely a matter of chance. In the same way, the word "person" does not contain the morpheme "son," and "history" does not contain "his." Both are shortened forms of Latin words—*persona* and *historia*. The women's liberationists who substitute "herstory" for "history" are quite wrong linguistically.

In other cases, however, a word which today is perceived as a single morpheme may be derived from two morphemes historically. The word "daisy," for example, is a shortened form of "day's eye." It was so named because people thought the daisy looked like a miniature sun, and the sun is certainly the "eye" of the day. "Alligator" is one morpheme in English, but it's derived from two morphemes in Spanish: *el lagarto*, "the lizard." One might be tempted to call "cranberry" a single morpheme on the ground that "cran" has no meaning of its own, but it's really another form of "crane." Very few people today perceive "breakfast" as the meal at which one breaks the overnight fast. By the twenty-first century, it will probably be considered one morpheme, just as "daisy" is today.

Affixes

Besides being classified by *position* into prefixes and suffixes, affixes may be classified by *function* into *derivational* and *inflectional*. *Derivational affixes* are those which enable us to obtain (or derive) more complicated new words from the simpler, older ones. The "-ly" which makes "friend" into "friendly" is a derivational affix. *Inflectional affixes*, or *inflections*, do not create new words, but instead affect grammatical features, such as changing singular to plural or present to past. The "-s" which makes "friend" into "friends" is an inflectional affix. (Oddly enough, we have two "-s" inflections: the noun inflection, which makes a singular noun plural, and the verb inflection, which makes a verb singular. This is a chance resemblance of unrelated morphemes.) Sometimes it's difficult to decide whether an affix is derivational or inflectional. Here are some guidelines that work most of the time:

1. The derivational affix often changes the word from one part of speech to another. Adding "ness" to "lively" changes it from adjective to noun. Adding "-ify" to "false" changes it from adjective to verb.
2. The derivational affix often changes a concrete noun or adjective to an abstract one. For example, "person" is more concrete than "personality" or "personhood."
3. The derivational affix may completely change the meaning of the base, so that "kind," for example, becomes "unkind."
4. The inflectional affix must be added to a word after all the derivational affixes. The plural of a derived word such as "unfriendliness" is "unfriendlinesses," not "unfriendsliness."

Inflections

Because of historical changes and the influence of other languages, the inflectional system of English contains a number of surprises. Let's examine the inflections of nouns, verbs, adjectives, and adverbs in detail.

English nouns are inflected for number and case. *Number*, in English, means whether the noun is singular or plural. (Other languages have other grammatical numbers such as dual, "two," or paucal, "a few.") *Case* refers to the use of the noun in the sentence. English used to have four cases: the nominative for subjects, the accusative for direct objects, the dative for indirect objects, and the possessive. Some of our pronouns still make a distinction between nominative and accusative: who-whom, he-him, they-them, for example; but our nouns have only two cases nowadays. They are the possessive case and the neutral case for everything else. The *paradigm* (pattern) for noun inflection is as follows:

friend (no inflection)	My *friend* is kind.
friends (plural inflection)	My *friends* are kind.
friend's (possessive singular)	My *friend's* dog hunts.
friends' (possessive plural)	My *friends'* house is large.

The use of the apostrophe to show singular and plural possession is another example of morphemic spelling in English, for the three inflected words are all pronounced exactly alike. The placement of the apostrophe is taught in elementary schools, but since it doesn't reflect the communicative structure of the language, many people find it difficult to remember. It's one of the largest sources of spelling errors.

Incidentally, the *sound* added to "friend" is not *s*, as it is spelled, but *z*. The pronunciation of some morphemes is determined by the preceding sound. Here are the rules for plural and possessive *s:*

1. If the preceding sound is *p, t, k, f*, or the *th* in "myth," the *s* is pronounced. Examples: tips, stacks, mitts, laughs.
2. If the preceding sound is a sibilant (hissing sound), the *z* is pronounced with a vowel to make an extra syllable. Examples: kisses, buzzes, wishes, churches, judges.
3. If the preceding sound is any vowel or any other consonant, the *z* is pronounced. For some words such as "knife," "wife," and "calf," the *f* in the original word is changed to *v* and the plural (but not the possessive) is pronounced with a *z*.

These rules seem very complicated, and people who are learning English as a second language have to master them by a painful combination of memory and practice. These same rules are seldom mentioned in ordinary English classes because native speakers learn them long before they ever attend school.

In addition to the common *-s* inflection, English has a set of irregular plurals left over from a different inflectional system in the morphology of Old English. Included in this group are tooth-teeth, man-men, mouse-mice. Each generation of new speakers tries to bring these words into line with the majority of plural words, and sometimes they succeed. "Book," for example, originally belonged to this group, but now we say "books" instead of "beek." Another minority plural which has been almost completely replaced by the *-s* is *-n*. About the only one still in common usage is "oxen." ("Brethren" and "children," for historical reasons, do not belong with "oxen.")

All of these various ways of forming plurals fulfill the same function. Therefore, instead of analyzing them as different morphemes, we call them *allomorphs* of the plural morpheme. (*Allo-* is a Greek morpheme meaning "other.") In addition to these fairly common allomorphs, we have the plural forms of nouns adopted from foreign languages. Thus the male graduates of a school are *alumni* and the female graduates are *alumnae* because the word comes from Latin, which has different inflections for different genders. Foreign plurals undergo different fates in English, as is illustrated by various Latin words which have *-um* in the nominative singular and *-a* in the plural: curriculum-curricula, gymnasium-gymnasia, medium-media, datum-data, agendum-agenda. If the word is used primarily by very scholarly, intellectual people, the foreign plural will be retained, as it is in *corrigenda*, "errors to be corrected." Sometimes the original plural and a "naturalized" plural will be used interchangeably; in the average faculty meeting, one hears both "curricula" and "curriculums," depending on the formality or informality of the speaker's style. Sometimes the foreign plural is completely replaced, as has happened with "gymnasiums." Surely no professor is stuffy enough to say "gymnasia" without laughing.

For "medium," two plurals are in common usage in different contexts. Biologists still grow their bacteria in the Latinate "media," but in conducting a seance, one calls more than one medium "mediums." In still another context "media" has become a singular noun meaning "way of transmitting information." "Data" has also ceased to be a plural noun for most people. They regard it as a mass noun like "information" and say "The data is. . . ." "Agenda" has so completely lost its plural meaning that people give it a second plural, speaking of "agendas." In general, we may say that the speakers of the language try to simplify and normalize the morphology as much as possible. The irregular plurals that survive are the ones used so often that we learn them as pre-schoolers, such as "feet," or the ones used so seldom that we learn them as exceptions, such as "corrigenda."

Verb Inflections

English verbs are inflected for *tense*. The paradigm for the majority of verbs is as follows:

walk—present tense, used with I, we, you, and all plural nouns

walks— present tense, used with he, she, it, and all singular nouns

walking—present participle, used with the *be* auxiliary or in an adjective slot

walked—past tense, used with all nouns and pronouns

walked—past participle, used with *be* or *have* auxiliaries[1] or in an adjective slot

This inflectional system is greatly simplified from the one used in Old English. The "-s" inflection in the present tense is all that is left of an elaborate set of distinctions based on *number*—singular-plural—and *person*—whether the subject of the verb is the speaker (I or we) the one spoken to

---

[1] See Chap. 4 for a discussion of auxiliaries and their role in the verb phrase.

(you) or the one spoken of (he, she, it, they, all nouns). Another simplification is that the past tense morpheme "-ed" is exactly like the past participle morpheme for most verbs.

Since the "-s" and "-ing" inflections are the same for all verbs, they are usually left out, so that the paradigm consists of present, past, and past participle. English, like the other Germanic languages, has two systems of inflection for these verb forms: the "-ed," technically called the *dental suffix*, which we have already seen, and a second system of changing the vowel within the word. The verbs belonging to this second system are called the *strong* verbs. One strong verb is "sing," with past tense "sang" and past participle "sung." Some of the strong verbs have both vowel change and an additional suffix "-n" or "-en" in the past participle, as in ride-rode-ridden. (Notice that the *i* spelling in "ride" and "ridden" represents two different sounds.) Sometimes there is no vowel change in the past participle, as in see-saw-seen.

The regular verbs are sometimes called *weak* verbs to contrast them with the strong verbs. *Regular* is more descriptive, because the greatest percentage of verbs in modern English are inflected by this method. The weak inflections are also *productive:* that is, when a new verb comes into the language, it invariably takes the weak inflections. Through the course of history, many strong verbs have become weak. Help-helped-helped, for example, used to be help-holp-holpen. Weak verbs seldom develop strong forms. The substitution of "dove" for "dived" in some dialects of American English is an example of a weak verb becoming strong. Sometimes the strong and weak forms develop slightly different meanings. For example, a person is "hanged" as a form of capital punishment, but a picture is "hung" in a gallery. English also has a few verbs which do not fit into either the strong or the regular systems, such as go-went-gone and do-did-done. As with the irregular nouns, these verbs are all very common words which one learns as a pre-schooler.

Adjective and Adverb Inflections

Adjectives and some adverbs are inflected for *comparison*. The "-er" inflection compares two things and the "-est" compares three or more, as in friendly-friendlier-friendliest. Some of our commonest adjectives have irregular inflections: good-better-best and bad-worse-worst. When the adjective or adverb is three syllables long, English speakers prefer to put "more" or "most" in front of the word instead of "-er" or "-est" at the end. We say "more beautiful" rather than "beautifuller." One-syllable words normally use "-er" and "-est." Some two-syllable words, such as "friendly," take "-er" and "-est." Others, like "slowly," require "more" and "most." The comparative words are considered to be allomorphs of the comparative morphemes.

Derivations

A *derivation* is a word formed by adding one or more derivational affixes to a base. Anyone may create a derivation at any time. For instance, knowing that adding "-ful" to "beauty" makes "beautiful," a speaker could add "-ful" to "paper" and describe the life of a minor bureaucrat as "paperful." Most people would understand the new word immediately, and if enough of them began to use it, especially in writing, it would be included in dictionaries. Sometimes people create a new derivation when an accepted one already exists. For example, students often make up "ableness" and use it instead of the standard word "ability." Often the new word becomes accepted and the two words will be used either interchangeably or in different contexts with slightly different meanings. For example, "sureness" has a slightly different meaning from "surety."

Often two different derivations with approximately the same meaning will arise in English because we have three sets of productive derivational affixes: a set of native English affixes such as "-ness," a set of Latin ones such as "-ity," and a set of Greek ones such as "-osis." Thus if we wanted to create a word to describe an item sold as a book but having no reading material in it, we could use native English and say "unbook," use Latin and say "inbook" or "nonbook," or use Greek and say "abook" or "dysbook." It's more usual, however, to combine Latin and Greek derivational affixes with Latin and Greek bases. A chart of the most common, useful Latin and Greek morphemes may be found on pp. 33–35.

Other Processes of Word Formation

Although most of us turn naturally to derivational affixes when we need a new word on the spur of the moment, there are several other methods of creating words. A derivational affix usually changes a word from one part of speech to another. "Winter" is a noun, and we make a verb from it by using "-ize." But we can also use "winter" as a verb without adding an affix as in the sentence, "The wild ducks commonly *winter* in Louisiana." This method of adding to our vocabulary is called *conversion* or sometimes *zero derivation*.

Back-formation is the process of subtracting a derivational affix to form a new word. For example, the word "obligate" came from subtracting the noun ending "-ion" from "obligation." Another verb meaning the same thing, "oblige," was already in existence. It's still used, but in different contexts and by different speakers. "Automatic," the adjective, became "automate," the verb, by back-formation. Perhaps someday the word "frantic" will spawn the verb "frant," and a woman will be able to say, "I divorced him because he franted me with his constant demands for perfection." Often the bit of language that is subtracted seems like an English morpheme but is not. "Escalate" was made from "escalator," "edit" from "editor," and "burgle" from "burglar" because people interpreted the endings as examples of the English "-er" morpheme meaning "doer of." Perhaps someday the verb "moth" will be made from "mother" by back-formation. Once such a pair of words is in common usage, it's impossible to tell whether the relationship occurred through derivation or back-formation. We just have to trust the dictionary-makers, whose profession it is to keep track of such things.

Compounding, putting together two already-existing words or base morphemes, is another way to create new words. "Bedroom" is a simple example. Notice that a compound word is stressed[2] on the first part. This is a characteristic phonological pattern for compound words; indeed it's this stress pattern which distinguishes between "a blackbird" and "a black bird." Not all compounds are written as one word. Some, like "entry-way," are usually hyphenated, and others, like "family room," are written as two words. There is no rule governing which is which. The federal government, publishing companies, and some businesses have their preferred forms, and these are made known to the workers by a list of rules known as a *style sheet*. If you don't have to follow a style sheet, you can simply guess, or look the word up in a dictionary if you care enough, or if your professor does.

Much of our compounding involves combining Greek or Latin bases. Without realizing it, all of us have acquired a fairly extensive Greek and Latin vocabulary, and when new diseases, procedures, or technological marvels appear on the scene, they receive Greek or Latin names. Some people feel that it's wrong to combine a Greek morpheme with a Latin one in the same word, but "automobile" is such a hybrid.

Clipping is another source of new words. "Gym" is a clipped form of "gymnasium," "phone" of "telephone," "quote" of "quotation." People normally use the clipped forms to express informality and the full words to express formality; but sometimes a clipped form will replace the full one. Only lexicographers and English teachers now remember that "bus" was originally *omnibus* (a Latin word meaning "for all"), that "mob" was *mobile vulgus* ("the crowd in motion"), and that "fan" was "fanatic."

A *blend* is formed by a combination of clipping and compounding. "Smog" is a blend of "smoke" and "fog," "motel" comes from "motor hotel," "bit" comes from "binary digit," and "transistor" comes from "transfer" plus "resistor."

Folk etymology occurs when non-linguists mistakenly analyze a word into morphemes. For example, the bikini swimsuit was named after an island in the Pacific on which an atomic bomb was tested, apparently with the implication that the swimsuit was more powerful than dynamite. By folk etymology the word was analyzed as bi-kini, so that a three-piece ensemble

---

[2]"Stress" means "spoken more loudly and forcefully." See Chapter 3 for a fuller discussion.

was advertised as a tri-kini,[3] and a topless suit was called a mono-kini. The classic example of the creation of a new morpheme by folk etymology is what happened to the word "hamburger," originally a shortening of "Hamburger steak" (a steak cooked the way they do it in Hamburg). Apparently, people assumed that the word meant "meat" plus "sandwich," because they began to use "burger" as an ending for various sandwiches: "cheeseburger," "beefburger," and "vegie-burger."

An *acronym* is a word formed from the initials, or perhaps the first syllables, of a phrase. "Radar," for example, comes from *r*adio *d*etecting *a*nd *r*anging. "Laser," "maser," "Fortran," "NASA," and "SALT" are all acronyms. In recent years organizations have begun to adopt names which spell a word suggesting the purposes of the organization: the National Organization of Women is NOW; the Colorado Language Arts Society is CLAS: the World Adoption International Fund is WAIF. Clever as it is, this custom spells the end of acronyming as a source of new words.

All of the processes discussed so far involve a perception of morpheme structure by the speakers. Some words, however, come into the language by *coinage*, or invention without the use of existing morphemes. "Quiz," "blatant," "scam," and "googol" are all *coined* words. A few of these words are *onomatopoeic*. That is, their sound suggests their meaning. "Buzz," "hiss," and "flop" are common examples.

Still other new words come into the language by *commonization*,[4] which involves using a proper noun generically. As already mentioned, "Hamburger" was such a proper noun. Another example is "bargello," a type of needlework named for a museum. Some products have become so popular that they have given their names to all products of the same type: "coke," "kleenex," and "xerox" are popularly used for all carbonated drinks, facial tissues, and photocopiers. Older examples of commonization involve naming something after a Greek or Roman deity: "mercury" the mineral from Mercury the god, "vulcanize" from Vulcan, "venereal disease" from Venus. Many units of measurement are named after scientists: volt, watt, ohm, fahrenheit, celsius, joule, newton, hertz, weber, decibel, and angstrom are all examples. Such words are called *eponyms*.

Borrowed Words

The most important source of new words and morphemes is *borrowing* (a neighborly process, since no one ever pays back) from other languages and subcultures. Whenever an item or custom used by one group is adopted by another group, the name is likely to be adopted also. The history of con-

---
[3]Thomas Pyles and John Algeo, *English: An Introduction to Language* (New York: Harcourt, Brace and World, 1970), p. 227.
[4]A widely-used term for this process is *antonomasia*. The person for whom something is named is an *eponym*, and such words are sometimes referred to as *eponymous*.

tacts between cultures can almost be written from a close study of vocabulary. Some of the oldest words in our language are borrowed. Before English even existed as a distinct language, when it was part of a group of Germanic dialects spoken by some tribes in Northern Europe, the conquering Roman soldiers introduced some items of civilization and also the names for them: "wine," "cup," and "kitchen," for example.

Both military and nonmilitary conquests lead to vocabulary borrowing. After the Germanic tribes were well settled in what came to be called England, the peaceful invasion of Christian missionaries brought Roman culture and such vocabulary items as "priest" and "angel." The military invasions of the Vikings brought Scandinavian words such as "sky," "skin," and "skirt." Another military conquest, that of William the Conqueror in 1066, introduced French, the greatest source of borrowed words into English. The two centuries during which speakers of Norman French and English coexisted resulted in drastic vocabulary change.

One nonmilitary conquest was the revival of interest in Classical Latin and Greek during the Renaissance. From this period comes our present-day custom of forming new words from Greek and Latin morphemes, especially in scholarly, scientific, and technological fields. During this period also, increased trade with other European countries led to an influx of French, Spanish, Italian and Dutch words into the language. In the 16th through the 19th centuries, when English speakers were invading other territories with both military and economic power, words from the Indian languages of America and from Africa, India, Australia, and China were adopted into English. Today, names of foods, garments, musical instruments, and institutions continue to be borrowed from other countries.

Vocabulary Loss

As English has expanded geographically from a handful of dialects spoken by some Germanic tribes to a worldwide language, its vocabulary has expanded enormously, so that a modern unabridged dictionary contains about 450,000 words. Of course, the language has been constantly losing words all this time. Many words cease to be used because the concept or object they name ceases to be used. "Wergild" (man-money) has fallen into disuse because murderers are imprisoned (or allowed to plead insanity) instead of being made to pay for the death. In a motorized culture, who remembers words like "felloe," "single-tree," and "sulky"? In an increasingly urban environment, the generic "bird" replaces the names of various species.

Some words are replaced because they sound too much like other words. In southern France, changes in pronunciation were causing both "cattus" (cat) and "gallus" (rooster) to become "gat." To eliminate confusion, people began calling the rooster "vicaire" (priest). In English, certain animal names have been replaced because they sound too much like offensive names for parts of the body. Thus "donkey" has replaced "ass," "rooster" has replaced "cock," and "rabbit" has replaced "coney."

Often a word used by a small group of people, a dialect word or slang word, will be replaced by a more general term. "Johnny cake," "hoecake" and "flapjack," for example, have been pretty well replaced by "pancake" or "hot cake." On the other hand, sometimes a dialect word or slang word will replace the more general one. The classic examples come from Late Latin, in which *testis* (modern French *tête*) replaced *caput* for "head" and *caballus* (modern English "cavalry") replaced *equus* for "horse."

Finally, there seems to be a steady attrition of words for no explainable reason. In our own lifetimes we can observe the disappearance of slang words. Basic words disappear much more slowly, but at a steady rate. In fact, an established linguistic theory is that we can determine how long two originally united language communities have been separated by calculating the number of basic words they still have in common.

Semantic Change

Besides the addition and subtraction of words, the vocabulary can become more responsive to the needs of the speakers through *semantic change*. Semantic change involves a shift in what a word refers to or in the feelings associated with it. Two of the most common semantic changes are *generalization* and *specialization*. What has happened to the word "go" over the years is a good example of generalization. Its original meaning was "to walk." Serfs had to go, while knights and other members of the nobility were able to ride. "Go" became generalized to include all means of transportation. In recent years it has become even more generalized and includes many sorts of nontransportation activities. In some contexts it can even mean "say." You may overhear a conversation like this: "So the boss goes, 'Why were you late?' and I go, 'My car broke down.' "

Specialization is the opposite process. "Meat," which used to mean "solid food," as in the phrase "meat and drink," now means one particular kind of food. "Starve," which used to mean to die from any cause, now means to die of hunger, or simply to be very hungry without actually dying. When the language contains two words which are very similar in meaning, often one or both will become specialized. At one time "deer" and "beast" referred to the same thing—a living creature which was neither fish, bird, nor reptile. "Deer" became specialized so that now it refers only to creatures belonging to the *Cervidae* family, and "beast" came to be used only in literary contexts, often with a derogatory connotation. At the time when "deer" and "beast" were general words, "animal," the present general word, was just coming into use as a scholarly, technical term meaning "any living creature that breathes." Thus a human being was an animal, but not a deer or a beast.

Two other semantic changes, *elevation* and *degradation*, involve changes in the feelings associated with the word. The commonest example of elevation is the word "minister," which originally meant "servant." But a king's servant might be an ambassador or an administrator of huge funds—a powerful and important person. A servant of the church such as a priest or bishop was also an important and respected person. Thus, the word acquired a very high connotation. Some specialization was also involved, since "minister" is no longer applied to a waiter or bellhop, but only to certain kinds of servants. The change in word connotation is often caused by a change in feelings toward the thing the word refers to. Thus many religious names, such as "Christian," "Methodist," and "Quaker," were originally derogatory terms; as the group became respected, the name underwent elevation.

The opposite process of *degradation* occurs when a person or thing named involves unpleasant feelings. The name becomes contaminated by the negative feelings toward the person or thing. Some old examples of degradation are "knave," which originally meant "boy" or "servant"; "villain," which originally meant "farm worker," and "hussy," which originally meant "housewife." We can speculate that the degradation of these particular words indicates the attitude of upper-class male courtiers toward people unlike themselves.

The process of degradation can be clearly seen in the history of *euphemisms*. A *euphemism* is a pleasant or neutral word applied to an unpleasant or embarrassing topic. Each euphemism becomes so degraded that another one must be substituted. In English-speaking countries, there has been a whole series of words to refer to the place where a certain physiological act is performed. One old word is "gong," from the word "go." Another word was "privy," meaning "private," as in "the king's privy council." (Notice that "privy" is now specialized to mean only an outdoor, non-flush convenience.) Another word was "closet," a closed-in place. At first spare clothes, if people had any, were kept there; in more prosperous and better-plumbed times, the clothes closet and the water closet came to be two separate places. "Toilet," "lavatory," and "bathroom" are other euphemisms, now more or less degraded in meaning.

The most important semantic change is by *transfer*. As methods of transportation have changed, the word "car" has been transferred from its original meaning of "chariot" or "wagon" to refer to the horse-drawn buggy, the railroad car, the trolley car, the gondola of a dirigible, and finally to the automobile. When the transfer of meaning involves the comparison of two unlike things, it is called a *metaphor*. "Legs" are what animals and people stand on. To speak of the legs of a table or chair is metaphorical. Because the legs "fork" from the trunk, a metaphorical comparison allows us to speak of the legs of a triangle or the legs of a compass. Some students of language have claimed that all language originates in the human ability to see likenesses in unlike objects and experiences. In other words, all language is metaphorical in origin.

Etymology and Style

Just as a painter chooses paints with different chemistries for different effects, cadmium red for warmth and alizarin for coolness, so also the skillful writer chooses words according to their etymologies. From Anglo-Saxon, the native Germanic base of the language, comes a large proportion of our common, everyday, short words. Words like "mother," "father," "heart," "bread," "good," "eat," and "love" have been in the English language from the earliest times. Almost as basic are the words added to English from French in the Middle Ages: words like "joy," "mercy," "city," "silence," "story," "arrive," "wait" and "pay." Words such as these are what Joseph Conrad has called the "fresh usual words."[5] They create a sincere, down-to-earth, plain effect. Words borrowed from French in later times, such as "chef," "chivalry," "enchantment," and "morale," are fancier. At the far end of the spectrum are the polysyllabic words from Latin and Greek, which create an objective, impersonal effect.

People who study etymologies have noted that for many of the things we want to talk about there are three word choices: one from the native Anglo-Saxon, one from French, and one from Latin or Greek; we choose one word rather than another according to the formality or intimacy of the occasion. For example, we have "hearty," "cordial," and "cardiac." A hearty welcome is somehow less formal, more deeply felt than a cordial welcome, while a cardiac welcome is unthinkable. That word is used only in medical and technical contexts. Other triplets are ask-question-interrogate and kingly-royal-regal.

During the 16th century there was a movement led by Sir John Cheke to "purify" English by getting rid of the borrowed words and using only Anglo-Saxon. Cheke wanted people to say "folk" instead of "people," "foresayer" instead of "prophet," and "leechcraft" instead of "medicine." His impassioned pleas for purity contained just enough borrowed words to destroy his credibility. Although Cheke went too far, it is true that most people's writing style can be improved by making an effort to choose fewer polysyllabic words from Greek and Latin. Using big words is a natural thing to do—it seems to make a person's ideas sound more profound and impor-

---

[5]Quoted by John Frederick Nims in *Western Wind* (New York: Random House, 1974), p. 146.

tant—but the sensitive word artist will seek for the mixture that produces the most effective tone and rhythm.

Because of the normal processes of semantic change, words mean what they mean. It's necessary to make this point because once people become aware of etymologies, they are apt to get carried away. For example, one pedant argued that no manufacturing is done in the modern factory, because "manufacture" comes from two Latin morphemes meaning "hand made." The same person would not use the term "dilapidated" for anything but a *stone* building. This insistence on the original meanings of words and morphemes is called the *etymological fallacy*. It's a denial of the process of semantic change.

On the other hand, poets often increase the vividness and power of words by referring to their original meaning along with the present one. Richard Wilbur writes, "Deliberately the drawbridge starts to rise." If we remember that "deliberately" contains the Latin morpheme "liber" which comes from *libra*, a scale or weight, we see the cleverness of Wilbur's choice of this word in describing the weighted mechanism of the drawbridge.[6] The transfer of meaning usually goes from concrete to abstract. When the poet reverses the transfer by returning the word to its original meaning, the effect can be startling.

Dictionaries

To keep up with etymologies and semantic changes in words is the study of a lifetime for a *philologist* (etymologically, a friend of words). Those of us who are not philologists must depend on dictionaries for our information. A collegiate (large desk) dictionary provides sufficient information for most needs. The etymology of a word is conventionally enclosed in square brackets and is found either before all the definitions or at the end of them. (The rather cryptic abbreviations of language names can be decoded with the help of a list usually found in the front of the book.) The dictionary will not specifically point out a semantic change as generalization, specialization, or transfer, but it will list all the meanings that are common at the time the edition goes to press, and it may omit or list as "archaic" or "obsolete" meanings which no longer apply to the word. Obsolete words and meanings may be retained when they occur in famous literature. For example, in Shakespeare's *Hamlet* the Prince exclaims, "By heaven, I'll make a ghost of him that lets me!—" (I, iv, 85) when his friends are trying to stop him from following the ghost of his father. From the desk dictionary we find that an old meaning of "let" is "stop." This meaning is not entirely obsolete, since it survives in tennis and ping-pong in the phrase "let ball," but we know that it is rare because so many people think the phrase is "net ball."

---

[6]Nims, p. 171.

To trace semantic changes more completely, and also to find changes in morphology and spelling, the best single source is the *Oxford English Dictionary on Historical Principles* (1884–1928) with its *Supplement* (1933). The *OED*, as the dictionary is usually called, supports each meaning of a word with dated quotations, so that one can determine when a word acquired a particular meaning and when that meaning was lost. For example, the *OED* shows that the word "girl" was used to mean "a young person of either sex" as illustrated with quotations dating from 1290 to 1450. The meaning "young female" is illustrated with quotations dating from 1530 to 1894. Until very recently, the usefulness of the *OED* was lessened by its lack of information about most of the twentieth century, but publication of a new supplement was begun in 1965. From it we can perhaps find out when the technical terms "inferiority complex" and "paranoid" from psychiatry and "input" and "interface" from computer technology began to have general, everyday meanings. Although no other dictionary provides as much and as many kinds of information about English words as the *OED*, the average desk dictionary contains much of what is known about the etymology and semantics of English words. People who consult their dictionary only to learn the correct spelling of a word are not getting the full benefit of this most common reference work.

Words are tools with which human beings come to grips with their world. It follows that knowledge of words can help us to understand and manipulate our environment. As psychologists have observed, people who have large vocabularies tend to be intelligent and well-educated, whether they have academic degrees or not. A knowledge of Greek and Latin morphemes is useful in that it gives us clues for interpreting the new technical words that we meet and also gives us a method for remembering and spelling such words. An awareness of the origins and histories of words gives us a feeling for their emotional overtones—their connotations and appropriate contexts. Of course, the power of words is sometimes misused. People think they understand a thing simply because they can apply a word to it; demogogues hypnotize people by using words which sound good but have little meaning; and sometimes people use words to avoid real contact and communication. But if a person's education is to be, as it should, a lifelong process, he must become a philologist, a lover of words.

Exercises

1. English Goes Ethnic

Find out from what languages the following words are borrowed into English. Consult the list of abbreviations in the front of the dictionary so that you can be sure of the language names.

1. taboo	8. zombi	15. caucus
2. macho	9. guru	16. shivaree
3. cinema	10. karate	17. kowtow
4. schlepp (shlep)	11. curfew	18. vodka
5. kabob	12. ciao	19. luau
6. clone	13. chigger	20. eureka
7. xerography	14. checkmate	21. graffiti

2. *Future Talk*

Here are some hypothetical new words and their meanings. These words have been made through processes of derivation, back-formation, conversion, compounding, etc. Try to determine what process was used to create each one.

1. She would quickly *door* an annoying salesman.
   "to door" = "to slam a door in someone's face"
2. Biofeedback is essentially learning to *autometer* bodily processes.
   "autometer" = "self measure"
3. *Curtainizing* a new home is certainly expensive.
   "curtainize" = "to provide with curtains"
4. She loved him, but found that he became a *spock* in a longterm relationship.
   "spock" = "a coldly logical person"
5. We had a leisurely *lupper*.
   "lupper" = "a meal eaten in mid-afternoon"
6. Since the husband and wife were both pilots, they enjoyed flying their small planes in *twomation*.
   "twomation" = "a pattern created by two airplanes"
7. The *bookation* of that film was certainly successful.
   "bookation" = "publication of a book based on a film"
8. They have a refrigerator full of beer in every room of their *contel*.
   "contel" = "a condominium that offers a number of hotel services"
9. The *davoth* gained popularity during the Seventies.
   "davoth" = "compact car," from the initials of four manufacturers

3. *One Morpheme or Two?*

Many words that look like a single morpheme are actually more than one in the original language; likewise, some words that seem to contain recognizable English morphemes consist of a single morpheme in the original language. Look up the etymologies of the following words and determine how many morphemes each word includes.

1. aardvark
2. algebra
3. chowder
4. cockroach

5. minion
6. nostril
7. window
8. woodchuck

4. Using the Oxford English Dictionary

The *OED* is harder to use than the collegiate desk dictionary, but the information it offers makes the additional effort well worthwhile. An entry contains the following parts:

1. The *listing* of the word in boldface type, followed by the part of speech (usually omitted for substantives—i.e., nouns).
2. The *pronunciation* (British), in parentheses.
3. Variant *spellings* and *inflections*, preceded by a number indicating the time of usage. 1 = 11th century or 1000's; 4-6 = 14th through 16th centuries (1300's through 1500's).
4. The *etymology* in square brackets.
5. The *meanings*, listed in roughly chronological order, and numbered. A dagger before the number indicates an obsolete meaning.
6. Illustrative quotations follow each numbered meaning and show the word being used in that sense. These quotations are preceded by date, author, and title (the latter drastically abbreviated).

Note: The meanings listed as current (without the dagger) are those in use when the volume was published (between 1884 for the first part of A and 1928 for the last letters of the alphabet).

A. Studying Semantic Change

For the following words, compare the specified meanings and then state what semantic change has occurred.

1. box, sb. 2—Compare Meaning I.1. with II.8, II.9, and II.10.
2. angel—Compare Meaning 1 with Meaning 8.
3. vulgar, adj.—Compare Meaning II.9 with II.13.
4. courtly—Compare Meanings 1 and 2.
5. sell, v.—Compare Meanings I.1 and I.3.
6. ether—Compare Meanings I.1 and II.6.
7. sidestep, v.—Compare the only definition given to a contemporary meaning especially common in political contexts.
8. starve—Compare Meanings I.1 and I.4.

B. Some Degradations

Names for females are especially likely to undergo degradation, as this list shows. Look up the more favorable original meaning in the *OED*.

1. spinster
2. mistress
3. maid
4. witch
5. gossip

C. Deservedly Little-Known Facts

Use the *OED* to answer the following questions about spelling and inflectional forms.
1. When did *helped* begin to replace *holp* as the past tense of *help?*
2. When did the past participle *holpen* for *helped* cease to be used?
3. What is the date of the earliest citation of the modern plural form *brothers?*
4. When did the plural *brethren* cease to be used?
5. What different spellings of *soap* were used during the 17th century?
6. Judging from the spelling, *raisin* was homophonous with what word in the 16th century?

5. The Word Factory

It's a common practice in science and industry to make up new words from Latin and Greek morphemes. For each of the following definitions, put together two or more morphemes from the morpheme list below to create a new word. Study the English examples and supply extra syllables to make the word sound English. For example, an awkward teenager who is all feet would be a *panipus*, not a *panpus*.
1. A person who talks so much that he or she seems to have more than one tongue.
2. The personality of one who looks outward rather than inward.
3. Unemployed.
4. A gossiper, one who carries speech everywhere.
5. A man who loves a woman only for her body.
6. The female counterpart of #5.
7. Beyond knowledge.
8. The wrong kind of person, not our kind.
9. An out-of-breath jogger.
10. Out of his or her mind.
11. A professor who loves to give surprise quizzes.
12. A roommate who takes more than her share of the space.
13. Someone who needs to borrow ten dollars.
14. A credit card limited to $1000 expenditure in any one month.
15. A debater.
16. A person who is unhappy because of receiving a bad horoscope reading.
17. An instructor who gives too much homework.
18. A film or other performance that is not worth seeing.

Now that you have the hang of it, make up some words of your own. Use each word in a sentence and see if your classmates can guess the definition you had in mind.

Morpheme List

Meaning	Latin	Greek	English Examples
A. Numbers			
1	uni-	mono-	university, monotone
2	duo-, bi-	di-	duologue, bicuspid, dichotmy
3	tres-, tri	tri-	triad
4	quart-, quat-	tetra-, tessera-	quarter, tesseract
5	quin-	penta-	quintuplets, pentagon
6	sexta-	hexa-	sexagenarian, hexameter
7	sept-	hepta-	September, heptarchy
8	octo-	octa-	October, octagon
9	novem-	ennea	November, ennead
10	decem-	deka-	decimal, decade
100	cent-	hekaton	century, hectare, hectograph
1000	millia	chilioi (kilo)	mile, kilometer
B. Amounts			
many	multi-	poly-	multitude, polygraph
large	magni-	macro-	magnificent, macrocosm
small	mini-	micro-, micr-	minimal, microscope
half	semi-	hemi-	semester, hemisphere
all	omni-	pan-	omniscient, pandemic
C. People, Body			
human being	homo, homin-	anthrop-	hominoid, anthropology
man	vir	andr-	virile, android
woman	femin-	gyn-	feminine, androgyne
body	corpus, corpora-	soma	corporal, psychosomatic
mind, life	anima-	psyche	animated, psyche
breath	spiri-	pneuma-	spirant, pneumatic
head	capit-	cephal-	capital, hydrocephalic
tongue	lingu-	gloss-, glot-	linguist, glossolalia
eye	ocul-	ophthalm-	oculist, ophthalmologist
hand	manu-	chiro-	manufacture, chiropractic
foot	ped-	-pod, -pus	pedestrian, cephalopod
D. Prepositions			
against	contra-	anti-	contradict, antithesis
down	de-	cata-	depress, catabolism

Meaning	Latin	Greek	English Examples
through, across	per-	dia-	persevere, dialect
upon, on	in-, im-	epi-	impose, episode
beyond, over	supra-	hyper-	suprasegmental, hyperactive
under, less	infra-	hypo-	infra-red, hypothryoidism
beyond	trans-	meta-	transfer, metaphor
beside	juxta-	para-	juxtapose, paramedic
around	circum-	peri-	circumspect, perimeter
with	co-, con-, com-	syn-, sym-	compassion, sympathy
not	in-, im-, il-, ir; non	a-, an-	imbalance, asymmetrical
far	ultra-	tele-	ultrasonic, telescope
out of, from	ex-, e-	exo-	evoke, exodus

E. Verbs

Meaning	Latin	Greek	English Examples
love, like, care for	am-, stud-, dilig-	ero-, phil-	amorous, student, diligent, erotic, philosopher
bear, carry	-fer	-pher	prefer, Christopher
look, see	-spect	-scope	circumspect, periscope
teach	doc-, doct-	dog-, -dox	doctrine, dogma
know	cogn-	gno-	cognitive, agnostic
work	labor-	erg-, urg-	laboratory, ergative
speak	locut-, loqu-	legein,	elocution, loquacious
word, speech, reasoning		logos, log-, -logue	philology, logical, dialogue
read, choose	leg-, lic-, lect-	leg-	college, (no word directly from Greek)

F. Nouns

Meaning	Latin	Greek	English Examples
race, kind, origin	gen-	gen-	genocide, genesis
light	luci-	phot-	lucid, photograph
measure	metri-	-meter	metrical, kilometer
end, limit	fin-, termin-	teleo-	finite, terminal, teleology

G. Confusing Look-Alikes

a- : reduced form of O.E. *on*, as in alike
a- : Greek prefix meaning *not*
a- : reduced form of Lat. ad, as in ascribe

| Meaning | Latin | Greek | English Examples |

anti- : against, Gr., as in "anti-war demonstrators"
ante- : before, Lat., as in "antebellum" (before the war)

inter- : between; intermural = School A plays School B
intra- : among; intramural = Frat 1 plays Frat 2 (both in School A)

nomen-, nomin- : name, Lat., as in nomenclature, nominate
-nomy, nomo- : law, Gr., as in gastronomy, nomothetic
onoma-, -onym- : name, Gr., as in anonymous, onomastics, synonym

loc- : place, Lat., as in locate
locut- : speak, Lat., as in circumlocution

chron- : time, Gr., as in chronometer
chrom- : color, Gr., as in chromatic

homo : man, Lat., as in Homo Sapiens
homo- : same, alike, Gr., as in homophone

mis-, miss-, mit- : Lat., send, let go, as in commission
mis- : hatred, Gr., as in misogynist
mis- : wrong, bad, O.E. or Fr., as in misspell

viti-, vic- : evil, bad, Lat., as in vice, vitiate, vicious
vice- : substituting for, Lat., as in vice-president

Writing for Insight and Review: Using Examples

An example is a specific instance of some concept or category. It plays an important role in persuasive and expository writing. In persuasive writing a number of examples may be cited to prove that what the writer says is true. When a political writer is trying to persuade people that his candidate is honest, he will cite examples of honesty: the business deal where Mrs. Torez took a loss rather than consent to a shady practice; her handling of the PTA treasury; the way she kept the campaign promises she made in the city council race. In explanatory writing the examples allow the reader to understand and follow what the writer is saying. This sort of example has been used extensively throughout Chapter 2. In the section on morphemes there is an example of each type of morpheme mentioned, and also examples of the various relationships between form and meaning. Each paragraph names a concept and then gives instances of that concept. The fifth paragraph of the section, beginning "To make things even more complicated," presents the idea that a morpheme may be unpronounced and then gives instances of it. The sixth paragraph's concept is "single morphemes derived from two morphemes historically."

Practice writing a simple paragraph in which the first sentence names a concept and the rest of the sentences provide examples. (Incidentally, this

sort of paragraph is useful in essay examinations.) If you have done the exercises, you have examples to illustrate the following concepts:
1. Many common English words have been borrowed from other languages.
2. Assuming that the common processes of word formation will continue to operate, the future vocabulary of English might contain several new words.
3. It's often difficult to determine whether a word contains only one morpheme, or more than one.
4. Words designating females are particularly likely to undergo degradation.
5. It's easy to make up new words using Greek and Latin morphemes.

Writing Projects

1. Make a new word using one of the normal processes of word formation discussed in the chapter. Use the word in casual conversations. What responses do you get? Write a paragraph explaining what you learned and using the responses you received as examples.

2. Science fiction authors sometimes create new words to enhance the strangeness of their stories. Analyze a portion of a short story or book for this feature. What processes of word-formation does the author use?

3. In order to avoid speaking of "breast" and "leg" or "thigh" in mixed company, people during the 19th century learned to ask for "white meat" or "dark meat." Pretend that a common word will similarly come to be avoided in the 21st century. For example, because of the association with toilets the word "bowl" might come to be avoided in all contexts. Other words, euphemisms, would have to be found for "cereal bowl," "the bowl games," "bowling ball," etc. Pretend that a common word becomes taboo in this way. Explain why it becomes taboo and give examples of the euphemisms people substitute.

4. In fiction, one of the easiest ways to characterize a person is to provide him/her with a favorite expression. For some of us, earliest memories include learning to say "Abadabadoo" like Fred Flintstone. In real life, politicians and performers also have such trademarks. Write a paper about such characterizing expressions. You will need to limit your topic in some way. You might choose to write about the favorite expressions of your friends, relatives, or professors, the characters in a single book, or the books of a single author. You might compare the favorite expressions of present-day celebrities to those of celebrities ten years ago. Needless to say, you will include many examples as you discuss your point.

3

Language Study on a Sound Basis

The phonology, or sound system, of a language provides the physical means by which speakers communicate. Lexical units (that is, words and morphemes) have a certain pronunciation by which we recognize them. It would seem reasonable that the exact reproduction of this pronunciation would be of the highest importance. Yet speakers differ widely in the way they pronounce the same words. You say *eye-ther*, I say *ee-ther;* Mrs. Smith says *raa-ther* (to rhyme with lather), Mrs. Jones says *raw-ther;* and little Bernie, who doesn't talk very well yet, says *free* when someone asks how old he is. How can all these people understand each other?

Linguists still don't know the precise answer to this question. In broad terms, we understand because we don't so much hear sounds as hear meanings through sounds. Think of a photograph blown up to poster size. When you stand too close all you see is dots of color. But move back halfway across the room and the eye uses the dots of color to create a picture.

Just as the eye creates a picture from dots of color, so also the ear creates a message from the bits of sound it receives. One author has explained the hearer's reception of a message this way: when you write a letter, the recipient reads the actual piece of paper that you wrote; but when you send a telegram, the recipient reads a re-creation of your message rather than what you actually wrote.[1] So also with the act of hearing: the hearer reconstitutes the message from hints and impulses provided by the sound waves. In this chapter we'll look first at the processes involved in producing and receiving sounds. Then we'll see how these processes are organized into the sound system of English. Finally, we'll consider how phonology is related to orthography, or spelling.

---

[1] Dennis Fry, *Homo Loquens: Man as a Talking Animal* (Cambridge: Cambridge University Press, 1977), p. 21.

First, a matter of terminology: *phonetics* is the study of sound itself, often without reference to any specific language; *phonology* is the study of the way sounds are structured in a particular language. In phonetics we learn what sounds human beings can say and hear. In phonology we learn how the possible sounds are used to signal meaning in a particular language. To study phonology requires, naturally, some knowledge of phonetics. Both phonetics and phonology are branches of linguistics. They should be distinguished from *phonics*, which is a method of teaching reading by showing the learners how to "sound out" words.

Phonetics

The branch of phonetics dealing with the production of sound is called *articulatory* phonetics, and the branch dealing with the reception of sound is called *acoustic* phonetics. Articulatory phonetics is older than acoustic phonetics. Until the development of the sound spectrograph shortly after World War II, the only way to define the properties of sounds was by the way they were produced. A knowledge of the mechanics of articulation is still basic to field linguistics: a field linguist attempting to crack the code of an unknown language relies on his ability to observe the informant's articulation and to imitate it using his own speech organs. Anyone wishing to study a foreign language will find that a little knowledge of articulatory phonetics makes a big difference in his ability to produce the sounds of that language accurately. It's also useful in studying the history of a language, for when sounds change, they change to something with a similar articulation. And finally, the person who wishes to specialize in speech and hearing problems will need to understand the mechanics of articulation.

The development of acoustic phonetics in the past thirty years has led to important practical applications also. Technicians can now analyze precisely the quality of sound transmissions by radio and telephone. Some efforts have been made to develop machines capable of synthesizing sounds in order to read aloud to blind people. Other machines synthesize sounds so that people who have lost their vocal cords can pronounce words. There are also experiments with the problem of enabling computers to respond to voice commands.

Even if we have no immediate application for the knowledge, the study of phonetics can reveal to us something of how our minds work by changing some of our perceptions. In the process of learning to speak and write, we have learned to hear only what we expect to hear, and to produce only those sounds which belong to the English language. An infant can make all the speech sounds of the world, joyously and without inhibition, but as we grow older this flexibility is lost. We begin to feel a reluctance, almost a sense of threat, about making un-English sounds. Studying articulatory phonetics restores some of this flexibility, enabling us to hear sounds more clearly and to make a variety of sounds freely. Aside from abnormalities, the vocal apparatus of every human being is like that of every other human being. If a Cheyenne Indian can pronounce a certain sound, so can anyone else. The unpronounceable sound—unpronounceable by everyone except native speakers—is a myth.

The Articulatory Process

The following description is intended to make you aware of the various parts of the articulatory process. Don't just read, but make the sounds and do the exercises. Allow yourself to become a child again, to play with your voice the way a baby does. And if your spouse or your roommates think you've gone crazy, that's their problem.

The Air Supply. Put your hands on your ribs. Breathe deeply and let the air flow out while saying "ah." Feel the contractions of the chest muscles which control the intake and outflow of air. Now breathe deeply again and let the air flow out as you say "Ha! Ha! Ha! Ha! Ha!" We control the outflow of air so that we can form syllables and words conveniently. Speech sounds are normally made while exhaling: speech is, literally, hot air.[2] It's possible to speak while inhaling, but not easy. Try it now. Say "Hello" while breathing in. It sounds strange, doesn't it? In some parts of the Philippines a young man may use such inhaled speech to conceal his identity from his girl friend's parents as he stands outside her house calling to her in courtship.[3]

When air is exhaled it moves out of the lungs, through the *bronchial tubes,* and into the *trachea* or *windpipe.* A small flap of tissue called the *epiglottis* closes off the windpipe when a person is eating so that bits of food do not get into the lungs, but rather go down the esophagus into the stomach. Thus we can not talk and swallow at the same time.

Voicing. The *larynx,* or voice box, is a cartilage container for the *vocal cords.* Because the larynx is most easily seen in men's throats, it is popularly called the "Adam's apple." The vocal cords themselves are like a pair of lips which can relax to let the air pass through freely or tighten to create vibration. The sounds made with the air passing through freely are *voiceless,* while the sounds made with the vocal cords vibrating are *voiced.* First put your hand on top of your head and make the noise you use to hiss the villain in a mellerdrammer: *sssss.* Then buzz like a bee: *zzzzzz.* The first sound is voiceless, and the second sound is voiced, since the vocal cords are vibrating. This vibration affects the whole column of air, and that's why you can feel it on top of your head.

In addition to relaxing and tightening, the vocal cords can close off the air completely to make a sound called a *glottal stop* (because the space be-

---

[2]Fry, p. 22.
[3]David Abercrombie, *Elements of General Phonetics* (Chicago: Aldine, 1967), p. 25.

tween the vocal cords is called the *glottis*). The glottal stop is not an "English" sound, but we do use it to separate two utterances of the same vowel. Say "three eagles" and you will hear a little grunt separating the two words. That's a glottal stop. In Arabic or Hebrew it's a consonant, one just as important as [p] or [g].[4] The glottis can also narrow to produce *whispered* speech. If you listen carefully, you'll find that you can hear the difference between [s] and [z] even when both are whispered. Whisper "sit" and "zit" to try it for yourself.

Most consonants come in pairs, one voiced and the other voiceless, but the glottal stop is always voiceless. Since the air is stopped to make it, the vocal cords cannot possibly be vibrating to produce voice.

The Velum. The column of air next comes to the back of the throat. If the *velum* (sometimes called the soft palate) is raised to block off the nasal passages, the air will go into the mouth to be modified there in various ways. If the velum is only partially raised, some of the air will go into the nasal passages. This physiological fact provides the means of classifying sounds as *oral* and *nasal*. There are three consonants in English which release air through the nose—the last sounds of *ram, ran,* and *rang*. It's also possible to *nasalize* vowels. All other sounds are *oral*. To contrast oral and nasal sounds, pinch your nostrils gently and say "see" and "mine." "See" contains all oral sounds; "mine," all nasal sounds. Many Americans habitually leave the velum partially relaxed while speaking, so that all their sounds have a nasal quality. To find out if you do this, pinch your nostrils gently and say, "I paid a high price for this hat, but the style is well worth the cost." If you nasalize any of the sounds, you'll feel a slight vibration in your nose.

The Mouth. In the mouth cavity, the moving air is modified in various ways to produce different sounds. The tongue assumes different positions, and sometimes the lips or teeth play a part. The different modifications provide natural classifications for the sounds, as follows:

1. Obstruents—made with the air stream obstructed in some way. There are three kinds of obstruents:

    stops (sometimes called *plosives*)—air stopped completely, then "exploded" suddenly.

      Examples: *p*in, *b*in, *t*in, *d*in, *k*in, *gig*

    fricatives (sometimes called *spirants*)—air obstructed so as to set up a strong friction.

      Examples: *f*in, *v*ine, *th*ick, *th*en, *s*it, *z*it, *sh*ell, equa*t*ion

    affricates—a stop with a fricative release.

      Examples: *ch*urch, *j*u*dg*e

2. Nasals—air is obstructed in the mouth, but goes out the nose.

      Examples: ra*m*, ra*n*, ra*ng*

---

[4]When sounds rather than letters of the alphabet are referred to, it's customary to enclose them in square brackets.

3. Liquids and Glides—air is relatively unobstructed, but there are special movements of the tongue.
   Examples of liquids: *roar, lilt*
   Examples of glides: *wow, yell*
4. Vowels—air is relatively unobstructed, but the shaping of the lips and tongue create different sounds. Examples will be given later.

Not only do the sounds fall into natural classifications according to the type of modification of the airstream, but also according to the part of the mouth where the modification occurs. Fig. 1 shows the voice mechanism with the place of articulation of some obstruents. The important classifications by place of articulation for English are as follows:
1. Labials—lips
2. Dentals—upper teeth
3. Alveolars—ridge behind the upper teeth
4. Palatals—hard palate
5. Velars—soft palate

To observe these places of articulation, pronounce these words: "mom," "nun," "song." The articulator (lip or tongue) meets the point of articulation to stop the flow of air from the mouth so that it goes out the nose. The [m] is a labial, the [n] an alveolar, and the [ŋ] (ng) a velar. Stops occur in these same places: "pop" and "Bob" begin and end with labial stops, "tot" and "did" with alveolars, "cook" and "grog" with velars.

It's convenient to list consonants within a matrix with the places of articulation arranged from left to right and the manners of articulation from top to bottom. As you study the chart (Fig. 2), you'll notice some differences between the phonetic symbols and the conventional alphabet. Here are some additional explanations of the chart:
1. Each of the boxes for stops has three symbols in it. The ones with the superscript *h* represent a stop followed by *aspiration*, or strong breathing. We pronounce the stops of "pin," "tin," and "kin" with aspiration. When these stops are preceded by [s], they are pronounced without aspiration, as in "spin," "stint," "skin." (Notice that the second [t] in "stint" is aspirated.) If you can't hear the aspiration, hold the corner of a sheet of paper about one inch from your mouth and pronounce the words. You will see the corner of the paper jump with the aspirated stops.
2. Voiced sounds are listed below voiceless ones with the same place and manner of articulation, so the third stop in each box is the voiced one, as in *b*ear, *d*og, and *g*oat. When the stops occur in certain positions within words and syllables, however, most Americans substitute the voiceless unaspirated stop for the voiced stop. More about this later. (Incidentally, English has no voiced aspirated stop, although it occurs in many other languages.)
3. The chart lists one other stop, the glottal stop. It's enclosed in parentheses to show that it's not considered part of the English sound system.

Phonetic Person

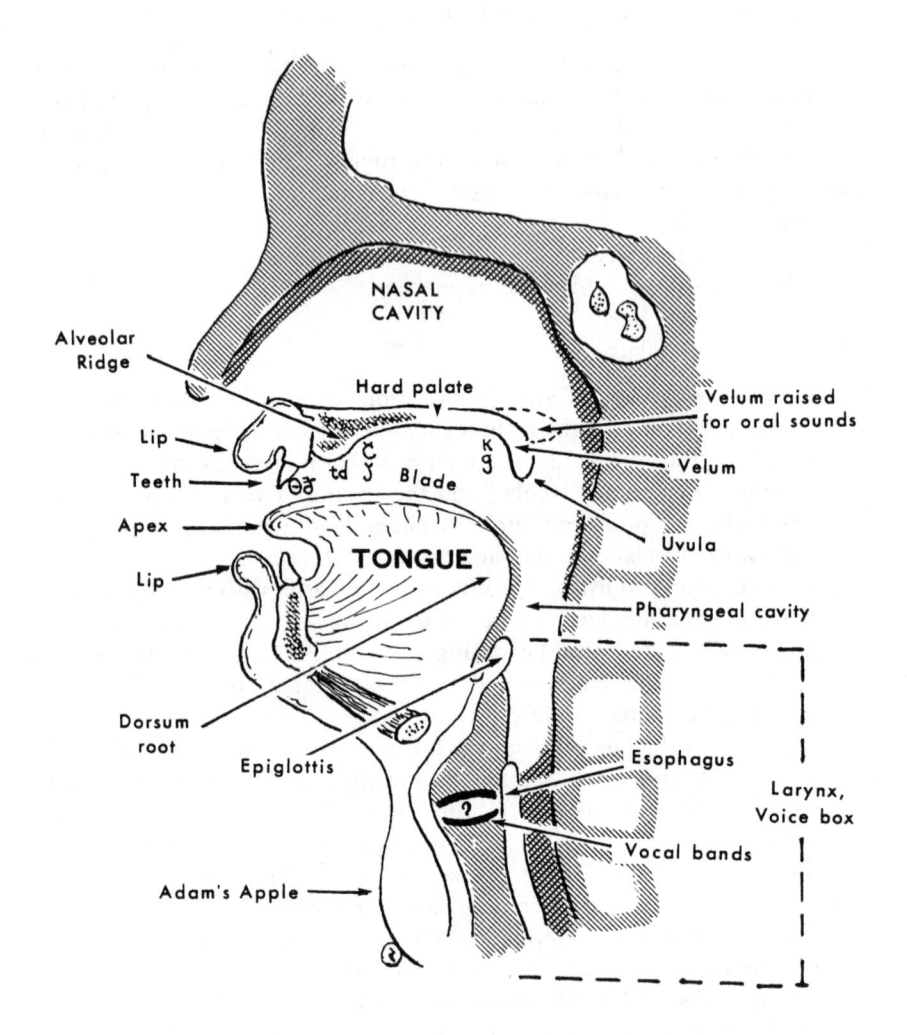

Fig. 1

CONSONANT CHART

Manner of Articulation	Place of Articulation					
	Bi-Lab	Labio-Dental	Inter-Dental	Alveolar	Palatal or Velar	Glot.
Stops	p^h p b			t^h t d	k^h k g	(?)
Affricates				č ǰ		
Fricatives	(p̓) (b̓)	f v	θ ð	s š z ž	(x) (g)	h
Nasals	m			n	ŋ	
Liquids				r l		
Glides	w				y	

IPA EQUIVALENTS

American	IPA	American	IPA
p̓	φ	č	tʃ
b̓	β	ǰ	dʒ
x	χ	y	j
g̓	ν		
š	ʃ		
ž	ʒ		

Fig. 2

4. English has only two affricates—the voiceless [č], and the voiced [ǰ], as in "chill" and "Jill." German has many other affricates. The middle sound of the name "Mozart" is an example.

5. The bilabial fricatives [p̓] and [b̓] are heard as replacements for [f] and [v] after [m], as in "triumphant" and "triumvirate."

6. Most students have difficulty in hearing the difference between the two kinds of *th*. The voiceless one, [θ], is the sound in *th*ick and dea*th*. The voiced one is heard in *th*e and brea*the* (the verb).

7. The difference between [s] and [š] is that the [š] is pronounced with the tongue drawn back a little further in the mouth, and also shaped a little differently. The voiced counterparts are made with the tongue placed exactly the same way. The [ž] is not really an English sound. It's heard in proper names and in learned pronunciations of words like "genre" and "ingenue."

8. Modern English has no velar fricatives, but the English of 1400 A.D. and earlier did. You can hear a voiceless velar fricative if you say the name "Hugh" with a very strong breath. It's also heard in the correct pronunciation of the name "Bach" and the Scottish word "loch."

9. The [h] sound in modern English is conventionally listed as a *glottal fricative,* because some of its phonetic quality is due to a slight modification of the air stream at the glottis. Actually, the place of articulation depends on the following vowel, as you can prove to yourself by noticing what happens when you pronounce the following words: heat, hoot, hate, hole, hat, haul, hot.

10. The [ŋ] is *ng* in conventional spelling. When people speak of "dropping the g," they are really referring to the substitution of the alveolar nasal for the velar one.

11. Although we list only one symbol for [l], the sound is slightly different in "kill" than in "call." Also, English [l] is normally classified as a voiced sound, but it may become voiceless when preceded by a voiceless stop. Try saying "clef" and see what you get. Other languages have voiceless l's—for example, the first one in a Welsh name like "Lloyd."

12. We also list only one r-sound, the *retroflexed* one. You can hear and feel this sound at the beginning of a word or syllable like "rain." It's a voiced sound made with the tongue bent backward, or retroflexed. Other languages, and some dialects of English, use other types of r's, including the following:
   a. The tongue-tip trill, a common sound in Spanish. The tip of the tongue taps repeatedly against the alveolar ridge.
   b. The flap-r. It's like the tongue-tip trill, except that the tongue taps only once. It sounds to our ears very much like a [d], and fiction writers will sometimes suggest this pronunciation by writing "veddy" for "very" in one dialect of British English.
   c. The uvular trill. It's used in a number of foreign languages, including French. This is the "tiger growl" made by vibrating the *uvula,* which is a little triangle of flesh hanging down from the velum.
   d. Finally, both American and British speakers of the so-called r-dropping varieties of English may signal the existence of an *r* by slightly lengthening or otherwise changing the preceding vowel.

13. The least consonantal of the consonants—in fact they often appear in vowel slots—are the *glides,* [w] and [y]. The term *glide* refers to the rapid movement of the mouth parts during the articulation. To make [w], we round the lips and raise the back of the tongue as if to say [u]. After the lips are rounded and the velum is poised, the tongue quickly slides into position to say the following vowel, and the lips unround. Try it by saying "we" while watching your mouth with a mirror. Then try saying "wow." Notice that your lips become rounded both initially and finally. The [w] is similar to

the [u] vowel as heard in "boo." Whether the sound is written [w] or [u] often depends on fine points of phonetic analysis, which are not appropriate to an introductory text (thank goodness). A whispered [w], used by people who do not pronounce "which" and "witch" alike, does not appear on the chart. It can be symbolized as [ʍ] or [hw].

14. The [y] glide is very similar to the [i] vowel as heard in "bee." However, we usually think of [i] as alveolar, while [y] is palatal. If you wish to prove this to yourself, position your mouth to say the [i] of "eek" and then say "yes" instead. Notice that the tongue changes position very slightly and quickly from [i] to [y]. Again, the distinction is such that the same sound may be written [y] by some linguists and [i] by others.

Phonetic Symbols

In dealing with consonants we have very little trouble with the phonetic symbols for sounds, for most of them are the same as our English letters of the alphabet. When we come to vowels, however, the phonetic symbols are just different enough from the alphabetical symbols to cause a problem. Most people resist learning a standard notation for sounds. It seems to them like an overly complex, bastardized version of the "regular" alphabet. We all learned the alphabet and spelling rules of English with a good deal of difficulty, and it seems unreasonable to ask us to start over. Nevertheless, the "regular" alphabet is simply not adequate to describe sounds. It works for us only because we already know pretty well how to pronounce the words. We read the word *house* and the Virginian pronounces it one way, the Nebraskan another way, and the Texan still a third way. The spelling does not tell us how to pronounce a word in any absolute sense, but only how to pronounce it according to the rules of our dialect.

The person trying to learn a foreign language from books, without a teacher, soon becomes aware of the alphabet's inadequacy. For example, one Greek textbook states, "The *ou* diphthong of Greek is pronounced like the ou of the English word *route*." Some people pronounce *route* to rhyme with *boot;* others pronounce it to rhyme with *kraut*. Which sound should be used in pronouncing Greek? Without standard phonetic symbols there's no way to tell.

The two most widely known systems of phonetic transcription are the International Phonetic Alphabet, or IPA, and the American system. IPA is especially useful for transcribing the sounds of European languages. The American system is better for doing field work on tribal languages with minimal equipment. It uses more of the symbols found on an ordinary typewriter, so that a person typing up a phonetic transcription need not constantly stop to put symbols in by hand. One version of the American system, called Trager-Smith after its developers, is especially designed to record all the variant vowel sounds of American English dialects. This book will use

Pike's version of the American system. The differences in consonants are as follows: American [š] and [ž] are IPA [ʃ] and [ʒ]; American [č] and [ǰ] are IPA [tʃ] and [dʒ]; American [y] is IPA [j] without the check on top.

Phonetic transcriptions differ greatly in the amount of detail they include. The symbols on the chart are adequate for a *broad* transcription of English and a few of the most noticeable regional differences in pronunciation. The *narrow* transcription needed to record more subtle regional and individual differences requires that the linguist use additional symbols. Some such symbols are widely known and accepted, but often the linguist simply makes up his own and provides a list, with phonetic descriptions, at the beginning of his presentation. No matter how narrow a transcription is, it still reflects the individual linguist's perception of what he heard. It's always more like an artist's drawing than a mechanically produced photograph. With this in mind, let's consider a description of the vowels.

English Vowels

Since vowels are spoken with a relatively unobstructed flow of air, it's impossible to classify them in terms of articulator and point of articulation. Instead we use these descriptive terms:

HIGH, MID, LOW—tongue height (how close it is to the roof of the mouth).

FRONT, CENTRAL, BACK —tongue retraction (whether it's raised in the front, middle, or back of the mouth).

ROUNDED, UNROUNDED—whether the lips are more like an O or more like a smile.

The front vowels, in order of descending height, are [i], [ɪ], [e], [ɛ], and [æ]. To observe these various tongue heights, fix your mouth and tongue to say *eek* and then say only the vowel. As you are saying it, let your tongue and jaw drop gradually. You will hear yourself make all these vowels in succession (though if you open your mouth as wide as it will go you will hear [a] instead of [æ]). Do the jaw-dropping exercise several times, correlating what you hear with the symbols on the chart. (See Fig. 3.) Use the key words with great caution, for people pronounce vowels quite differently. For example, you may use not [æ], but [ɛ], in the key word. So it's safer to think of these vowels in terms of their phonological descriptions: high front vowel [i], lower high front vowel [ɪ], mid front vowel [e], lower mid front vowel [ɛ], and low front vowel [æ].

To observe the degrees of tongue retraction, use a mirror and flashlight to look into your mouth as you say *he, hurt* and *who*. You will see the tongue bunch up first in the front of the mouth, then in the midsection, and finally in the back.

The back vowels are harder to distinguish by the jaw-dropping exercise. The jaw doesn't open as far at the back as it does at the front. But try it

VOWEL CHART

Phonetic Description	Key Words	Text	Trager-Smith	Others
High Front	beet, e̲asy	i	iy	i:
Lower High Front	bit	ɪ	i	ɪ
Mid Front	great	e	ey	ei, e:
Lower Mid Front	debt, says	ɛ	e	
Low Front	act, cat	æ	æ	
High Central (centralized high fr.)	just (quickly), ros e̲s	ɨ	i̇	
Mid Central Stressed	sun, butt, burred	ə	ə	ʌ
Mid Central Unstressed	sof a̲, ab o̲ut	ə	ə	ə
Higher Mid Central	bird (if not pronounced like burred)			ɜ
High Back Rounded	ooze, boot	u	uw	u:
Lower High Back R.	book, butcher	ʊ	u	ω
Mid Back Rounded	boat, go, own	o	ow	ou, o
Low Back Rounded	ca w̲ed, bought	ɔ	ɔh	ɔ:
Low Back Unrounded	pot, f a̲ther	a	a	ɑ
Diphthong—low to high front	wife, bite	ay	ay	ɑɪ, æɪ
Diphthong—low to high back	how, ab o̲u̲t	aw	aw	ɑʊ, æʊ
Diphthong—low rounded to high back	boy	ɔy	ɔy	ɔɪ

Fig. 3

anyway. Fix your mouth to say the vowel of *boo* and gradually let your jaw drop, ending up with the sound you make when the doctor says, "Say 'ah,'" please." You may hear yourself make most of the back vowels of English: [u], [ʊ], [o], [ɔ], and [a]. Notice that your lips are rounded more for [u] than for [ɔ], and not rounded at all for [a]. It's a general principle that English back vowels are spoken with the lips rounded, English front vowels with the lips unrounded.[5] For that reason, [a] is often called a central vowel, even though the tongue is not doing anything at the center area of the mouth. The [a] designates the sound that most Americans use in pronouncing *father*

---

[5]Examples of rounded high front vowels are French *tu* and German *über;* rounded mid-front vowels are French *feu* and German *schön*.

and *not*. Many New Englanders, however, pronounce *father* with a vowel similar to [a], but with the tongue slightly more retracted (backed), and in some British dialects the vowel of *father* is closer to [ɔ] than to [a]. Some Americans do not have the [ɔ] vowel, so that they pronounce *cot* and *caught* alike.

The midcentral area has an equally troublesome variety of vowels. Students of phonology disagree about what they hear and how it should be analyzed, leading to a variety of symbol systems. The basic midcentral vowel is the *schwa*, symbolized by an upsidedown *e:* [ə]. This is the sound usually spelled "uh"when dialog is written out in books, and the sound we use in pronouncing the italicized letters in *a*lone, *e*lement, *a*troc*i*ty, and s*u*ppose. It also occurs frequently before an [r], although some people, in some words, use a sound just slightly higher in the mouth, symbolized [ɜ]. If you do not pronounce *hurt* and *bird* with the same vowel, you probably use [ɜ] for *bird*. As previously mentioned, some people pronounce the [r] so lightly that it hardly seems like a separate sound, and some phoneticians record this by attaching a small script *r* to the vowel. You will not be able to record all the variant sounds that you hear in the midcentral area with the simplified phonetic alphabet we are using.

Just as the obstruents came in voiced and voiceless pairs, so the vowels often come in pairs. One member of the pair will be described as *tense, close, long*, or any combination of these terms. The other will be *lax, open*, or *short*. In English, these three characteristics go together. Tense vowels are spoken with perceptible muscular tension in the tongue. When the tongue is tense it's naturally positioned a little higher in the mouth, so that the tense vowel is also close (because the tongue is *closer* to the roof of the mouth). The tense vowels usually take a little longer to say, also. We will call the vowels with these characteristics *long*. They are [i], [e], [o] and [u]. Since vowels are made with a relatively unobstructed air stream, it's quite common to glide quickly from one to another in the time it would take to pronounce a single vowel. This combination of vowel plus glide is called a *diphthong*. Our long vowels are actually dipthongized because we add a glide to the original tongue position. If you say the word *boat* slowly while looking in a mirror, you'll see your lips come together for the [b], become round for the [o], and then round even more for [w] as you begin to say [t]. If you speak like most Americans, you really say [bowt] rather than [bot]. Similarly, as you say *make*, the front part of the tongue moves upward to say [y] as the back part moves upward to say [k], so that you pronounce [meyk] and not [mek]. Even the [i] and [u] the highest front and back vowels, have a little glide in most words. Glides onto the [u] are interesting in that sometimes the glide actually distinguishes between words, as in boot [but] and *butte* (or *beaut*) [byut], and sometimes merely represents a difference in pronunciation habits, as in *news* [nuz] and [nyuz].

The diphthongal glides on the long vowels are ignored in a broad phonetic transcription. We have three other diphthongs that must *not* be ignored because they are part of our vowel system: the [ay] in *night*, the [aw] in *brown*, and the [ɔy] in *boy*. People pronounce these diphthongs in various ways. For some speakers, the first part of the diphthong is not [a] but [æ] in words like *night* and *brown*. Others pronounce the first part more toward the midcentral area. For some speakers, the vowel of *night* is not a diphthong at all, but a monophthong: [nat]. For some speakers, the first part of the *boy* diphthong is higher in the mouth, between [ɔ] and [o]. And there are many other subtle differences depending on the sounds that precede and follow the vowel.

At this point someone usually asks anxiously, "But what is the correct way to pronounce these sounds?" The answer is that sounds are neither correct nor incorrect—they just are. What the person is really asking is "Which pronunciation has prestige?" The answer to that question varies according to region. One simply has to listen so as to find out what gentlefolk say "around here." For a survey of the different regions of the United States, see Chapter 8, but realize that the general information there must be supplemented by personal observation.

The Phoneme

So far we've been discussing the phonetic properties of sounds; now let's move to the function of the sound as a signal. A sound considered only as a set of phonetic properties is called a *phone*. A sound considered as the smallest signal in a language system is called a *phoneme*. The function of a phoneme is to make a meaningful contrast. The phone is set off by square brackets [p], and the phoneme is set off by slashes, like this: /p/. Since all the sounds we have described except the glottal stop are phonemes of English, the difference is not obvious, but perhaps this story will help clear up the confusion: A woman carrying on an affair devised a signaling system to let her lover know when the coast was clear. She would hang either red clothes or green clothes out on the line. When she hung out green clothes, her lover would park the car around the corner and come back. When she hung out red clothes, he would drive on, knowing that her husband was at home. The husband, suspecting something because his wife was doing so much laundry, confiscated all the red clothes and locked them up. So the wife hung out pink clothes. Did the lover park the car or drive on?

Of course he drove on. Although pink is a different color from red, it contrasts well with green. So does orange. In the woman's signaling system, red, pink, and orange are all ways to signal the "coloreme" meaning "danger." Another way to define the phoneme is this: a phoneme is a sound that contrasts with other sounds in a particular language. In English, /k/ is a phoneme. We have described it as a voiceless velar stop, but that's not always true. If you pronounce *kick* and *cook* together and notice how your mouth feels, you'll find that the k's of *kick* are palatal stops, while the k's of *cook* are velars. Another variation of the /k/ phoneme involves *aspiration*, a soft additional puff of air which is articulated when the stop is released. We use aspirated /k/ in *kin* and unaspirated /k/ in skin. Just as red, pink, and orange belonged to the same coloreme in the woman's signaling system, so also the aspirated and unaspirated voiceless palatal stops and the aspirated and unaspirated voiceless velar stops all belong to the phoneme /k/ in the English signaling system. We have difficulty hearing the different *allophones* (variants) of /k/. Because the allophonic variation is not significant, we have trained ourselves to ignore it. We don't hear sounds, but rather we hear meanings through sounds.

A phone is never a phoneme in isolation, but only with respect to a particular language. In English, [r] and [l] are separate phonemes. The use of one rather than the other signals the difference between *reek* and *leek*, *rink* and *link*, *rake* and *lake*, and, for some speakers of English, between *root* [*rut*] and *loot*. But in the various Chinese languages they are members of the same phoneme, and that's why Charlie Chan says "velly solly" and "flied lice" on the Saturday reruns. Because these sounds are not contrastive units for them, the Chinese have trained themselves not to hear the difference.

In order to establish the phonemes of a language, the linguist must set up such contrastive utterances as *reek* and *leek*. Everything in the two utterances is the same except for one sound, the initial consonants in this case. The two consonants *contrast in identical environment* and thus form a *minimal pair*. The palatal stop and the velar stop are not two different phonemes in English because they do not occur in identical environments. Instead the palatal stop is used with a front vowel (as in *kick*) and the velar stop with a back vowel (as in *cook*). They are found in *complementary* environments. In practice, the field linguist uses an intuitive, guess-and-check procedure instead of hunting for minimal pairs, which can be hard to find in a language one is just learning. For example, /š/ and /ž/ are called separate phonemes in English on the basis of the minimal pair *mesher-measure*, but many of us have never heard *mesher* and would deny that it's a real word. Furthermore, there are other complications.

In English, the voiceless stops and the voiced stops are separate phonemes, since we have such minimal pairs as /pɪn/-/bɪn/, /tel/-/del/ and /kəm/-/gəm/. But, as we noted previously, many Americans do not voice their voiced stops. How, then, can the contrast be maintained? To answer the question, consider these facts:
1. The voiced stops are not aspirated in English.
2. The voiceless stops are always aspirated except when preceded by /s/ (and in a few other environments).
3. The voiced stops are never preceded by /s/.

Elementary, my dear Watson! As long as the /p/ and /b/ phonemes contrast, it makes no difference whether the contrastive feature is voicing or aspira-

tion. With this, the difference between *phonetic transcription* and *phonemic transcription* becomes clear. Phonemic transcription is not, as some people think, simply a broad phonetic transcription, but rather one based on the contrasts of the language, as follows:
Phonemic transcription: /kɪt/, /skɪt/, /gɛt/
Broad phonetic transcription: [kʰɪt], [skɪt], [kɪt]
Narrower phonetic transcription: [kʰɪtʰ] [sk̟ɪtʰ], [k̟ɪtʰ]

The broad phonetic transcription picks up the first aspiration, since it's necessary for contrast, and also records that the dialect of the speaker includes the pronunciation of "get" as "git." The narrower phonetic transcription includes the aspirations whether necessary or not, and a sign to show that the [k] is palatal rather than velar.

Larger Units of Sound

Our study of phonology thus far has shown us two aspects: the processes of articulation, which are determined by our physiology, and the patterning of these processes to form a system of phonemes. The facts of articulation are the same for all human beings all over the world; the phonemic systems show many differences. The number of phonemes in a language differs widely—from a minimum of about 13 to more than 70. English has about 36, depending on the dialect and the method of counting. Languages also differ in the way they combine phonemes into larger units. Some books say that phonemes combine into morphemes, but strictly speaking, this is not true. The morpheme is a unit of the syntactic component of the language. Phonemes belong to the phonological component, and they combine to make syllables. If you have read Chapter 2, you know that some morphemes are manifested by a single sound, such as the [s] or [z] of the noun plural, and so are less than one syllable. Other morphemes, like the word "mother," are more than one syllable. The morpheme is the smallest unit of meaning. The phoneme is not a unit of meaning, although it is a meaningful signal.

With the syllable, like the other units, there are two aspects: the physiological and the slot-and-filler patterning. The physiological basis of the syllable is the chest pulse. Air does not flow from the lungs in a steady stream, but is propelled by contractions, or pulses, of the chest muscles. Each pulse constitutes one syllable. The center, or *peak*, of the syllable is a sound that has a greater *sonority*, or audibility, than other sounds. It's usually a vowel, but occasionally nasals or liquids function as the peak of a syllable. Although these facts are the same all over the world, languages have quite different inventories of allowable syllable structures. In English a syllable may consist of any of the following:

1. a single vowel or vowel-like sound, as in *O!* or *a*-bout.
2. as many as three consonants preceding the vowel, as in spray [spre]. (If

there are three consonants, the first must be /s/, the second a voiceless stop, and the third a liquid.)
3. as many as three consonants following the vowel, as in /wants/.[6]

English does not allow a syllable to begin with /ŋ/, or with a consonant combination like /vr/. Such combinations are not impossible to say: the youngster reading a comic book or playing with his cars says "Vroom, Vroom" with no trouble at all. It's just that each language has its own pattern. Japanese, for example, does not allow a consonant after the vowel or more than one consonant before the vowel. Thus the borrowed word /bes bɔl/ is pronounced [ba su ba ru] in Japanese. English has borrowed many words beginning with unEnglish consonant combinations, such as *tzar*, *psychology*, and *ptomaine*. We Anglicize them by leaving out one sound.

Syllables are grouped into the next larger unit, the *stress group*. At intervals one syllable is spoken with a stronger chest pulse than the ones preceding and following it. Such a syllable is said to be *stressed*. In addition to using a stronger chest pulse, we stress a syllable by raising the pitch of the voice, holding the syllable a little longer than usual, and perhaps by making the vowel a little more tense. English, like other languages, has strict rules for the placement of stressed syllables—rules which are complicated for linguists to state, but easy for native speakers to follow.

The stress group gives English its particular rhythmic quality. In English we take a long time, comparatively speaking, to say the stressed syllable and then skate quickly over the unstressed syllables to get to the next stress. We take the same amount of time to say several unstressed syllables as we do to say the one stressed syllable. Consider this nursery rhyme:

TWO little MON keys JUMP ing on a BED,
ONE fell OFF and BUMPED his HEAD.
MOM my called the DOC tor and the DOC tor SAID,
HAD no BUS iness JUMP ing on the BED.[7]

Each one of these lines takes the same amount of time to say, for each one contains four *primary* stresses (shown by capitalization). The shortest line contains seven syllables (four stressed and three unstressed); the longest line contains eleven syllables (four stressed and *seven* unstressed). Yet the lines match.

Because English rhythms work this way, English is a *stressed-timed* language. Spanish, instead of being stress-timed, is *syllable-timed*. If the nursery rhyme were Spanish, then line 2 would take only two-thirds as much time to say as line 3, because there are only two-thirds as many syllables. Because of this difference in rhythm, English poetry and Spanish poetry produce quite different effects.

---

[6]Words like *glimpsed*, which might appear to have more than three consonants in the post-tonic slot /glɪmpst̪/, are simplified in pronunciation: /glɪmst̪/.
[7]Example from Robbins Burling, *Man's Many Voices: Language in Its Cultural Context* (New York: Holt, Rinehart and Winston, 1970), p. 138.

One or more stress groups make up the next larger unit, the breath group, or *intonation contour*. The phonetic basis of the breath group is that a person can't keep exhaling speech sounds forever. Sooner or later he has to breathe in. The end of a breath group is marked by certain changes in the pitch, stress, and timing of the utterance, and these are features of the intonation contour. The breath group also coincides with the end of some syntactic unit. When speaking (or singing), a person inhales quickly and exhales gradually, timing the outgo of breath so that it will last until the end of a phrase, clause, or sentence. For a linguist who's trying to analyze an unknown language, the breath groups provide the first clue to its phonological and syntactic units.

In English, if the end of the breath group is also the end of a sentence, the voice pitch rises sharply and then falls gradually over the last one or two syllables. The highest pitch comes on the stressed syllable. If the end of the breath group is not the end of a sentence, but of some other syntactic unit, there's a different but still distinctive pattern of pitch, intensity, and timing. You can observe this distinctive pattern in a radio or television taped quotation. Often the editor cuts the tape in the middle of a sentence; the result is that the quotation makes sense, but it sounds a little strange because it doesn't have the pitch pattern of a complete sentence.

Each stress group, spoken in isolation, contains a primary stress. Each intonation contour also has a primary stress. Thus, when two or more stress groups are combined into a contour, the primary stresses of all groups but one must be downgraded and the necessary adjustments made in pitch and timing also. Again, the rules for accomplishing this are exceedingly complicated when a linguist writes them out specifically, but we all obey these complex rules without a thought.

One interesting difference in languages has to do with the significance of the pitch pattern. In English, the pitch pattern is operative over a whole intonation contour. It can make the difference between a statement and a question: "You want a drink." as contrasted with "You want a drink?" (Our punctuation system hints at intonation but doesn't really record it.) In many languages, the same word, spoken with different pitches, or tones, will have quite different meanings. Languages with this feature are called *tone languages*. A Navaho student once related that his Anglo friend, proud of knowing a little of his language, intended to say, "Bring me a cup of coffee," but used the wrong tone, so that he said, "Bring me a diaper." When words in a tone language are combined into contours, the tones are adjusted accordingly, in complex patterns. No wonder the Anglo made a mistake.

In summary, the units of the phonological component of a language are as follows:
1. phones, structured as phonemes, or units of contrast;
2. chest pulses, structured as syllables;
3. stress groups, structured as phonological words or phrases;
4. breath groups, structured as intonation contours.

Phonology and Spelling

The first people to make a phonemic analysis of a language by providing it with an alphabet were the Greeks. The Phoenicians from whom the Greeks obtained the symbols wrote only consonants, because the vowels in their language were fairly predictable. Thus, their system represented a syllabic analysis rather than a phonemic one. The Greek language lacked many of the consonants found in Phoenician, so people began using the unneeded symbols to write vowels. The aleph, for example, representing the glottal stop, was used to record the low back vowel in Greek, and a true alphabet came into being.

An ideal alphabet would have a *grapheme*, or unit of spelling, for every phoneme. No language of the world has ever achieved this ideal, although several have approximated it more nearly than English. Our spelling system has been the despair of school children and the butt of jokes for two centuries. George Bernard Shaw once put together the letters *ghoti* and maintained that the word was *fish:* gh as in *laugh*, o as in *women*, and *ti* as in *nation*. Right? Wrong: *gh* never spells /f/ at the beginning of a word, and *ti* spells /š/ only when it's part of a syllable like *-tion*. Actually, our phoneme-grapheme match is pretty good for the consonants. In learning the phonetic alphabet, we have to learn only a few new consonant symbols, and for some of those we have graphemes that work quite well.

Our grapheme for the velar nasal /ŋ/ is *ng*. The fact that it doesn't have an alphabet symbol of its own, but adds *g* to *n*, reflects the fact that it's rather a marginal phoneme. We can prove that it's a phoneme by citing the minimal pair *sin-sing*, but it's an allophone of /n/ in words like drink [drɪŋk]. Also, [n] and [ŋ] occur in complementary environments inasmuch as [ŋ] never occurs at the beginning of a word or syllable. Maybe not having a separate letter for this sound makes sense after all.

The same thing is true of the *th* grapheme. Although, phonetically speaking, there are two sounds, the /θ/ and the /ð/, in most situations they function as allophones of each other. The /θ/ occurs at the ends of nouns, the /ð/ at the ends of corresponding verbs, as in *mouth, mouth; sheath, sheathe, cloth, clothe; breath, breathe*. The /θ/ occurs at the beginnings of lexical (meaningful or vocabulary) words, such as *thick, thorax, thousand*. The /ð/ occurs at the beginning of grammatical marker words such as *the, that, then, there*. It's possible to find minimal pairs which show /θ/ and /ð/ in contrast: *ether* and *either*, for example; but this is a contrast only for the people who say /iðər/ rather than /ɑyðər/. Even for them, the chances of these two words being confused is wildly improbable, since they are used in completely different contexts.

We have a grapheme for /š/—*sh*. We have no grapheme for the corresponding voiced sound, /ž/. Are they ever in contrast? One linguist has suggested the minimal pair *mesher-measure*, but again, the chances that anyone would need to contrast these two words is wildly improbable. The /ž/ sound occurs mostly in borrowed words: *genre, rouge, garage;* and many people make even these sound more "English" by substituting a /ǰ/. The suffix *-tion* or *-sion*, usually pronounced /šən/, is pronounced /žən/ in such words as *equation* and *vision*. Thus the status of /ž/ as a phoneme is weak. We're not surprised to see that the spelling system lacks a separate grapheme for it.

Although the phonemic status of other fricatives such as /f/, /v/, /s/, and /z/ is firmly established, in many cases they function as variants of each other. The alternation we pointed out of /θ/ for nouns and /ð/ for verbs holds for other fricatives also: *half-halve, wife, wive* (meaning to take a wife); *house-house* (/haws/, /hawz/). A word spelled with the voiced fricative is pronounced with the voiceless fricative in some environments, and vice versa. For example, *have* may be pronounced /hæf/ in an expression like "I hafta do it." Between two voiced sounds, such as vowels, a voiceless fricative becomes voiced: the name *Susan*, for example, is pronounced /su' zn/; *with*, pronounced quickly, becomes /wɪð/ rather than /wɪθ/.

We've just seen that the lack of an alphabetical symbol for certain consonants shows something about their importance as phonemes in the language. Certain other sounds are closely related to one another within the phonemic system of English, and these close relationships are similarly expressed in the spelling system.

One such relationship is the alternation between the voiced velar stop, /g/, and the voiced affricate /ǰ/. The spelling system reflects this relationship by calling the two sounds "hard g" and "soft g." The /ǰ/ functions as a variant of /g/ in certain positions: 1) between two voiced sounds (usually vowels), as in *region;* 2) in final position following a voiced sound, such as /larǰ/ or /barǰ/; and 3) at the beginning of a word before the graphemes *i* and *e*, as in *gene, gesture, gin, genius, gelatin*. Most of these words have come into English from Latin or French, and the graphemes *i* and *e* represent the front vowels of those languages. Thus, we see that the substitution of /ǰ/ for /g/ is environmentally conditioned—by voiced sounds or front vowels. This fact may help you distinguish between *angel* and *angle*. In *angel*, the g has to be followed by *e*, since it is pronounced /ǰ/. It will also help you remember which words are spelled *-able* and which ones *-ible*. If the word has a "hard g" sound, it must be spelled *-able*, since *-ible* would cause the g to be pronounced as /ǰ/.

A parallel relationship exists between the voiceless velar stop, /k/, and the fricative /s/. The spelling system reflects this in the familiar terms "hard c" and "soft c." In Latin the /k/ sound was normally spelled *c*. In the course of history the /k/ developed an /s/ pronunciation before the (Latin) front vowels /i/ and /e/. That's why *city* and *cent* use *c* to spell the /s/ phoneme, and *cape, code,* and *cup* use *c* to spell /k/. When English first began to be written down, the *c* of the Latin alphabet was used to express /k/, as in *cene* (keen), but the relationship between "soft c" and *i* and *e* has become so well established in people's minds that the original spelling had to be changed.

If the graphemes *g* and *c* appear at the end of a word, they have the "hard" sound—/g/ and /k/. When followed by a "silent e" they have the "soft" sound—/j/ and /s/. Compare *rag, sag, stag,* and *wag* with *rage, sage, stage,* and *wage.* The *c* in *attic* is pronounced /k/; add the "silent e," as in *lattice,* and the *c* is pronounced /s/. The silent *e* is also used this way, as we have seen, to distinguish between /θ/ and /ð/, as in *breath* and *breathe.* The silent *e* isn't very silent after all, is it?

Another important relationship is the one between /t/ or /s/ and /š/, as seen in words ending in *-tion* or *-sion*. These endings, which come into our language from Latin or Latin through French, were originally pronounced as two syllables: /ti on/, /si on/. When pronounced rapidly, the /i/ becomes a /y/-glide. Since /y/ is a palatal sound, the preceding consonant becomes "palatalized" to /š/. Thus, these suffixes are now pronounced /šən/. Since the spelling did not change when the pronunciation changed, the spelling now seems a little illogical until you get used to it. Incidentally, the high back vowels, because they are pronounced with a [y] on-glide, can also cause palatalization of /s/ or /t/, and that accounts for the relationship between spelling and pronunciation of such words as sugar /šʊg r/, sure /šʊr/ and literature /lɪt' rəčʊr/.

This discussion has shown us that many of the so-called illogicalities of English spelling are derived from the regular sound changes in the obstruent system of Latin and Latinate languages. Another source of apparent illogicality is that we have several different spelling systems competing with one another, because our language has borrowed words wholesale from other languages (and their foreign spellings). Thus, knowledge of etymology may be helpful in guessing how to spell a word. This point is discussed more fully in Chapter 2.

Turning to the vowel spellings, we find a much more difficult problem. The pronunciation of various vowel sounds differs widely from dialect to dialect, and different dialects actually have different sets of vowel contrasts (phonemes). Words which form minimal pairs in one dialect may not do so in another. The spelling system of the vowels is related to the pronunciation, but in an indirect and abstract manner.

English has more vowel phonemes than many languages. The Latin alphabet which we use has five vowel graphemes, but the English language has to spell fourteen or fifteen vowel phonemes with them. One way we solve the problem is to set up a pairing of short vowels and long vowels. All of the short vowels are phonetically short in pronunciation (i.e., lax and open). Some of the long vowels are phonetically long (tense and close), but at least "long i" and "long u" (and the others in some dialects) are phonetically diphthongs. As you can see on the chart (Fig. 4), the short vowels are usually spelled with the letter which names them. The long vowels are spelled in various ways, mostly according to the way they were pronounced at the period in history when their spelling became standardized. One of the most common ways to spell long vowels is to add a "silent e" after a single

VOWEL SPELLINGS

Spelling Item	Dict Symbol	Most Common Spellings	Common Pronun.	Variant Pronunciations
short a	a	a (cat, bad)	/æ/	/ɛ/, /ɪ/ before nasals (ex. any)
short e	e	e, but ap. 40 words sp ea as in bread	/ɛ/	/ɪ/ before nasals (ex. pen)
short i	i	i, except build, women, busy, been y in a few foreign words	/ɪ/	
short o	o	o	/ɑ/	/o/, /æ/ in some dialects, esp. before /r/
short u	u	u, except oven, love, of	/ə/	of may be /əv/
long a	ā	aCe; ai, ei inside word; ay, ey at end of word; a in open syllable (ex. fa-vor)	/e/, /ey/	
broad a	ä	a except sergeant, etc.	/ɑ/	/a/ in New Eng, as in father
long e	ē	eCe, e in open syllable (ex. Me); feet, meat, piece, receive, finally	/i/, /iy/	/ɪ/ in creek, /aɪ/ in either
long i	î	iCe, i in open syllable (fi-nal) lie, my	/ɑy/	/ay/, /æy/, /ɛy/ /ɑ/
long o	ō	oCe, on in open syl (Lo-gan) oa in closed syl (coat) oe at end of one-syllable words ow at end of word (ex. low)	/o/, /ow/	
long u	ū	uCe, u in open syl (ex. u-nite) cue, few, feud, you	/yu/, /u/	
short oo	oo	wood, look, put	/ʊ/	/e/
long oo	o͞o	fool, rude, glue, fruit, grew	/u/	
au, aw	ô	au, aw initially, au within aw finally; other two digraphs follow same principle	/ɔ/	/ɑ/
oi, oy	oi		/ɔy/	/oy/, /ay/
ou, ow	ou		/aw/	/æw/

Fig. 4

consonant, as in rap-rape, pet-Pete, bit-bite, not-note, cut-cute. The *e* (but not the other long vowels) may be doubled to show length, as in *seek*. All the long vowels can be combined with another vowel to show length. The chart shows the most common combinations.

Perhaps three-fourths of the most commonly misspelled words could be spelled correctly if we English-users would just adopt the schwa as a grapheme. It's the most common vowel sound in English, because the vowels of unstressed syllables tend to be "reduced" to schwa, no matter what letter they are spelled with. If we could use schwa, we could unhesitatingly spell *definite* as "defənət," *calendar* as "calendər," and *grammar* as "grammər." For many words, however, we would lose the advantage we presently have of being able to see at a glance what words are related in meaning. Our present spelling shows that *definite* is related to *finite*, *photograph* to *photography*, *economy* to *economical*. Since no one shows signs of adopting the schwa, our best strategy is to learn these related words together. It's easy to spell *finite*, and if we remember the connection, we can spell *definite* just as easily.

One way to show that a vowel is short rather than long is to double the consonant following the vowel. This is especially useful when adding suffixes. Study the short-long contrasts in the following examples: latter-later, betting-beating, dinning-dining, clotting-cloning, cutter-cutie. This doubling rule commonly applies only to stressed syllables. In spelling unstressed syllables, doubling the consonant is considered unnecessary, since an unstressed vowel normally becomes schwa anyhow.

In some words ending in a /k/ the grapheme *ck* is used to show that the vowel is short. This is a kind of doubling, since *c* is a way to write /k/. Thus we have *sick, trick, brick, lick*. Earlier in the history of English, people spelled *music* with the *ck*, but this was later thought to be unnecessary, since it would be unnatural to pronounce the *i* as a long vowel. For the same reason, *t* and *d* are often added to the spellings of the two affricates. Thus *itch*, with a short vowel, has a *t; each*, with a long vowel, does not. *Knowledge*, with a short vowel, has a *d; college* does not. At this point you may want to object that both these words have the same syllable—/əǰ/. You're right. Unstressed vowels, no matter how they're spelled, tend to be pronounced with a schwa. But if you then look at words derived from these two, you see a contrast between long and short vowels. *Knowledgeable* is pronounced /nɑl'əǰəbl/, but *collegiate* is /kəliǰ'ət/. Here, then, is another reason for learning to spell by associating words which have the same base.

There are many other complex sound-spelling relationships in the English system. Most of us have unconscious knowledge of these relationships, knowledge we acquired by seeing the words in print over and over, and by rote memory of the weekly spelling list in elementary school. Elementary language teachers present a few spelling rules to their students, but not many. Just as the baby constructs the phonological patterns of the language from the evidence around him, so literate people seem to construct the spelling rules. Why, then, don't we spell as well as we pronounce?

Perhaps we do. Our spelling system is the focus of a great deal of emotional energy and social control, and we require high standards of correctness. If a person mispronounces a word, nobody makes a federal case of it; but a misspelled word in a resumé can cost an applicant the job. Even the worst speller on the college level will not misspell more than twenty words in a 500-word essay, and that's a 96% accuracy—worth an A in any other subject.

Exercises

1. Articulation

1. The ordinary English [f] is a labio-dental fricative, but we often substitute a bi-labial [ɸ] after [m], as in *triumphal*. Try reciting "Fee, fie, fo, fum" from the old nursery rhyme, substituting the bi-labial fricative for the [f]. Then try alternating, using the labio-dental for one syllable and the bi-labial for the next. Have a partner try to tell which sound you are using, first face-to-face and then with the speaker's back turned.
2. Practice the nonsense phrase, "Round the rugged rock the ragged rascal ran," first using the normal English retroflex *r*, then a tongue-tip trill, and finally a uvular trill.
3. In English, all front vowels are unrounded and all back vowels are rounded. To hear what an unrounded back vowel sounds like, first pronounce the word *kook* normally. Then fix an unworried Alfred E. Neuman smile on your face and pronounce it again. Be careful not to let your lips move into a rounded position as they want to do.
4. The taco is served both north and south of the border. First order it in English: /tʰa kʰow/; then in Spanish: /ta ko/. Use the corner of a sheet of paper to make sure that you don't aspirate the stops, and avoid diphthongizing the /o/. Now order a Coca-cola to go with the taco, first with aspiration, then without.
5. Read a sentence or so of easy prose while a partner taps a pencil to mark every primary stress. Is the rhythm of the tapping more or less even, as we would expect in a stress-timed language? If it's not, why not? (Some possible explanations: the material is poorly written and has an awkward rhythm; the reader is performing in a hesitating, halting manner; the tapper is performing inaccurately; etc.)
6. Say the following sentences with different intonation patterns. Have your partner determine what the difference in meaning is.
    a. Why did you do that?
    b. He nearly died. (Also say it as a question.)
    c. Just a minute.

d. May I help you?
e. I'll do that tomorrow.

2. Reading Phonetic Transcriptions

The following words are written in phonetic symbols. Rewrite them in conventional spelling. There are some proper names, and words may be written in a dialect unfamiliar to you. Some may have more than one conventional spelling.

1. [hɪz[
2. [hɪs]
3. [hiz]
4. [rid]
5. [red]
6. [rɛd]
7. [rayd]
8. [mæǰ]
9. [blɛd]
10. [bled]
11. [bləd]
12. [blud]
13. [mæθ]
14. [spak]
15. [mak]
16. [mɔk]
17. [wel]
18. [hwel]
19. [rowd]
20. [rad]
21. [θɪn]
22. [ðɪn]
23. [čɛk]
24. [əv]
25. [ðə]
26. [ði]
27. [mæš[
28. [kəlaž']
29. [šɛf]
30. [ke'as]
31. [rɔy]
32. [maws]
33. [mays]
34. [led]
35. [lɛd]
36. [layd]

3. Making Phonetic Transcriptions

Here are some commonly misspelled words. Look at the conventional spelling carefully, and then write the word in phonetic symbols.

1. loose
2. lose
3. where
4. were
5. there
6. their
7. receive
8. relieve
9. achieve
10. grammar
11. sponsor
12. traveler
13. definite
14. psychology
15. defense
16. prophecy
17. prophesy
18. weird
19. potato
20. separate (two pronunciations)
21. among
22. category
23. benefit
24. necessary
25. opinion
26. paid
27. precede
28. proceed
29. procedure
30. quiet
31. studying
32. practical
33. writing
34. occurred
35. desirable

4. Reading Dictionary Symbols

The pronunciations of the following words are indicated by dictionary symbols. Rewrite each pronunciation in standard phonetic symbols. Also write your pronunciation of the word, if it seems radically different from the one given by the dictionary. Check your work by referring to Fig. 4.

Conventional Spelling	Dictionary Spelling	Phonetic Spelling
1. alveolar	al vē′ələr	_____
2. amateur	am′əchoor, am′ətyoor	_____
3. American	əmer′ə kən	_____
4. stanch	stônch, stanch, stänch	_____
5. angel	ān′ jəl	_____
6. angle	ang′gəl	_____
7. covet	cuv′it	_____
8. mirror	mir′ər	_____
9. mirage	mi räzh′	_____
10. butte	byo͞ot	_____
11. office	ô′ fis, of′is	_____
12. chinook	shi nook′, shi no͞ok′	_____
	chi nook′	
13. schnook	shnook	_____
14. syrup	sir′əp, sûr′əp	_____

5. Phoneme-Grapheme Relationships

George Bernard Shaw's spelling of *fish* as *ghoti* is completely unEnglish. He ignored the fact that the grapheme *gh* spells /f/ only at the ends of words, never at beginnings; that *o* spells /ɪ/ only in *women;* and that *ti* spells /š/ only within words, usually those ending in the morpheme *-tion*.

The following spellings are equally impossible. Choose the reason from the list, and then supply the normal spelling.

Phonetic Spelling	Impossible Spelling	Reason	Normal Spelling
1. /hɪuǰ/	hooge	_____	_____
2. /dɹɪǰ′əbl̩/	dirigable	_____	_____
3. /ɛks pərt/	eckspert	_____	_____
4. /kæf/	caph	_____	_____
5. /kæn/	chan	_____	_____
6. /bayk/	bic	_____	_____
7. /bayk/	bice	_____	_____
8. /kɪt′ ən/	kighten	_____	_____
9. /kway′ nayn/	choinine	_____	_____
10. /kwɔwt′ ə/	quoata	_____	_____

List of Reasons:

A. *c* followed by *e* spells /s/, not /k/.
B. *ch* spells /k/ in words derived from Greek, not native English words.
C. The English spelling system avoids three vowels in a row.
D. The *gh* suggests that the preceding vowel is long.
E. The Latin morpheme is spelled *ex*.
F. A *g* followed by *a* spells /g/, not /j/.
G. *ph* spells /f/ only in words derived from Greek, not native English words.
H. *oi* spells /way/ only in *choir* (a pseudo-etymological spelling).
I. The *oo* grapheme spells /u/ or /ʊ/, not /ɪu/.
J. Without following silent *e*, the vowel is short.

6. Phonetics and Poetry

Poets often intuitively arrange their words in interesting patterns according to phonetic features. Here's a list of poems that are probably available in your library, together with notes concerning what phonetic features to look for. Your instructor can suggest others.

1. e.e. cummings, "in Just-spring"
   Notice the use of high-front vowels and mid-central vowels for contrast and emphasis. Notice the pitch patterns also.
2. Elizabeth Bishop, "The Fish"
   Notice the high percentage of labials in the description of the fish's lip.
3. William Carlos Williams, "The Dance"
   Notice the contrasts between tense and lax (long and short) vowels on the stressed syllables.
4. Alfred, Lord Tennyson, "The Eagle"
   Notice the way stressed syllables begin with similar consonants and consonant clusters.
5. John Milton, "On the Late Massacre in Piedmont"
   Notice the use of "long o" to emphasize words and to imitate the sounds of grief.
6. Gerard Manley Hopkins, "God's Grandeur"
   Notice both vowel and consonant patterns in stressed syllables.
7. Alexander Pope, the famous passage from *Essay on Criticism* beginning "True ease in writing."
   Notice the contrast between obstruents and liquids.

Writing for Insight and Review: Processes

The description of a process is one of the most difficult, yet one of the most necessary types of writing. It's used in science to describe an experiment; in history, sociology, and economics to set forth the development of trends; and in psychology to discuss learning theory and the formation of attitudes. The discussion of articulatory processes in the first part of Chapter 3 was extremely difficult to write, and I'm still not satisfied with it. There are two sources of difficulty: first, the speech process involves movement in time, so that I needed to identify significant stages of the action; second, the different components of articulation are functioning simultaneously and affecting each other. One solution is to trace the movements of one component from beginning to end, then go back and repeat the tracing for another component. Another is to describe a stage completely and then go on to another stage. Often a writer tries to present an overall view of the process before (or after) describing various components and stages. There's no one good way to do it, and the conscientious writer resigns himself to making two or three drafts using different methods. The first drafts clarify the process for the writer himself and enable him to produce a final draft which will actually be useful to a reader.

Practice writing process paragraphs. Here are some projects that will provide a review of the chapter at the same time.

A. Say the following phrases several times and notice exactly what happens to the jaw, tongue, and lips. Then write a paragraph explaining the articulatory process of one of the phrases:
1. neat car
2. cool weather
3. Molly Brown
4. yeah, man!

B. If you have studied a foreign language, write a paragraph explaining how to produce one of the sounds of that language that isn't found in English. If you haven't studied a foreign language, write a paragraph giving a foreign student directions for pronouncing the following sounds: /θ/, /ð/, /f/, /v/. Assume that the foreign student's language has /t/, /d/, /p/, and /b/, pronounced like the English sounds.

C. Use writing to help you master the information from another course: write a description of a chemical, biological, or geological process; of a sociological, psychological, or political phenomenon; of a procedure you have studied in an educational methods class; of how to perform a certain technique on a musical instrument.

4

What Petey Forgot

Along with the breakfast food commercials on Saturday morning there is, or was, a commercial break called "Grammar Rock." With smooth lyrics and humorous cartoons, it tries to indoctrinate the Bugs Bunny set with the slogan, "A noun is the name of a person, place, or thing." What the young viewers are supposed to do with this information is never made clear, but apparently it's important. I knew a sixth grade teacher who used to spend quite some time in conversations like this:

Teacher: Petey, a noun is the name of a person, place or thing.
Petey remains silent.
Teacher, encouragingly: Petey, what's a noun?
Petey, after a long pause: I done forgot.

This definition of a noun and seven other such definitions make up a body of wisdom called "the parts of speech." It's a traditional part of childhood, like spelling and orthodontia. Most people resist learning them, though perhaps not as stubbornly as Petey did.

Petey's resistance, however, was perfectly justified: the whole complex mechanism of language works best when we're unaware of what we're doing. We resist analyzing the parts of speech because doing so makes the easy matter of talking seem strange and difficult. The person who wrote "Please engage brain before putting mouth in motion" just didn't understand how important it is for language to be automatic.

We also resist studying the parts of speech because there seems to be no security in them. The "right answer" changes mysteriously. The following sentences, for example, show that the word *down* can be used as five different parts of speech:

Noun: Life has its little ups and *downs*.
Verb: He can *down* more beer than any other man in his club.

Adjective: She was depressed when she received her *down* notices, because she hadn't realized that her grades were *down*.
Adverb: Jump *down*, now.
Preposition: Little Red Riding Hood ran *down* the path.
It's no wonder that Petey "done forgot."

Nevertheless, being able to name parts of speech does have value, as we find when we begin to acquire a second language. In English we say "tomato sauce," but French reverses the order: "sauce tomate." If we know such terminology as "adjective," "noun," and "attributive" we can formulate this difference very simply and learn it once and for all. (At least some of the traditional part-of-speech names are used for every language of the world.) In fact, it's easier to learn the parts of speech for a foreign language than it is for English because we lack the automatic, "natural" ability to use the foreign language. This is the reason you sometimes hear people say, "I never understood English grammar until I took French (or German, or Arabic, or Japanese)."

If a person doesn't plan to learn a foreign language, then, why bother with the parts of speech? Why not just leave well enough alone?

First, one goal of linguistic study is to understand language competence—what people know about their language. Apparently one thing we all know intuitively is a rough classification of our lexicon into parts of speech. Second, English is a world language with a complex history and a sophisticated literature. It consists of much more than the routine phrases and sentences with which we conduct our daily affairs. In attaining this broader understanding, a knowledge of terminology is helpful, if not absolutely essential. In this chapter we'll discuss how English words are classified into parts of speech and the way these parts are combined into phrases. In Chapter 5 we'll look at the way phrases are related to larger units called sentences and clauses.

If part-of-speech classifications are to be useful in describing sentence structures, the words must be classified on the basis of *syntax* (arrangement) rather than *semantics* (meaning). In classifying anything into categories, you get different groups if you use different criteria. If you classify the members of your class on the basis of sex, you'll get one grouping; if you classify them on the basis of whether they live on-campus or off-campus or whether they pay in-state or out-of-state tuition, you'll get entirely different groupings. The same thing is true of linguistic classifications. If we classify *no, not, un-,* and *-less* on the basis of semantics, they all belong in the same category because they all have a negative meaning; but if we classify them on the basis of syntax, they all belong in different categories because they fit in different arrangements. *No* goes with nouns, as in "No solicitors"; *not* goes in groups like "not at home" and "could not see"; *un-* is a prefix, *-less* a suffix.

Much of the difficulty in learning part-of-speech categories comes be-

cause textbooks do not always emphasize sufficiently the distinction between syntax and semantics. There is some correlation between meaning and syntactic class, but the relationship is unreliable. Petey once said that *run* is a verb in the sentence "Robin hit a home run" because he had learned the definition, "A verb is an action word." Semantically, *run* is certainly an action, but in that sentence the syntactic pattern makes it a noun. Likewise, two words can belong to the same syntactic category but not the same semantic category. Consider these sentences:
1. The child *hits* the new kid on the block.
2. The child *knows* the new kid on the block.

Syntactically both "hits" and "knows" are verbs, but "hits" is an action word while "knows" is not, except in a very figurative sense.

Besides the difficulties caused by the confusion between syntax and semantics, there are difficulties caused by the unnecessary assumption that there are eight and only eight parts of speech. The ancient Romans first classified their words into three categories: (1) those which change form to show number and case; (2) those which change form to show person and tense; and (3) those which do not change form. Class 1 included what we today would call nouns, pronouns, adjectives, and participles; Class 2 included verbs; and Class 3 included prepositions, adverbs, conjunctions, and interjections. During the Middle Ages the number of parts of speech for Latin—no other languages were being analyzed—varied between seven and ten. Finally, one medieval grammarian asserted that eight was the proper number because there were eight kinds of clergy in the Church.[1] (This reason is just as sensible as many of the rules Petey failed to learn.)

To have eight parts of speech works pretty well for Latin and languages like Latin, but when linguists began to work on American Indian, African, and Oriental languages, new parts of speech had to be defined and named. For example, in Thai an important unit of syntax is the classifier, a word which comes before a noun and tells what kind of noun it is. English has something like classifiers in phrases like "a *pair* of pants," "a *game* of tennis," and "twenty *head* of cattle," but we analyze them as nouns rather than classifiers because of the way they fit into our noun phrase pattern.

How many parts of speech are necessary for English? More than eight, certainly. The traditional class of adverbs needs to be broken up because it contains such a wide variety of words: descriptive words like "slowly," the negator "not," intensifiers like "really," "hardly," and "almost," and transition words like "however," "thus," and "therefore." The traditional class of pronouns also contains a wide variety of words: personal pronouns like "I" and "we," pointers like "this" and "that," and question words like "who" and "which."

---

[1] Karl W. Dykema, "Where Our Grammar Came From," *College English* 22 (1961), 455–65. In *Language: Introductory Readings*, ed. Virginia P. Clark, Paul A. Eschholz and Alfred F. Rosa, 2nd ed. (New York: St. Martin's Press, 1977), p. 281.

In an ideal situation, all the words of one class would fill the same slot and have the same inflectional and derivational forms. But human languages are never ideal, and English is especially hard to classify. Because we have so few inflections, we're able to use a noun as a verb or an adjective (or any other combination of those three categories). It becomes the new part of speech just by the place it occupies in the sentence. Because the language has changed so much over the centuries, even members of the same category do not behave alike. Thus "we" is used for subjects and "us" for objects, but "you" is the correct form for both subjects and objects. And some words—"that" for example—have so many functions that they have to be classified several ways.

Although it's confusing to have too many different types of words in one class, it's equally confusing to make unnecessary distinctions. For example, in describing English it's not necessary to have separate parts of speech for abstract and concrete nouns because the two types of words occur in the same patterns. We say, "I admire her *determination*" (abstract noun) or "I admire her *garden*" (concrete noun).

One of the most successful efforts to get away from the traditional eight parts of speech was made by linguist C. C. Fries (rhymes with *freeze*) in the 1930s. Fries ended up with nineteen classifications, but he called only four of them "parts of speech." The other fifteen were structure words, words that communicate how the sentence units are related. To emphasize the freshness of his analysis and get away from traditional associations, Fries numbered his parts of speech as Classes 1 through 4 and lettered his structure words as Groups A through O. Theoretically it doesn't matter what a class of words is called as long as the definition is clear, but in practice we find grammar easier to tolerate when the names are familiar. So we'll use Fries's definition of the "Class 1 Word," but call such words "nouns."

The four parts of speech which Fries defined coincide pretty well with what we might call nouns, main verbs, adjectives, and descriptive adverbs. These are the content words of our language. They're also called the *open* classes because the new words we add to our vocabulary always belong to one of these classes. The noun class is the most open one. We're constantly inventing or discovering new things, and of course they have to have names. The verb class is less open than the noun class, but, as Chapter 2 shows, we make new verbs freely by adding verb suffixes such as *-ify* or *-ize*. Adjectives and adverbs are somewhat less open than the verb class, but occasionally we find a new adjective like *humongous*, and almost any noun can become an adverb by the addition of the suffix *-wise*.

The open classes are also called *form classes*, because all of them have inflectional forms. The nouns change form by adding *s* to show plural and possessive. The verbs change form to show tense, as in start-starts-started-starting. Some adjectives and adverbs change form by adding *-er* and *-est*, as in sweet-sweeter-sweetest, although many of them use "more" or "most" instead. Many members of the form classes can also be recognized by their

COMPARISON OF PART-OF-SPEECH CATEGORIES

Traditionally Defined	Syntactically Defined
NOUN—the name of a person, place, or thing.	NOUN—recognized by plural inflection, derivational affixes, determiners
VERB—a word that shows action or state of being.	VERB—recognized by tense inflection, derivational affixes, auxiliaries
ADJECTIVE—a word that modifies a noun.	ADJECTIVE—recognized by comparison inflection, derivational affixes, ability to fit this slot: It was very _____.
ADVERB—a word that modifies a verb, adjective, or another adverb.	ADVERB—same comparison inflections as adjective, different derivational affixes. Fits slot in verb phrase; never modifies adjective or adverb.
PRONOUN—a word that takes the place of a noun. Personal—I, mine, me, etc.	PERSONAL PRONOUN—Occupies a noun phrase slot.
Demonstrative—this, that, these, those	DEMONSTRATIVE—Same list. Also classed with determiners.
Indefinite—one, someone, nothing, none, etc.	INDEFINITE—inflected for possessive like nouns; otherwise patterns like personal pronouns.
Relative: who, whose, whom, which what, that	RELATIVE—Same.
Interrogatives—who, whose, whom, what, which	QUESTION WORD—introduces questions and noun clauses. Same list plus where, when, why, how.
PREPOSITION—a word that shows the relationship between a noun and the rest of the sentence.	PREPOSITION— defined by slot, distribution.
CONJUNCTION—a word that joins two parts of a sentence. Types: Coordinating—and, but, etc.	COORDINATOR—Same list.
Subordinating—words like if, because, after; also relative and interrogative pronouns.	SUBORDINATOR—words like if, because, after; relatives, question words not always included.
INTERJECTION—a word that shows strong feeling.	Not listed, since the word has no syntactic relationship to the rest of the sentence.

Comparison of Part-of-Speech Categories (cont.)

Traditionally Defined	Syntactically Defined
Classified with adjectives or pronouns.	DETERMINER—defined by position in noun phrase.
Classified with adverbs.	INTENSIFIER—precedes adjectives, adverbs; may occur within verb phrase; not inflected like adverbs.
Classified with verbs.	AUXILIARY—occurs in VP's according to a definite formula.
Classified with adverbs; sometimes called "conjunctive adverbs."	TRANSITION WORD—occurs at beginning or parenthetically within clause; discourse-level connectives; examples: thus, therefore, then, furthermore, consequently, however.

Fig. 5

derivational affixes, such as *-tion* for nouns, *-ify* for verbs, *-ous* for adjectives and *-ly* for adverbs. Thus the four biggest classes of words—nouns, verbs, adjectives, and adverbs—may be referred to as the content words, the open classes, or the form classes.

Fries defined fifteen classes of structure words. Some of these, such as "well," the sentence opener, seemed of marginal usefulness to later analysts, so that Fig. 5 shows only twelve structure classes.

Another good name for the structure words is syntactic markers, because they signal what syntactic category the content words belong to. For example, it's impossible to know whether "run" is a noun or verb in isolation. But if it's preceded by "the" in "the run," we know it's a noun. If it's preceded by "will" in "will run," we know it's a verb. Structure words also signal the relationships of larger units of syntax, as in the sentence, "*While* I am gone, don't run *after* other women." "While" and "after" introduce important groups of content words. The structure words do not have inflections or derivational affixes. Thus, the only syntactic basis for classifying them is *distribution*—what slot they fit into. As Fig. 6 shows, many of them can fit into a number of slots, so that all classifications of them are somewhat confusing.

The classes of structure words are all *closed* classes, because we seldom add any new ones to the language. Although some advocates of women's liberation have tried to create a new non-gendered pronoun to replace *he* and *she*, the various suggestions have been slow in catching on. Instead, people who wish to avoid specifying sex use a pronoun we already have, *they*, to mean "he or she." "They" was a new addition to the language in the Mid-

DISTRIBUTION OF RELATIVES AND QUESTION WORDS

Words	Determiner	Pronoun (NP Slot)	Relative (in Adj. Cl.)	Introducing Noun Cl.	Subordinator (Adv. Cl.)	Question
who, whom		✓	✓	unusual		✓
whose	✓		✓	unusual		✓
which	✓	✓	✓	unusual		✓
what	✓	✓		✓		✓
that	✓	✓	✓	✓	in phrase "so that"	
when			✓	✓	✓	✓
where			✓	✓		✓
why			✓	✓		✓
how				✓		✓

Fig. 6

dle English period, borrowed from Scandinavian. And lately I've noticed people using "plus" as a conjunction instead of "and." So it is possible to add to the closed classes.

Thus, various names for these small classes of words are structure words, the closed classes, and syntactic markers. They are also called *function words* in some texts because they are classified according to function—i.e., the slot they fill.

Some of the structure words have traditionally been put into one of the large open classes. For example, noun markers like *a* and *the* were classified with the adjectives, or described as "a special kind of adjective, the article." To make a strict separation of the open classes from the closed classes clarifies the way English syntactic structure actually works.

Comparing the Classifications

Noun

   Traditional: A noun is the name of a person, place, or thing.
   Syntactic: A noun can be recognized by these characteristics:
   1. inflection for *plural* and *possessive*
   2. derivational affixes: -ness, -ment, -hood, -ation, -ship, -ity, -ism, -ist, -er, -ee, -ance
   3. the headword of a noun phrase
   4. may be preceded by a determiner

Since the traditional definition of a noun is based on meaning, it's necessary to know the meaning of a word in order to classify it as a noun. With the syntactic approach, one can be sure that "toves" in Lewis Carroll's "the slithy toves" is a noun by the determiner and the plural inflection, without having the slightest idea what a tove is. The traditional definition also fails to identify as nouns such words as "poor" in "The poor you always have with you" and "run" in "He scored a home run." "Poor" is, according to the definition, an adjective rather than a person, and "run" is an action (verb).

The syntactic classification also has its problems. Words like "scissors" and "tennis" have no plural inflections, and apparently no inflection for possessive. Should they still be called nouns? Most of us would vote yes, since either one can be a headword in a noun phrase, but at least one textbook votes no.

Verb

Traditional: A verb is a word that expresses action or state of being.
Syntactic: A verb can be recognized by these characteristics:
   1. inflection for *tense*
   2. derivational prefixes and suffixes such as be-, for-, fore-, em-, in-, re-, -ify, -ize, en, -ate, etc.
   3. the headword, or main verb, in a verb phrase
   4. may be preceded by one or more auxiliaries as structure words

Again, the traditional definition of the verb is based on meaning, while the syntactic definition allows one to recognize a verb without knowing what it means. The only problem with this category has to do with the auxiliaries, words such as "will," "can," "am," and "do." The traditional approach merely distinguishes them as "helping verbs." The syntactic approach puts them in a category of their own, but this isn't entirely satisfactory. Occasionally a sentence comes up in which one of them is the main verb: for example, Popeye's "I am what I am and that's all I am" and "She cans peaches every year." With "can," the meaning is so different that the main verb "can" and the auxiliary "can" probably ought to be considered homonyms, but there's no such clear difference between Popeye's use of "am" as a main verb and its use as an auxiliary.

Adjective

Traditional: An adjective is a word that modifies a noun.
Syntactic: An adjective can be recognized by these characteristics:
   1. inflection for *comparison* by the use of *-er* and *-est,* or *more* and *most*
   2. derivational affixes such as -ful, -less, -ly, -y, -like, -ish, -esque, -able, -some, -ic, -ical, -al, -ive, -ous, etc.
   3. fits between determiner and noun in a noun phrase
   4. can be a predicate adjective in a sentence like this:
      The thing was very _____ .

Although the traditional definitions classify nouns and verbs by meaning, with adjectives the basis of classification switches to *function*—what the adjective does. Also, the traditional approach cannot differentiate between descriptive adjectives and determiners. Articles, for example, are often mentioned as "a special kind of adjective." The syntactic approach has a minor problem with adjectives that cannot be compared, such as "pregnant." (It makes no sense to say "more pregnant" or "most pregnant.") However, the syntactic pattern is so dominant in people's minds that many "uncomparable" adjectives are compared. The preamble to the U.S. Constitution calls for "a more perfect union" and we hear people say that a tourist attraction is "one of the most unique," even though "unique" means "one of a kind" and therefore logically can have no comparison. Despite these problems, there's no major difference in results between the traditional and the syntactic approaches.

Adverb

Traditional: An adverb is a word that modifies a verb, adjective, or another adverb.

Syntactic: An adverb can be recognized by these characteristics:
1. inflection for *comparison* by the use of *-er* and *-est* or *more* and *most*
2. derivational affixes such as -ly, -ward, -wise, -fashion, -style, a-, etc.
3. movability: the adverb can be placed in or near the verb phrase, at the beginning of the sentence, or at the end.

It's in dealing with the adverb that the traditional and the syntactic approaches are most at odds. The syntactic approach identifies as adverbs only those words that modify the verb phrase. The words that modify "verbs, adjectives, and other adverbs" are, according to the newer system, *intensifiers* (sometimes called *qualifiers*). The intensifier changes the intensity with which a statement is made, as in "The hand of the artist is particularly adept." The syntactic approach puts intensifiers in a separate class because they lack the movability of the open-class adverbs. On the other hand, the traditional approach has something in its favor: some words can be used both as intensifiers and as open-class adverbs. "Particularly," for example, can mean "in a fussy manner," as in "He examined the tomatoes *particularly*, turning each one over and over."

The characteristics of the open classes are summarized in Fig. 7.

Pronoun

Traditional: A pronoun is a word that takes the place of a noun.
Syntactic: The *personal* pronouns are a small class of words inflected for person, gender, number, and case that can occupy a noun phrase slot. Other

THE OPEN CLASSES

Inflectional Forms	Derivational Affixes	Positions	Structure Words
NOUNS Plural: -s Possession: -'s, -'	-ness, -ment, -y, -hood, -ation, -ship, -ity, -ism, -ist, -er, -ance, -ee, -dom, -ure	Head word in Noun Phr.	Determiners
VERBS Pres: walk, walks see, sees Past: walked saw ing Participle: walking, seeing Past Participle: walked, seen	be-, for-, fore-, em-, in-, re-, -ify, -ize, -en, -ate	Head word in Verb Phr.	Auxiliaries
ADJECTIVES Positive: ∅ Comparative: -er Superlative: -est	-ful, -less, -ly, -y, -al, -like, -ish, -esque, -ic, -able, -some, -ical, -ive, -ous	1. Between det., noun in noun phrase 2. After Be-verb as predicative adjective 3. As post-modifier (rare)	Intensifiers
ADVERBS Same as adjectives	-ly, -ward(s), -wise, -fashion, -style	1. Within verb phrase 2. Beginning or end of clause	Intensifiers

Fig. 7

types of words traditionally called pronouns should be put in other categories.

To say that the personal pronouns are inflected does not mean that they add endings, as nouns and verbs do. Instead, they change form completely. Also, they have changed over the centuries, so that the inventory of inflections is not complete. The differentiations of *person* have to do with viewpoint. First person is the speaker (I, we), second person the person spoken to (you), and third person the person(s) spoken about (he, she, it, they). Some languages have additional distinctions in person, such as first person inclusive (speaker and hearers) and first person exclusive (speaker only). In all its history English has never had inclusive/exclusive distinctions in pronouns. The differentiation of *gender* is, in English, a matter of sex, and it's made only in the third person (he, she, it). In Arabic, there are gender distinctions in first and second persons also. *Number* is the distinction between singular and plural. It's made in all the personal pronouns except the second person. *Case* is the distinction between subjects, possessives, and objects, such as I, my, me, and he, his, him.

The words other than personal pronouns which are traditionally called pronouns are put into categories of their own when a syntactic basis of classification is used. No classification is entirely satisfactory.

For example, the *indefinites* (words like "one," "someone," "somebody," "anything," etc.) are like pronouns in that they sometimes "take the place" of a noun phrase. But they form possessives like nouns: somebody, somebody's. They can also appear in a typical noun phrase with a determiner and adjective, as in "the lonely one." (See the discussion of noun phrase structure further along in the chapter.) Thus the traditional approach of calling them pronouns has some validity, but they act a lot like nouns.

The *demonstratives* (this, that, these, those) are traditionally called pronouns, and they "take the place" of a noun phrase in such sentences as "*This* is my kind of place." But they also fill the same slot as words like *a* and *the*, which is a justification for putting them in a class of their own.

The *relatives* (who, which, what, that) are so called because they relate one part of a sentence to another, as in "I saw the child *who* stole the magazine." This group overlaps with a category of *question words*. All of the relatives except *that* can be used to introduce a question. In addition, there are some question words that cannot fill a noun phrase slot as the relatives do. Fig. 6 shows the various functions these words can have. In "*Who* stole the magazine?" "who" is a pronoun because it fills the noun phrase slot, but it's a question word because it introduces a question. How did our language get into such a mess?

Preposition

Traditional: A preposition is a word that shows the relationship between a noun and the rest of the sentence.

Syntactic: Prepositions are words like *of, in,* and *to* which are usually followed by a noun phrase called the object of the preposition.

The two approaches to classification here result in exactly the same list of words. The traditional approach defines the preposition (as it does the adjective and adverb) by *function.* The syntactic approach defines it by *distribution.* All the words that fit into the same slot in a particular sentence make up a distribution class. For example, in the sentence, "The clue to the murderer's identity was _____ the desk," the list of words that can fill the blank include "in," "on," "inside," "within," "outside," "under," etc. They're all prepositions. They're also related semantically, since all express some kind of physical position, although the early attempts to classify parts of speech syntactically tried to ignore semantics. This was a practical policy, since a word like "with" would not fit the slot only because of the noun's meaning. Change it to "The clue to the murderer's identity was_____ the other papers," and additional words like "with," "between," and "among" are revealed as prepositions.

The big problem of classification—one that nobody can make easy—is that many words belong to three distribution classes. They not only appear in the preposition slot before a noun phrase, but also as conjunctions to introduce a clause or as adverbs modifying a verb. Consider the word "after." In "The baby bear scampered *after* its mother," the word fills the same slot as other prepositions such as *before, with, to.* In "*After* the bears had left, we began to assess the damage to our camp," it fills the same slot as other conjunctions such as *when, although,* and *since.* In "The mother bear left, and the baby followed *after,*" it fills the same slot as other adverbs such as *quickly, clumsily,* and *immediately.* If the three lists of words coincided completely, we would have only one classification, but they don't. Thus, the categories cannot be neat and logical, for the structure of the language isn't.

Also, classifications may change as the language changes. In addition to introducing the prepositional phrase, certain prepositions are used more and more to complete or intensify the meanings of verbs. For example, we say that someone will "head up" a committee, "finish up" a task, "do in" an enemy, or "pig out" at the pizza parlor. Not all prepositions are used in this way. "In," "out," "up," and "down" are the most common. Perhaps in the future, linguists analyzing the English language will feel that these words should be put in a class of their own, since their distribution into syntactic patterns is so different from that of other prepositions.

Conjunction

Traditional: a word that joins words or groups of words.

Syntactic: Since classification is made on the basis of distribution, the traditional conjunction becomes two separate categories: *coordinators*—that is, joiners of syntactically equal elements—and *subordinators,* joiners of unequal elements. The distinction is somewhat confusing because a number of

coordinators and subordinators are almost identical in meaning. *But,* for example, is a coordinator and *although* is a subordinator. They have about the same meaning (and even the same position) in the following sentences:
1. They gave a concert in Reno last year, *but* I didn't attend.
2. They gave a concert in Reno last year, *although* I didn't attend.

The distribution is different, however, in that *although* can introduce the first clause in the sentence while *but* can't:
1. **But* I didn't attend, they gave a concert in Reno last year.
2. *Although* I didn't attend, they gave a concert in Reno last year.

(The asterisk shows that the first sentence is ungrammatical.) Another difference in distribution is that *but* can be used to introduce a single clause and relate it to the rest of the paragraph. *Although* can't be used in this way:
1. *But* I didn't attend. (complete sentence)
2. **Although* I didn't attend. (sentence fragment)

In the first example, *but* is apparently being used as a sentence adverb (see explanation below) rather than as a conjunction. Since *although* can't be used this way, the two words differ in distribution. Why? As the bureaucrat said

JOINING WORDS

Coordinators	Subordinators (can begin sentence)	Transition Words
And but or for so	Time: after, before, since, when, until, as soon as	Time: then
	Concessive: although, even though, while	Concessive: however, still, nevertheless
	Cause or reason: since because, as, so that	Cause or reason: thus, therefore, consequently as a result
	Purpose: in order that, so that, that, that . . . not	
	Comparison: as, as if, as though, as . . . as, so . . . that	Comparison: instead
	Universal conditions: whether, whatever, wherever, etc.	
		Additive: furthermore, moreover

Fig. 8

to the citizen, "There's no reason for it—it's just our policy." See Fig. 8 for a list of joining words most often used as coordinators, subordinators, and sentence adverbs.

Interjection

Traditional: a word that shows strong feeling.

Syntactic: If language is being analyzed syntactically, the interjection is ignored, since it stands by itself, never combining with other words to make phrases. It doesn't really fill a slot, so analysts have no interest in it.

Determiner

Traditional: no definition; all these words are classed with adjectives or pronouns.

Syntactic: Determiners are words that can be substituted for *the*, or that fill the same slot as *the*.

The determiner is an important structure word in English, because it enables us to turn any word into a noun. For this reason it's sometimes called a *noun indicator,* but in some ways that's an unsatisfactory classification. Only the articles, *a, an,* and *the,* invariably fill the determiner slot. Other determiners simultaneously belong to other classifications, such as demonstratives (*that* book, *That* is silly), question words (*What* amount would you accept?), and possessive nouns (*Jerry's* bike is broken) or pronouns (*My* phone bill is too high). Despite the remaining classification problems, it has been an improvement to take them out of the adjective class.

Intensifier

These are the words which, in the traditional definition, modify "verbs, adjectives, or other adverbs." The open-class adverb modifies only verbs, or perhaps the sentence as a whole. The words that can modify adjectives or other adverbs are the intensifiers, and their syntactic function is quite different from that of open-class adverbs. The most common intensifiers are *more, most, very, pretty, rather, really, fairly, somewhat, too, quite, less, least, hardly, scarcely.* See the previous discussion of adverbs for additional comments on intensifiers.

Auxiliary

In traditional grammar, these are classified with the verbs, but their function in the verb phrase is quite different from that of the open-class verbs. Open-class verbs are always the headword, or main verb, of the verb phrase; auxiliaries are the "helping verbs." See the heading "The Verb Phrase" below for a fuller discussion of the auxiliaries.

Transition Word

Another name for these is *conjunctive adverbs*. They appear within a sentence but they don't modify the verb or whole sentence as an adverb does, and they don't join one part of the sentence to another as a conjunction does. Instead, they join sentences to other sentences or even paragraphs. Some examples of transition words are *thus, therefore, nevertheless, furthermore, consequently, however, still, moreover, as a result, then,* and *instead*.

As this comparison of traditional and syntactic classifications has shown, there's nothing sacred about any particular analysis of language. Traditional classification is useful because it provides a rough-and-ready tool for the native speaker to use in handling many language problems. Most dictionaries use the traditional terminology as set forth here, although the *Oxford English Dictionary* follows an even older tradition by recognizing one class, the noun, and then further dividing it into *substantives* and *adjectives*, so that you may see references to "noun substantives" and "noun adjectives." Syntactic classification is useful because it helps us focus on the grammatical machinery of English—features like the determiner, the auxiliary, and the transition word—which we might otherwise ignore. For a closer look at that language machinery we'll now examine the structure of phrases.

The Noun Phrase

The easiest way to recognize the noun phrase is to look for three slots: determiner, adjective, and noun: *the sneaky snake*. Each of the words is the filler of a different slot, and each filler has the same distribution (pattern of occurrence) as the other words which can fill that slot. We can think of the slot as a point of choice and the different fillers as the list of choices for that slot. In the adjective slot, we can choose "slimy," "scaly," "green," or "little." In the noun slot we can choose "grasshopper," "ocelot," or "professor," or any number of words. (Remember that both adjective and noun are open classes.) The determiner class includes *a, this, no, which, my, John's,* and *each*. Any one of these can substitute for *the* in the typical noun phrase.

The syntactic pattern for the noun phrase may be stated, for convenience, in an algebra-like formula. Since the noun phrase pattern consists of determiner, adjective, and noun, the formula is as follows:

NP = Det + Adj + N

The formula says that there are three slots in the noun phrase and specifies the part-of-speech category for the fillers of each slot. The formula is a first effort to understand the patterns of the English language. If we're unable to apply this pattern to a sample of the language, it doesn't mean that the writer or speaker is using language wrongly. Instead, it means that the formula is somehow wrong or incomplete. We can test the formula by applying it to a passage of ordinary English prose:

The recent evolution of man certainly begins with the advancing development of the hand, and the selection for a brain which is particularly adept at manipulating the hand. We feel the pleasure of that in our actions, so that for the artist the hand remains a major symbol: the hand of Buddha, for instance, giving man the gift of humanity in a gesture of calm, the gift of fearlessness.[2]

The recent evolution, the advancing development, and *a major symbol* fit the formula precisely. But we also want to call *selection* and *fearlessness* nouns, since they have typical noun suffixes, *-tion* and *-ness*. Since the formula is intended to state what English-speaking people do when they produce a noun phrase, rather than what they "should" do, we revise it to show that the adjective is not always present, as in *the selection,* and that the determiner also is not always present, as in *fearlessness.* We can use parentheses to mean "optional slot." "The formula becomes: NP = (Det) (Adj) N. Now we're able to identify as noun phrases *man, the hand, the selection, a brain, the pleasure, our actions, the artist, Buddha, the gift, humanity, a gesture, calm,* and *fearlessness.* Since the noun slot is the only one in the NP which must be filled, the noun is called "the *headword* of the noun phrase."

There's another type of noun phrase in the passage which the formula doesn't cover. *We* in the second sentence and *which* in the first sentence are both called noun phrases because they fill a noun phrase slot in a higher level of syntax, the clause. (Clauses are discussed in Chapter 5.) Both these words belong to the class traditionally called the *pronoun.* We can correct the formula to include the pronoun as follows:

NP = (Det) (Adj) N
or
Pro

As it stands, the formula still fails to deal with compound structures like "the quiet, well-mannered girls and boys" and noun phrases containing different kinds of determiners like "all the many annoyances." We could set up a formula to cover these structures also, but it's more practical to use an oversimplified formula while remaining aware of its limitations. After all, the oversimplified formula does apply to the majority of noun phrases.

Much of Petey's discouragement with English syntax came from trying to analyze sentences with oversimplified formulas and categories, and then assuming that he was a failure because the analysis failed. We can avoid such discouragement by constantly remembering that we are using an inadequate formula.

---

[2]Jacob Bronowski, *The Ascent of Man* (Boston: Little, Brown, 1973).

The Prepositional Phrase

Now that we have the noun phrase pattern, the formula for the second basic pattern, the prepositional phrase, is easy:
PrepPh = Prep + NP

The preposition slot is filled by a small group of words that all have original meanings of space relationships. Some examples of prepositions and their space relationships are as follows:
1. The runner walked *to* the starting line.
2. The cake is *in* the oven.
3. The book is *by* the vase.

Since we think of time as a sort of pseudo-space, it's natural to use prepositions to express time relationships:
1. The class meets from eleven *to* twelve.
2. The secretary can type five pages *in* an hour.
3. I expect the boss to arrive *by* four o'clock.

By extending the meanings of the prepositions still further, we can use them to express many other relationships, some of them quite surprising:
1. I gave the plant *to* Mary. (*To* shows that Mary is the receiver.)
2. Alphonse is *in* business for himself. (*In* introduces Alphonse's activity.)
3. The best ad presentation was created *by* Rhoda. (*By* shows that Rhoda is the doer, or agent.)

If you ever find yourself with some thumb-twiddling time, you might look up one of the prepositions in the dictionary. The great range of meanings will astonish you, and you can derive a certain sly satisfaction out of seeing what a hard time the dictionary-makers have in writing definitions for such a "simple" word. You will also see the futility of trying to define the preposition as a part of speech on the basis of semantics.

Here's the same prose passage with the prepositions italicized:
The recent evolution *of* man certainly begins *with* the advancing development *of* the hand, and the selection *for* a brain which is particularly adept *at* manipulating the hand. We feel the pleasure *of* that *in* our actions, so that *for* the artist the hand remains a major symbol: the hand *of* Buddha, *for* instance, giving man the gift *of* humanity *in* a gesture *of* calm, the gift *of* fearlessness.

The passage contains five prepositions; and some of them are repeated, so that there are actually 14 prepositions in all. Each preposition is followed by a noun phrase. (The construction, "at manipulating the hand," which seems to be an exception, will be discussed later.) Notice that the prepositional phrases tend to be attached to the word that comes immediately before them in two ways:
1. Semantically: they complete, specify, or add to the meaning of the

preceding word. For example, *of man* specifies what creature is evolving with respect to the noun *evolution*.
2. Phonologically: they are attached to the preceding word by the melody and rhythm of your voice when you read the sentence naturally.

Thus *the recent evolution of man* hangs together as a semantic and phonological unit. Furthermore, we can replace these five words with *it* and say "*It* certainly begins . . ." Since *the recent evolution of man* is a unit of some sort, and since it contains a phrase *(of man)* not mentioned in the formula, we must either find a new name for it or revise the noun phrase formula. When we study clause-level units (in Chapter 5), we find that either *the recent evolution* or *the recent evolution of man* can appear in the same clause-level slot, indicating that these two word groups belong to the same unit category. Therefore, it will make sense to revise the noun phrase formula to account for both. The following seems logical: NP = (Det) (Adj.) N (PrepPh). However, the language unit after the noun is not always a prepositional phrase. Sometimes it's a unit like this: *which we have studied*, as in *the recent evolution which we have studied*. Therefore, we need a more general term for the unit after the noun. One common name is *post-modifier*. The revised noun phrase formula, then, is this:

NP = (Det) (Adj.) N (Post-Mod.)

The noun of any prepositional phrase may have its own post-modifier, and the headword in that post-modifier may have its own post-modifier. This is normal. Language has wheels within wheels within wheels. It's like the old bit of doggerel:

And so we see that all the fleas
Have smaller fleas to bite 'em
And so it goes, and so it goes,
Ad infinitum.

The Verb Phrase

The verb phrase is the most difficult word cluster to recognize because it comes in such a great variety of patterns. Also, it's easily confused with the *verbal phrase*, which we'll attack later. Traditional terminology adds to the difficulty, as you see in the confusing similarity between the names *verb phrase* and *verbal phrase*. A further difficulty is the subtle and complex relationship between syntactic and semantic categories which apply to verb phrases. Finally, our English-speaking ancestors made a hopeless mess of the morphology. But with reasonable attentiveness and good cheer we can learn to recognize some important regularities within the verb phrase pattern. To do so, we'll use separate formulas for different parts of the total range of verb phrase possibilities.

The verb phrase must have at least one word called the *main verb*. It may also contain one or more *auxiliaries*, which Petey's teacher called *helping words* or *helping verbs*. Open-class adverbs, a few of the intensifiers, and the negator *not* may also be tucked into the verb phrase. These may or may not be considered part of the verb phrase, depending on the purpose or whims of the grammarian. In the sentence "The tour guide was not speaking comprehensibly," it's correct to say that the verb phrase is "was not speaking comprehensibly"; but since our purpose is to understand the way main verbs and auxiliaries work together, we'll leave out the "not" and the open-class adverb and say that the verb phrase is "was speaking."

The simplest verb phrase consists of two slots—a main verb such as "speak" and another slot called *tense*. The two slots are often combined in a single word. "Walked," for example, consists of only one word, but it contains the main verb *walk* and the tense marker *-ed*. The verb phrase "walks" also has two slots, *walk* and *-s*, a present tense marker. "Walk," as in "The companions *walk* as far as Moria together," also has a tense slot. The absence of any other tense marker shows that the verb is in the present tense. (As anyone waiting for the phone call that never comes could tell you, the absence of a signal communicates just as emphatically as the presence of one.) We can state this simplest verb phrase in a formula as follows:

Basic formula: VP = Tns + MV
Example: Jughead *laughed*.

For historical reasons, English has many verbs which use something other than *-ed* as the past tense marker—a vowel change, as in *speak-spoke*, or a change of the whole word form, as in *think-thought* or *go-went*. (See Chapter 2.)

As in other processes of syntactic analysis, we must distinguish carefully between syntax and semantics. When we speak of the tense slot or tense markers, we're speaking of syntactic forms rather than meaning. *Tense* is not the same thing as *time*. Tense is a syntactic category while time is semantic. In the sentence "I *speak* whenever and wherever I am invited," *speak* has the syntactic form of present tense, but the meaning refers to a recurrent action. It's a peculiarity of English verb morphology that there are only two syntactic tenses, *present* and *past*.

Besides the two obligatory slots of main verb and tense, the verb phrase may have the following optional slots: modal, perfective, progressive, and passive. The presence of each of these slots is signaled by a combination of morphemes.

Modal: The term *modal* (pronounced / mow dəl/) is related to the word mood, and the modal auxiliaries, generally speaking, express moods—things like politeness, determination, hope, regret. The list of modal auxiliaries includes *can*, *will*, *may*, *shall*, and *must* in the present tense and *could*, *would*, *might*, and *should* in the past tense. Since *must* has no past tense, we use *had to* as a past tense form of it. To say that *could* is the past tense of *can* etc. is a convenience of syntactic analysis. It has nothing to do with time. For example, "You can go now" and "You could go now" both refer to the present time, but they convey subtle differences in mental attitude. The justification for listing the modals into present and past categories is this: every verb phrase must have a tense slot. When there's a modal in the verb phrase, the tense marker can not appear anywhere else in the phrase. It seems easier to put the tense slot in every verb phrase and call the modals present and past than to make a rule that every verb phrase has a tense marker unless it begins with a modal. Since the kind of rule we make doesn't change the way people speak, we might as well construct rules which have as few exceptions as possible. When the modal option is chosen, the formula looks like this:

Modal formula: VP = Tns + Modal + MV
Example: Jughead *will pay* for all of us. (Is the mood hope—or determination?)

Perfective: The presence of the perfective slot in the verb phrase brings into focus the whole scope of an action. It's so named because the original meaning of the word "perfect" is "complete." To say "I *had sung* in the choir for two years," focuses on the fact that the whole action took place in the past. "I *have sung* in the choir for two years" emphasizes that the whole action extends up to the present time. To say "I sing" or "I sang" avoids emphasis on the wholeness of the action. Two morphemes are required to express perfective: the *have* auxiliary (*have* and *has* in the present, *had* in the past) and an inflectional ending called past participle. For most verbs, the past participle is the same as the past tense marker: *-ed*. Other verbs have other past participle forms, often the *-en* or *-n* endings.

Perfective formula: VP = Tns + Have + Past Part. + MV
Examples: Jughead *had shown* talent in goofing off, his chosen field.
He *has received* honorable mention.

Notice that the *Past Part.* morpheme is listed *before* the MV, even though in the actual verb phrase it appears on the end of the MV. When several of the optional elements are chosen, Past Part. combines with the following word, whatever it may be.

Progressive: In addition to the perfective option, which focuses on the wholeness of an action, English has the progressive, which focuses on the continuousness of an action. It shows that the action is or was a process, something extended in time. If we say "The child was squeezing the tooth paste out of the tube," we are focusing on the fascinating process of producing a long worm. To say "The child squeezed the toothpaste out of the tube" leaves undetermined whether it came out slowly or in a big squirt. The progressive option is expressed by some form of the *be* auxiliary (is, am, are, was, were, etc.) plus the present participle (*-ing*).

Progressive Formula: VP = Tns + Be + -ing + MV
Example: Jughead *is learning* English grammar. (If you believe that,

maybe you would like to buy the Brooklyn Bridge.) Notice that the form of be is combined with the tense, and the *-ing* attaches to the MV.

Both progressive and perfective are technically called *aspects*, because they express a focus, a way of looking at the action. Textbooks often list such things as "present perfect" or "present progressive" as tenses in a tabular presentation of verb forms, but technically speaking, these "complex tenses" are a combination of tense and aspect.

Passive: The passive option shows that the subject of the verb phrase, instead of doing, had something done to it. The passive option is expressed by some form of the *be* auxiliary (is, am, are, was, were, etc.) plus the past participle (-ed, -en, -n, etc.) Both progressive and passive use the *be* auxiliary, but they use different participle forms. "The scouts were seeing" is progressive, while "The scouts were seen" is passive.

Passive Formula: VP = Tns + Be + Past Part. + MV

Examples: Jughead *was seen* by teachers as a disruptive influence.

The meeting *was chaired* efficiently.

All four of the options—modal, perfective, progressive, and passive—can appear in the same verb phrase. Consider the sentence "The client *could have been being seen* for the past six weeks if the referral system had been working properly." *Could* fills the optional slot of modal and the obligatory slot of tense. *Have* is the sign of the perfective. There are two *be* verbs, one for progressive and one for passive. And *seen* is the main verb. Very few verb phrases use all the options at once. Although such long phrases are within our language *competence*, in actual *performance* we avoid verb phrases of more than three words.

Now that we've examined the verb phrase structure, let's look again at the passage from Bronowski. In the previous analyses of the passage we identified all the noun phrases and prepositional phrases. What we have left are the following:

      certainly begins   and
      is particularly adept   so that
      feel
      remains

The word groups in the left-hand column all contain one word which is inflected for tense: *begins, is, feel* (with the ∅ inflection) and *remains*. *And* and *so that* in the right-hand column do not and could not have a tense inflection. By morphology we can recognize *certainly* and *particularly* as *-ly* adverbs, and the appearance of adverbs is a good indicator of verb phrases. It's safe, then, to call the left-hand word groups verb phrases.

The word *adept* presents a problem. Morphologically, it's an adjective, since it can take the *-er* and *-est* inflections: "more adept," "most adept." In syntax it often fills the adjective slot in a noun phrase: "the adept mechanic." Yet we feel that "to be adept" is an action. But whether a thing is an *action* is a matter of semantics; whether it's a *verb* is a matter of syntax. Since we're studying syntax at the moment, we delete "adept" from the verb phrase. The second verb phrase is not "is particularly adept," but merely "is."

Before leaving the verb phrase, let's look at some additional syntactic patterns not covered by the formulas we've discussed, such as the use of the auxiliary *do* and its inflections, *does* and *did*. When a verb phrase needs to have two words and has no other auxiliaries, one of the forms of *do* fills the slot. When does a verb phrase need two words? One instance is the negative. The structure of English doesn't allow us to say, "I not studied." The negative must be associated with an auxiliary, as in "I could not study" or "I have not studied." When there's no other auxiliary, *do* must be supplied: "I did not study." If there's more than one auxiliary, the negative normally comes after the first: "I could not have done it." Placing the negative after the second, as in "I could have not done it," creates a subtle difference in meaning. This, incidentally, is the kind of rule that native speakers of English automatically obey. To foreigners, it seems awkward and arbitrary, and they must practice to get it right.

There's a further complication: the auxiliaries *have, has,* and *had; do, does, did,* and *done;* and *be, being, been, am, is, are, was,* and *were* are sometimes not auxiliaries at all, but main verbs. When used as a main verb the various forms of *have* mean "to possess" or "to be associated with" as in "I *have* a new car" (possession) and "I *have* a cold" (association). Sometimes a word can appear in both auxiliary and main verb slots at the same time, producing correct but awkward-sounding sentences such as, "The stereo was stolen before he *had had* it even a week." Such sentence may make the speaker feel, "Wait a minute! That can't be right." But it is. The forms of *do* are used when a generalized verb is needed, as in "He *does* interior decorating and landscape design." This sentence is smoother and clearer than saying "He interior decorates and landscape designs." The forms of *be*, when used as lexical verbs, mean "to exist" or "to equal" or "to have the quality of." The slogan, "Love is," means "Love exists." "Mary is the boss," expresses equality: Mary and the boss are the same person. "War is hell" means that war has the quality of hell.

A third complication in analyzing verb phrases involves a special use of prepositions. Consider the sentence, "The revolutionaries blew up the street." The action is "to blow up," not "to blow." "Blow up" is an idiom,[3] because the two words combine into a new meaning which is quite different from the meaning they have separately. Contrast the first sentence with this one: "The wind blew up the street." We can see that semantically the two actions are not the same. Must we analyze them the same way syntactically? The answer is "No," because the first sentence can be restated "The revo-

---

[3]See Chapter 6 for more about idioms.

lutionaries blew the street up." The second cannot be restated this way. We have found a syntactic difference. We solve the problem by creating a new part of speech. When a preposition combines with a verb in this way we call it a *particle*. If a preposition can be moved to the end of the sentence, it's not a preposition but a particle. Some writers eliminate the extra term by calling the particle an adverb, but it's not an adverb like "noisily" as in "The toddler blew noisily into his cereal bowl." Another test of the particle is that the idiomatic combination of verb plus particle can often be replaced by a single wood. "Exploded," for example, can replace "blew up."

Verbal Phrases

The final complication is that verb phrases are often difficult to separate from verbal phrases. Consider this sentence: "The young women planned to go skiing." When asked to state the verb phrase, Petey's first impluse was to say "planned to go skiing," because the whole thing makes up a single action; but according to syntactic rather than semantic analysis, only "planned" is the verb phrase. "To go skiing" fills a noun phrase slot. It's a verbal phrase, not a verb phrase.

A verbal phrase is a word cluster containing a verb form which fills a noun phrase, post-modifer, or adjunct slot in a clause. There are three kinds of verbal phrases: the infinitive, the *ing*-participle, and the past participle. Let's look at the infinitive first.

The infinitive is easy to recognize because it has a clear structure word, *to*. (It would be logical to give *to* its own part-of-speech category, but no grammarian ever does.) The verb part of the infinitive phrase can be a single word, as in "to go," or it can include perfective, progressive, or passive options as in "to have gone," "to be going," and "to be seen." The modal option is expressed by a double infinitive phrase such as "to be able to go" for "can go" and "to have to go" for "must go." When a noun phrase or a prepositional phrase completes the thought of an infinitive (or of any other verbal phrase), then it's considered part of the phrase, as in "His purpose was *to see the world by himself.*" The infinitive phrase can have adverb modifiers just as verb phrases do: "to be easily seen." (Incidentally, this phrase is wrong according to Petey's teacher, who told Petey to say "to be seen easily" because one should "never split an infinitive." This is the one rule Petey learned thoroughly. It's also the one rule he didn't need. The best writers and speakers of English have always split infinitives when it pleased them to do so. The writers of "Star Trek" were entirely correct, and stylistically sensitive, in choosing to say "To boldly go where no man has gone before" rather than "To go boldly.")

The *ing*-participle contains a main verb ending with *-ing*, and it usually has a noun phrase or prepositional phrase to complete the thought. If the

ing-participle fills an adjective or post-modifier slot, it's traditionally called a *present participle*, as in the following sentences:
Adjective: the *skiing* criminal was chased by helicopters.
Post-modifier: The criminal *skiing along the ridges* contributed some dramatic photography to an otherwise dull film.

The present participle can also appear before or after the main clause of the sentence, loosely connected with the thought:
Finding himself in a tight spot, the criminal surrendered.

When the *ing* participle fills a noun phrase slot, it's traditionally called a *gerund*. Here the gerund phrase is the subject of the sentence, and the whole thing could be replaced by *it*:
Skiing in well-run competitions is not particularly dangerous.

The Bronowski passage contains two *-ing* verbals—"advancing" and "manipulating." Can you tell the present participle from the gerund without a score card?[4]

The past participle contains a main verb ending with *-ed* or a special past participle form such as *seen* or *written*. Like the other verbal phrases, it may have a noun or prepositional phrase to complete the thought. It can appear in the same slots as the present participle, but it cannot be a gerund. Unless there is a special past-participle form like *seen*, telling the difference between it and a simple past-tense verb can be tricky. Consider this sentence: "The money, advanced under a low-interest loan plan, simply disappeared." "Advanced" is the past participle, and the whole past participle phrase is set off by commas. (Not all past participles are set off in this way.) "Disappeared" is the verb phrase. The key to identifying them is to ask which one needs a passive auxiliary. The money did disappear; no extra auxiliary is needed. But the money did not advance; it *was* advanced by someone, presumably the banker. Thus "advanced" is the past participle.

There are more problems with part-of-speech categories and their combination into phrases than the ones we have discussed. If, however, we pay attention to inflectional endings and the formulas for phrase types, we can classify most of the words in a particular sentence and pick out most of the phrases. When we can't classify a word or group of words, the unit may belong to a different level of syntactic structure—clause, sentence, or paragraph—or it may represent a dialect or speech style not covered by the analysis. A person ought to be content to leave these unclassifiables as unknowns instead of confusing the issue by making a wild guess. In many cases, two or three classifications might be equally valid, and it could be fun to discuss the reasons for choosing one rather than another. Perhaps one reason Petey decided to forget the whole thing was that he had too many teachers who insisted that there was one and only one way of looking at a problem

---

[4]"Advancing" is a participle and "manipulating" a gerund.

in analysis. Let's hope that someday he'll meet a teacher who agrees with linguist Edward Sapir that "All grammars leak," and who will accept "I don't know" as a valid answer.

Exercises

1. Identifying Morphemes

By comparing one word with another you can identify three separate morphemes. Notice that the English translation does not have precisely the same number of morphemes. List the morphemes and state the meaning of each one. The language is Huichol (Mexico).

1. kʌye 'tree'
2. kʌyezi 'trees'
3. pʌkʌye 'It is a tree.'
4. pʌkʌ̂yezi 'They are trees.'

Morphemes:

_____ means_____
_____ means_____
_____ means_____

Do you agree that Huichol has a structure word (syntactic marker) that English doesn't have? If so, what would you call it?

2. Part-of-Speech Categories

Determine the meanings of the Apinaye' words. How many part-of-speech categories do you need to explain the data—three or four? Why?

1. kukrę kokoi
2. kukrę kra
3. ape kra
4. kukrę kokoi rač
5. ape kra mɛč
6. ape mɛč kra
7. ape rač mɨ mɛč
8. kukrę rač kokoi punui
9. ape ŋre mɨ punui
10. ape punui mɨ
11. kukrę mɨ ŋre

1. The monkey eats.
2. The child eats.
3. The child works.
4. The big monkey eats.
5. The good child works.
6. The child works well.
7. The good man works a lot.
8. The bad monkey eats a lot.
9. The bad man works a little.
10. The man works badly.
11. The few men eat.

3. Noun Phrases

For each of the nouns in the list, perform the following steps:
1. Add a determiner.
2. Add one or more modifiers before the noun.

3. Add a post-modifier.
4. Write a sentence using the whole noun phrase *before* the verb.
5. Write a sentence using the whole noun phrase *after* the verb.

Example: lover. Step 1: that lover. Step 2: that intrepid lover. Step 3: that intrepid lover of poetry and fine whiskey. Step 4: That intrepid lover of poetry and fine whiskey *is* none other than the city's best motorcycle cop. Step 5: The children *admire* that intrepid lover of poetry and fine whiskey.

Steps 1, 2, and 3 cannot be applied to one of the nouns. Why not? Hint: Notice how determiners and modifiers make a noun more specific.
1. classes
2. money
3. David Letterman
4. player
5. star
6. time
7. turkey

4. Prepositional Phrases

Underline (or list on a piece of paper) all the prepositional phrases in the following sentences. Circle the preposition for each prepositional phrase. Ignore prepositions which do *not* occur in a prepositional phrase—that is, prepositions which are not followed by a noun phrase.
1. Writers of science fiction should learn a few simple facts about the nature of language.
2. It is ridiculous when the star ship crew contact the inhabitants of a planet orbiting around Vega, speak to the aliens in English, and are able to communicate perfectly.
3. Another ridiculous error is to depict all the intelligent creatures of a planet communicating in a single language.
4. Our present knowledge about the mechanisms of language suggests that the inhabitants of another planet would have languages differing from each other as much as ours do.
5. It is equally ridiculous to have the aliens communicating telepathically with the humans, without any explanation of the semantic basis for such communication.

5. Verb Phrases

The following pairs of sentences differ only in verb form—that is, whether certain options of tense, mood, aspect, and voice have been taken. Underline each verb phrase and explain briefly the different contexts implied by the different options.

Example: He hasn't acted in a Broadway production.
He didn't act in a Broadway production.

The verb phrases are *hasn't acted* and *didn't act*. The first one implies that he may get the opportunity to act in a Broadway production in the future. The second one seems to imply that he got an acting job, but it was not in a Broadway production.

1. A. The children had watched the parade.
   B. The children could have watched the parade.
2. A. After finding the dollar, the child bought a cold drink.
   B. After finding the dollar, the child had bought a cold drink.
3. A. I could not find my keys.
   B. I can not find my keys.
4. A. Why would someone do a cruel thing like that?
   B. Why did someone do a cruel thing like that?
5. A. He was cheerfully baiting everyone's hook.
   B. He would cheerfully bait everyone's hook.
6. A. The teacher will be judged by a jury of his peers.
   B. The teacher would be judged by a jury of his peers.
   C. The teacher shall be judged by a jury of his peers.
7. A. George studied the statistics carefully.
   B. George did study the statistics carefully.
8. A. Tami may study in Europe next year.
   B. Tami might study in Europe next year.
9. A. Dr. Spock should have understood the problem immediately.
   B. Dr. Spock would have understood the problem immediately.
10. A. The spiritual master was working in his garden.
    B. The spiritual master worked in his garden.
11. A. He should have seen that the approaching car was out of control.
    B. He must have seen that the approaching car was out of control.
12. A. Sarah had long talks with her most annoying subordinate.
    B. Sarah has long talks with her most annoying subordinate.
13. A. The children can sleep outdoors under the stars.
    B. The children could sleep outdoors under the stars.

6. Particles

Rewrite the following sentences, using a verb + preposition construction instead of the italicized verb.

You may need to look up the etymology in the dictionary.

1. When Dad saw the poor grades on my brother's report card, he *exploded*.
2. The principal *interposed* in order to keep the boys from fighting.

3. Let us *depose* the stupid tyrant!
4. Under his management the company has steadily *retrogressed*.
5. She *revoked* her promise.
6. George wanted no part of the controversy, so he *exited*.
7. The County Commissioners were upset because the new building *collapsed*.
8. In order to stay within the law, you must *reject* fish less than ten inches long.
9. The girls cruelly *excluded* anyone who could not dress according to their standards of fashion.
10. Ellen *extracted* the juice from the persimmons for her special persimmon wine jelly.

7. Finding the Verb Phrase

Underline the verb phrase of each sentence. (Remember that a verb phrase must have a tense and a main verb.) Most of these sentences also contain verbal phrases. Don't underline the verbal phrases—just ignore them.

1. Peacefully reading my magazine, I missed my bus stop.
2. Disgusted by the arbitrary requirements, Jim is leaving the university.
3. A live dinosaur, trying to escape observation, may have been spotted in the African jungle.
4. The teacher had failed to understand the child's problem.
5. To be happy, I need three things: a book of verse, a jug of wine, and thou beside me, singing in the wilderness.

8. Verbal Phrases

A. Underline all infinitive phrases (to + verb + other words).
   1. Metaphor seems to express deep feelings better than literal words.
   2. We may as well recognize that human beings are able to make metaphors because of their ability to perceive resemblances in unlike things.
   3. To bring in a metaphor refreshes and clarifies thought.
   4. Sometimes metaphor causes language to undergo semantic change.

B. Underline all participial phrases. These are present (-ing) participles.
   1. Coming into the city, we saw the cloud of pollutants hanging over the foothills.
   2. We turned our heads away from the disgusting sight, wishing it would go away.
   3. The single factor causing the most pollution is the automobile, not the industries.
   4. Pollution can be controlled by societies having the necessary motivation.

C. Underline all participial phrases. These are past participles.
   1. Controlled by his maker, the monster strode toward toward the doomed city.
   2. But in mid-stride he paused, attracted by the usual beautiful girl clothed in white.
   3. He picked her up, limp and faint, and looked for the boy friend hidden in the lilac hedge.
   4. The boy friend, revealed as a coward, dived for his car.

D. The following are -ing participles used in noun slots (gerunds).
   1. I hate leaving before the film is over.
   2. Learning what happened to the monster is not that important to me, but it is still one of life's little annoyances.
   3. Just once I wish I could see a monster movie without having to worry about that dumb girl in white.
   4. Although I am not a sexist, she is a pest and a waste of footage, if you understand my meaning.

9. *Identifying Phrase Formulas*

Identify the morphemes, using the same method of comparison that you used for Exercises 2 and 3. Then write formulas to represent the noun phrase and the prepositional phrase. Write out your longest phrase and then determine all the words that can fit in each slot. The language is Guajajara (Brazil). The & = schwa.

1. oho kuz& ko pe
2. oho kwez kuz& taw pe
3. ur kuz& kwez taw we
4. ur mokoz awa ko we
5. uata kwez awa taw rupi
6. uata mane
7. uata mane pehu rupi
8. oho mokoz mane reimaw ko pe
9. oho kuz& mane rupi

1. The woman went to the field.
2. That woman went to town.
3. The woman came from that town.
4. Two men came from the field.
5. That man walked around town.
6. Manuel walked around.
7. Manuel walked along the road.
8. Two of Manuel's dogs went to the field.
9. The woman went along with Manuel.

Writing for Insight and Review: Classification

Classification, putting objects and concepts into categories, is one of the most important processes of language learning, and of human thought in general. Chapters 4 and 5 both emphasize classification, for one of their purposes is to encourage you to take another look at the traditional categories of grammar. In Chapter 4 we saw that some of the traditional parts of speech—nouns, verbs, and interjections—were classified according to their meanings. Others—adjectives, adverbs, prepositions, and conjunctions—were defined primarily according to their function in the sentence. And the pronouns seemed to be defined first according to function (a word that takes the place of a noun) and then subcategorized according to meaning (personal, indefinite, demonstrative).

This traditional method of classification was contrasted with the syntactic method, which first divides English words into those belonging to the *form* classes and those belonging to the *structure* classes. The structure classes are then defined by distribution, and the form classes by inflections and distribution. This classification turns out to be very useful, because the form classes have other characteristics in common, features that are not shared by the structure classes. A good classification is a learning device.

The classification determines what features of the item will be most noticeable. For example, the classification of nouns, verbs, adjectives, and adverbs by inflectional affixes makes us notice that we can change the category of one of these words simply by changing the inflection on it. Furthermore, no matter what classification system is used, some items will always be borderline. As you probably noticed, pronouns share some of the characteristics of both form classes and structure classes. And a good argument could be made for putting prepositions, conjunctions, and some adverbs in the same class, calling them the *relationals*, perhaps.

If a classification is to be logical, all the categories must be related to a single feature. Phrases might be classified by length (short, medium, long) or by their function in the sentence (naming, describing, predicating), but you couldn't have a classification of short phrases, verb phrases, and phrases containing "the." Clothing might be classified as day wear and evening wear, or casual and formal, but you wouldn't classify it as sportswear, evening wear, and name brands. You may think that this principle is so obvious that it hardly needs discussing, but in practice it's very difficult to find a feature of classification that neatly categorizes all your items, and the more complicated the phenomena you're discussing the more difficult logical classification becomes.

One rather curious aspect of classification is that people seem to like triads. The components of language and linguistic study, for example, are listed in this book as phonology, syntax and semantics. An earlier classification listed phonology, morphology, and syntax. Morphology covered some syntactic matters like parts of speech and the use of affixes, and also some of the material that we now present as semantics. A more recent classification divides linguistics into semantics, syntactics, and pragmatics, with syntactics covering the arrangement of all kinds of units—phonological, morphological, and syntactic.

Here are some writing projects based on classification:
1. We normally divide the sounds of English into vowels and consonants. If you classified them into three categories rather than two, what would those categories be? What sounds would be difficult to classify? (Don't attempt this one unless you've studied Chapter 3.)
2. Put the following list of Latin words on cards or slips of paper. Have a person who doesn't know Latin make several groups, putting words together that are alike in some way. Record the words grouped together and the reasons. Write a report of your experiment. How much was your subject influenced by the inflectional endings? By other resemblances in form? To what extent did his or her categories match the actual Latin parts of speech?

    1. bonus
    2. ab
    3. ad
    4. peritus
    5. amo
    6. flecto
    7. canto
    8. novus
    9. amicus
    10. sed
    11. et
    12. fraudo
    13. sine
    14. qui
    15. sinus
    16. quod
    17. quando

    (*Note:* -*us* is a Latin noun or adjective ending; -o is a verb ending. Word meanings are listed below.)

    1. good
    2. from
    3. to
    4. experienced
    5. love
    6. bend
    7. sing
    8. new
    9. friend
    10. but
    11. and
    12. defraud
    13. without
    14. who
    15. fold
    16. what
    17. when

    You may wish to expand the project by putting English words on cards and asking the same subject (or a different one) to classify them. See how the results are different when the person knows what the words mean.
3. Discuss the way information is organized and classified in another subject you're studying. What sort of facts does this method of classification emphasize? Has the method changed during the history of this subject as the researchers or scholars learned more about it? (Brief histories of various subjects can be found in encyclopedias.) Is there another discipline that classifies the facts in another way? (For example, a psychology text and a sociology text might set up different classifications for types of families.)

5

Those Red-Pencil Blues

One of the hazards of academic life is the theme or essay. The student submits one, thinking that it's excellent—or at least O.K.—only to get it back pock-marked with symbols in red: RO, CS, SS, and the fatal FRAG. These symbols, standing for run-on, comma splice, sentence sense, and fragment, show that the student has incomplete understanding and control of the syntax of written English on the clause and sentence level. In speech, our language community allows us to combine phrases, which are the units of clauses and sentences, very freely; but in writing, language is expected to meet rigid norms, norms so difficult that even professional writers have trouble with them at times. Thus, a person who speaks quite fluently may have difficulty in meeting the standards of written English.

When spoken language appears in print, it's usually restructured and edited to conform to the rigid standards of written English. When it's not edited, the lack of coherence is surprising. The following passage has been taken from a tape transcript of the proceedings of a local governing body. It was printed without the usual editing because of the great controversy aroused by the meeting, and gives us a good example of the extent to which unstructured sentences are tolerated in speech, even in this fairly formal situation.

Member 1: . . . they get responsible job and considerable pressure is brought against them by their people. And, some will bend to that pressure no matter (pause) that's another you gotta consider.
Member 2: Don't they all
Member 3: Yea
Member 4: They?—Why don't we say "we" (pause)
Member 1: I think there's all their pressure is usually always there but some of 'em will I guess we all bend to some pressure to a certain extent (pause) but I'm talking about a specific group of people and a specific problem that is not relative just to this area. . . .

It's said that the press can make a public figure appear stupid just by printing the person's exact words without editing. Normally, of course, spoken material is edited for print. If the preceding conversation had been edited, it would have appeared in the newspaper something like this:

Member 1: When a member of this group gets a responsible job, his own people will bring pressure against him to favor their group. Some members of this group will bend to pressure no matter how hard they try to be responsible. In choosing an appointee, we must consider the effect of this pressure.

Member 2: Don't they all bend to the pressure?

Member 3: Yes, they do.

Member 4: Why don't we say, 'Don't *we* all bend to pressure?'

Member 1: Pressure is always involved in decision-making, and all of us bend to it sometimes, but the members of this group are always subject to pressure.

The process of editing this passage involves filling the slots which are considered "necessary" to English clause and sentence norms, and of rearranging these slot-filler constructions in "normal" order. The difference between the edited sentence and the actual sentence is comparable to the difference between the "real" sounds which make up a word and the word as it's sometimes spoken. A person who was asked to write "started" in phonetic symbols would probably write /startəd/ or /statəd/. Supposedly, the word has seven sounds—or six in an r-less dialect. But in actual speech, especially rapid speech, people often say /stard/ or /stad/, thus leaving out a sound or two. The spoken word may also have the sounds in the wrong order; for example, people often say "revelant" for "relevant." In speech, especially rapid speech, people do the same thing to sentences. They leave out items or get them in the wrong order. If you've studied Chapter 3, you're aware that no phonetic analysis ever captures all the features of sound which actually issue from people's mouths. The phonetic analysis is an abstraction and regularization of what people actually say. The same is true on the sentence and clause level of syntax: no method of analysis can ever capture all the complex variations of what people say and write. This survey of English clause and sentence patterns will give you a basic understanding of the most common structures, but it won't necessarily enable you to analyze a sentence from one of your textbooks, or one that you write yourself. It might, however, help you correct your sentences before the red pencil slashes them.

Some Definitions

In describing the most common patterns of English syntax we need three kinds of units. These units are the phrase, the clause, and the sentence.

The *phrase* is a group of words bound together by syntactic relationships. In Chapter 4 the following kinds of phrases were described:
Noun Phrase—a noun and its determiners and modifiers
Verb Phrase—a main verb, its tense, and any auxiliaries
Prepositional Phrase—a preposition and a noun phrase
Verbal Phrase—a verb in participle or infinitive form and its modifiers and/or completers

These four kinds of phrases are primarily syntactic units, but they coincide with phonological units, for in speaking we use patterns of stress, pitch, and timing to show that they belong together. A phrase usually has one strongly-stressed syllable, as in the following examples:
Noun Phrase: the little house′
Verb Phrase: may have stood′ (or maý have stood)
Prepositional Phrase: for a ceń tury
Verbal Phrase: accuḿ ulating happy meḿ ories

(Notice that the verbal phrase has two stresses because "happy memories" is also a phrase—a noun phrase.)

Although we have defined the phrase as a construction, or group of words, a single word may fill a phrase slot. "It" is a noun phrase, "stood" a verb phrase, "accumulating" a verbal (for some reason it's not customary to call it a verbal phrase unless it consists of more than one word), and "memories" another noun phrase. The prepositional phrase always has at least two words—the preposition and the noun phrase called the object of the preposition. The four phrases can be combined into a clause as follows: The little house/ may have stood/ for a century/ accumulating happy memories. With minimal phrases in each position it reads: It stood for a century accumulating memories.

The *clause* is a syntactic unit centering around some kind of verb. In its fullest form the clause has four slots: Subject, Predicate, Complement, and one or more Adjuncts. Here's a clause with the slots labeled:

   S   P   C   A
The fat lady/ hid / the box of chocolates / in the toaster oven.

Only one of the four slots, the predicate, is absolutely necessary, and in extreme cases a clause may consist of only one word: "Go!" This one word is simultaneously a morpheme, a word, a verb phrase, and a clause. When a clause has two slots, they may be subject and verb, as in "Grammar stinks," verb and complement as in "Play ball!" or verb and adjunct as in "Now, go!" When we use such clauses as these, the intonation pattern shows that it's a complete clause, and not merely a phrase. For example, "Going out?" has the complete normal intonation of a question, even though it lacks a subject and part of the predicate.

Let's look at the clause slots in a little more detail, since you may know them by different names:

Subject—normally a noun phrase, a pronoun, or some other noun-like group of words.

Predicate—a verb phrase.

Complement—something that gives "complete-ment" to the predicate. The type of complement required depends on the meaning of the main verb, so that the complement is closely attached to the predicate. In fact, some books use the term "complete predicate," meaning the verb phrase plus the complement. The most common types of complements are *direct objects, predicate nouns,* and *predicate adjectives.*

Direct objects are used with "transitive active" verbs, as in the following:

    S   P   Direct Object
The next batter / hit/ the pitcher's fast ball.

Predicate nouns and *predicate adjectives* are used with "intransitive linking" verbs, as in the following:

    S   P   Pred. Adj.
The witness/seemed/ quite positive.

    S   P   Pred. Noun
She/ had been/ a waitress.

The classification of verbs as transitive and intransitive, and of verb complements as direct objects and predicate nouns or adjectives is one of those rules of grammar that works just fine until you look at it closely. A lot depends on semantics—the meanings of the lexical items involved. For example, in "Jerry received the pass" the verb certainly expresses action and "the pass" is clearly a direct object. In "Stacy received a suspended sentence" the action is not nearly so clear. She probably did nothing but stand there and look sulky. And how about "The costume was red"? Is *red* a predicate noun or a predicate adjective? What difference does it make? For the purpose of avoiding the red-pencil blues, it's more important to recognize the complement than to know what kind it is.

Adjunct—a word, phrase, or clause that's added to the clause almost as an afterthought. It's often an adverb or some kind of adverbial phrase. Because it's not syntactically necessary to the rest of the sentence, it's often set off by commas (if written) or intonation (if oral). Normally, adjuncts occur at the beginnings or ends of sentences, but they can also be inserted into the sentence as an interrupter, as in the following example:

    S   A   P   C
The apartment,/ though small,/ is / quite convenient.

Because adjuncts are optional, many grammar books do not list them, concentrating instead on the other three clause elements. But a thorough knowledge of adjuncts is helpful to people who wish to develop a mature writing style.

All of the clause slots can be doubled or even tripled as in the following examples:
Two subjects: *Tom* and *Jerry* are cartoon characters.
Multiple predicates: They *caught, cleaned,* and *cooked* the fish.
Two complements: She sells *real estate* and also *business franchises.*
Each predicate with its own complement:

       P   C   P   C

They *drank beer* and *told dirty stories* all night.
Two adjuncts: *Within a short time,* the cowboys had branded all the cattle *without any particular difficulty.*

The clauses of all languages have these elements, but not all of them use the same order. In Old English (the version of our language spoken before about 1000 A.D.) the most common order was Subject-Complement-Predicate. In many languages the predicate comes first, in a Predicate-Subject-Complement order. The other three orders that are theoretically possible seem not to occur.

The *sentence* consists of one or more clauses. A sentence with only one clause is traditionally called a *simple sentence,* but that's not a very good name. It implies "uncomplicated," and nothing in grammar is ever uncomplicated. Actually, the distinction between simple (one-clause) sentences and others is less important than the distinction between coordinated and subordinated elements.

Coordination

Coordination means the joining of two or more elements that have the same syntactic rank. The examples given above of clauses with two or more subjects, predicates, or other clause elements are examples of coordination. When two otherwise complete sentences are joined together, the result is a coordinate sentence. In carefully written material, sentences are joined this way for a specific reason—either because they are alike in thought, or because one is the opposite of the other. This semantic relationship is emphasized by making the sentences similar in syntactic structure. Example:

The spaceship was damaged while landing on the moon,
  but
the satellite was saved by the quick action of the crew.

Notice that the two clauses are alike in having subject, predicate, and adjunct elements.

The structure words used to join coordinate clauses are called coordinating conjunctions, or simply *coordinators.* They are *and, but, or, for, nor,* and *yet.* If the coordinator is omitted, a semicolon (;) is usually necessary. When three or more coordinate clauses are put together, the coordinator is necessary only before the last one in the series, but sometimes an author will use more coordinators than needed to produce a sonorous, poetic effect:

There was a little city with few men in it, *and* a great king came against it and besieged it, building great siegeworks against it; *but* there was found in it a poor wise man, *and* he by his wisdom delivered the city; *yet* no one remembered that poor man. (Ecc. 9:14–15).

This effect is called *polysyndeton*, "many conjunctions." Short, vivid clauses may be joined without coordinators, producing an *asyndeton:*

I came, I saw, I conquered.—*Julius Caesar*

Writers also join together two thoughts in a loose coordination, just because a full stop would break the flow of thought, and this is perfectly acceptable if it's not overdone. But to express complex ideas briefly and clearly, the skilled writer inserts *subordinate* elements into a *base clause*.

Subordination

Subordination involves attaching or inserting an element of lower syntactic rank into an element of higher rank. Instead of joining two base clauses (sometimes called *main* or *independent* clauses) with a coordinator, you reduce the rank of one, either by turning it into a verbal phrase or by using a subordinator. First let's look at the process of busting a clause down to the rank of verbal phrase. Consider this one-clause sentence:

```
   S              P              C                  A
```
The mother/ was spanking/ her runaway child/ all the way home.

When the element of tense, expressed in the auxiliary *was*, is eliminated, the construction is no longer a full clause. It becomes a *verbal phrase.*

the mother spanking her runaway child all the way home

(The lack of punctuation shows that the construction is a verbal phrase rather than a sentence.) The change of verb form allows the item to become part of another clause. Here it is filling the adjunct slot of a larger unit:

```
   A                                              S            P
```
Spanking her runaway child all the way home,/the mother/was ex-
```
   C
```
pressing/both relief and frustration.

(Notice that the subject of the verbal phrase is omitted because it's the same as the subject of the full clause.)

If the tense is deleted from the new clause, it too can fill an adjunct slot:

```
   A                                                  A
```
Spanking her runaway child all the way home,/expressing both re-
```
           S         P        C
```
lief and frustration,/the mother/ignored/strangers who stared.

Verbal phrases can also fill subject and complement slots in the base clause:

    S   P   C
Spanking the child/was/a poor solution to the problem.

    S   P   C
The mother/regretted/ spanking the child.

Since the verbal phrase fills some slot in the base clause, the sentence is still regarded as a simple sentence in traditional grammar.

The second common way to subordinate a clause is to keep the subject and the verb tense while adding a structure word called a *subordinator*. Thus our little domestic crisis could be expressed this way:

When the mother was spanking her runaway child, she was expressing both relief and frustration.

Common subordinators include *when, while, after, before, if, although, because*, etc. Most clauses that fill the adjunct slot begin with subordinators like these. But it's also possible to fill the adjunct slot with a subordinate clause beginning with *who* or *which:*

They wouldn't cancel my traffic ticket, *which* was another example of bureaucratic pettiness.

They wouldn't listen to Greg, *who* saw the whole thing.

The most common subordinator for a clause that fills a subject or complement slot is *that*, as in the following sentences:

That the mother spanked her runaway child was a poor solution to the problem.

The mother thought *that strangers should mind their own business.*

The clause that fills a subject or complement slot is traditionally called a noun clause. As a subject, the clause must be introduced by *that*, but when the clause is a complement, the *that* is optional. (Try rereading the sentences without *that* to prove this point to yourself.)

In addition to clauses that fill adjunct slots and clauses that fill subject or complement slots, there are the clauses that fill a post-modifier slot within a noun phrase. If you've studied Chapter 4, you may remember that the noun phrase sometimes has a constituent following the noun as in "the recent evolution *of man.*" In this case the constituent, called a post-modifier, is a prepositional phrase, but it can also be a *relative clause*. It's introduced by one of the structure words called relatives. The most common ones are *who, which,* and *that.* Consider the following example:

    S   P
The cancellation of the traffic ticket *which I requested*/seemed/
C
reasonable.

Compare "which I requested" to "which was another example of bureaucratic pettiness." The one about bureaucratic pettiness is an adjunct. It's loosely related to the base clause. But "which I requested" is incorporated into the noun phrase, and, in fact, it's absolutely necessary to the meaning. You are not saying that the cancellation of all traffic tickets is reasonable, but only the one you requested. Such a construction is called *restrictive*, because it restricts the scope of the noun phrase.

Since clauses that fill post-modifier slots in noun phrases and clauses that are merely adjuncts can both begin with relatives, sometimes it's important to distinguish between them by punctuation. Consider the following examples:

1. Professor Blake enjoys the company of stockbrokers who are fabulously wealthy.
2. Professor Blake enjoys the company of stockbrokers, who give him a change from a narrowly academic point of view.

The first sentence restricts the scope of "stockbrokers." That is, it specifies precisely which stockbrokers Professor Blake enjoys. Not all stockbrokers are fabulously wealthy, but he chooses as companions only those who are wealthy. The second sentence does not restrict the scope of "stockbrokers." Professor Blake is not selective in his associations with stockbrokers, because any of them can give him a non-academic point of view. In the first sentence, the relative clause is a post-modifier. In the second, it's an adjunct. The difference is diagramed in Fig. 9.

Failure to control the distinction between restrictive (essential) and non-restrictive (adjunctive) information is one cause of the red-pencil blues.

Professor Blake enjoys the company of stockbrokers who are fabulously wealthy. (The clause restricts the scope of the noun phrase.)

Professor Blake enjoys the company of stockbrokers, who give him a change from a narrowly academic point of view. (The clause does not restrict the scope of the noun phrase.)

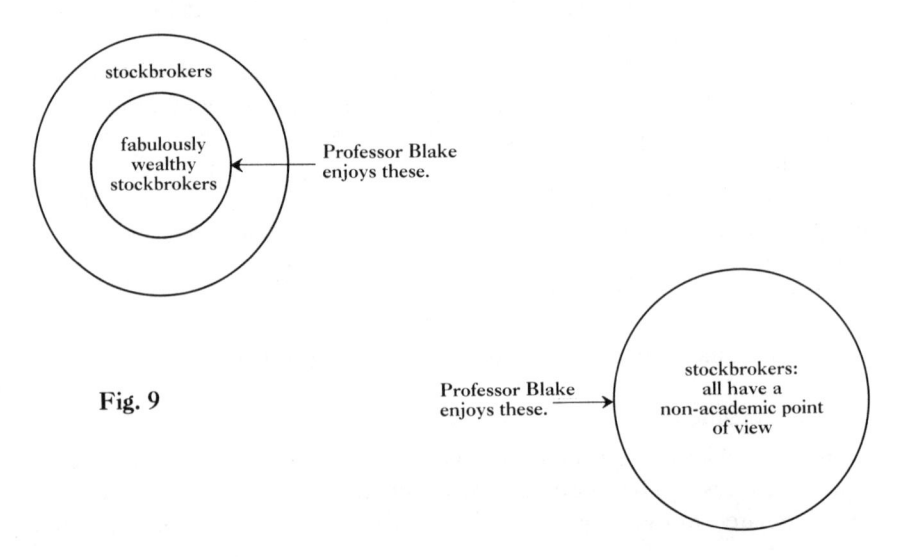

Fig. 9

Clauses filling the adjunct slot are set off by commas, except that the commas can be omitted if the adjunct comes at the end of the sentence. Clauses that fill the subject, complement, or post-modifier slot are always an integral part of the base clause. They must *not* be set off by commas.

The relative clause, like others, can be reduced to a verbal phrase by eliminating the subject and the verb tense. Example:

The men of the village *who were caught in the hiring freeze* turned to crime.

The men of the village *caught in the hiring freeze* turned to crime.

When a briefer expression is needed, you use the verbal phrase; but if your theme is supposed to be 500 words and you have only 498, you can add "who were" to the verbal phrase and make it a relative clause.

Transformational Relationships

We began by defining three levels of analysis: the phrase, a group of words related syntactically; the clause, a unit of predication (that is, a unit centered around a verb); and the sentence, one or more clauses. As we've seen, the verbal phrase is both a phrase and a clause, since it's centered around a verb. We've also seen that the verbal phrase and the subordinate clause are interchangeable; as is shown in Fig. 10, both can be used in the subject, complement, and adjunct slots of a base clause. Exploration of the relationship between syntactic structures like these is only one aspect of an approach to language called *transformational grammar*.

For quite a while linguists went along quite happily, dividing sentences into clauses and clauses into phrases. Then Noam Chomsky of M.I.T. began to ask some questions that revolutionized linguistics. Consider the following examples:

```
     S    P    C
John/ is/ easy to please.
     S    P    C
John/ is/ eager to please.
```

These two sentences have the same structure, and indeed the same lexical items except for one word. Yet as native speakers of English we know that the two instances of reduced clauses—that is, the two verbal phrases—have been reduced from completely different originals. In the first instance, the original clause must have been "Somebody pleases John." In the second, it was "John pleases someone." Chomsky asked himself, "How do we do that?" He hypothesized that the syntax of the sentence we read or hear must be derived from a more abstract pattern of knowledge. He spoke of the overt sentence as the *surface structure* and the abstract pattern as the *deep structure*. The deep structure consists of certain lexical items and their relationships to each other. The surface structure is the lining up of those lexical

FILLERS OF BASE CLAUSE SLOTS

Adjunct	Subject	Predicate	Complement	Adjunct
Adverb -ing Verbal Past Participle Absolute Infinitive Relative Clause Subordinate (Adv.) Clause	Noun Phrase -ing Verbal Infinitive Noun Clause	Verb Phrase	If Comp. is Pred. Noun or Direct Object: Noun Phrase -ing Verbal Infinitive Noun Clause If Comp. is Pred. Adj.: Adjective	Same as adjuncts preceding base clause.

If Noun Phrase has Post-Modifier, possible fillers are:
(Adjective)
Prepositional Phrase
-ing Verbal
Past Participle
Infinitive
Relative Clause

Fig. 10

items, plus appropriate syntactic markers, to make the kind of sentence we are used to. Consider the following examples:

Jeanette kicked the soccer ball.
The soccer ball was kicked by Jeanette.

We know that these two sentences mean the same thing. Both are surface structures which have been derived from the same deep structure. Furthermore, they are related in a way that can be expressed in a formula. Because of his mathematical orientation, Chomsky called the second sentence a transformation of the first. He and his students set out to define precisely (they used the term *generate*) all the syntactic structures of English and, indeed, other languages. They did not achieve the degree of precision that they originally hoped for, but they did open the way to a clearer understanding of the complicated syntactic options we all manipulate so unthinkingly. Certain clauses and verbal phrases can substitute for one another within a base clause because they are derived from the same deep structure. Here is a list of the transformational equivalents that are most important to good writing style.

1. Relative Clause with Active Verb = -ing participle
   Relative Clause:

   The girl *who is dancing on the table* brought delicious enchiladas to the party.

   Participial Phrase (-ing participle):

   The girl *dancing on the table* brought delicious enchiladas to the party.

   Note: Since the -ing participle has no tense, any sort of active verb phrase (such as *who danced, who had danced, who was dancing, who can dance*) is reducible to *dancing*. There may be a loss of precision, or even a change of meaning, since the reader will assume that the action of the participle takes place at a time logically consistent with the time of the base clause.

2. Relative Clause with Passive Verb = Past Participial Phrase
   Relative Clause:

   The cars *which were washed by members of the 4-H Club* sparkled in the sunlight.

   Past Participial Phrase:
   The cars *washed by members of the 4-H Club* sparkled in the sunlight.

   Past Participles ending in *-ed* must be carefully distinguished from main verbs; failure to do so is one of the chief causes of red-pencil blues. Compare the following sentences:

> Main Verb: The angry mother *grabbed* her child, glaring at the social worker.
> Past participle: The T-shirts *grabbed* by the greedy bargain-hunters. . . .

Here "grabbed by the greedy bargain-hunters" is part of the noun phrase—a post-modifier. This group of words lacks a predicate.

Not all past participles end in *-ed*. Many irregular verbs have separate past and past participle forms. Compare these:

> Irregular past tense verb: The carolers *sang* lustily as they walked through the snow.
> Irregular past participle: The carols *sung* by the youngsters pleased the old people.

3. Noun Clause = Gerund Phrase (same as *-ing* participle) = Infinitive Phrase

> Noun Clause: *That the teacher often (or frequently) kept students after school* was noted in his performance record.
> Gerund Phrase: *The teacher's frequent keeping (of) students after school* was noted. . . .
> Gerund Phrase, less specific: *Often keeping students after school* may indicate that a teacher is having trouble with discipline.
> Infinitive Phrase: *(For a teacher) to (frequently) keep students after school (frequently) (or often)* may indicate problems with discipline.
>
> *Notes:* The gerund phrase is an *-ing* verbal, just like the present participle. Someday we English teachers will overcome our natural conservatism and eliminate the term *gerund* completely, because the construction can just as well be described as "a present participle filling a noun slot." According to old puristic grammar, the subject of the gerund ("The *teacher's* keeping") was always a possessive, but many people do not follow that rule. Finally, notice the alternations between *often, frequent,* and *frequently.* Your ears will guide you in choosing the word which fits.

4. Subordinate Clause = Present or Past Participle = Absolute = Infinitive Phrase

> Subordinate clause: *Because it was denied permission to land,* the jet proceeded to Jakarta.

Past Participle: *Denied permission to land,* the jet proceeded to Jakarta.

Absolute: *The jet having been denied permission to land,* the pilot proceeded to Jakarta.

Infinitive: *For the jet to be denied permission to land,* a special government document was required.

Notes: Notice that all the above constructions fill adjunct slots. Also notice that all the verb forms cited happen to be passives. The same relationships exist when they're actives. (See Chapter 4 for a discussion of active and passive verb forms.) Finally, notice the difference between a participle and an absolute: the semantic subject of the participle is "jet," the same as the subject of the main verb "proceeded," while the subject of the absolute is different from that of the main verb. One cause of the red-pencil blues is the *dangling participle,* which occurs when the participle has an unstated subject different from the subject of the main verb:

Flopping on the grass, the fisherman quickly rebaited his hook.

Presumably the fish, not the fisherman, flopped. The dangling participle passes without comment in the quick give and take of speech; in written communication it's a grievous error, almost a crime. Most dangling participles can be corrected by changing them to absolutes.

5. Nominalization

A verbal phrase, or even a clause, can be turned into a noun phrase by changing the verb to a related noun.

Noun clause as subject: *That the child failed math* was disappointing to the parents.

After nominalization: *The child's failure in math* was disappointing to the parents.

Notice the use of the possessive, "child's," and the preposition, "in," to express the subject and complement relationships.

6. The Extraposition Transformation

When a noun clause or a long phrase of any sort fills the subject slot, the extraposition transformation may be used for better rhythm and readability. The subject slot is filled with the dummy subject *it* and the long subject is moved to the end of the sentence. Consider the following examples:

Noun clause as subject: *That he has to leave before the holiday is over* is a shame.

After extraposition: It is a shame *that he has to leave before the holiday is over.*

In some cases extraposition is needed with long complements:

Infinitive phrase as complement: The psychiatrist considered *to give the patient a major tranquilizer* advisable.
After extraposition: The psychiatrist considered it advisable *to give the patient a major tranquilizer.*

Writing Mature Sentences[1]

Unskilled writers are likely to express their thoughts in a Dick-and-Jane style, with one simple sentence after another. When the teacher uses the red pencil to comment "short, choppy sentences" in the margin, these writers go to the other extreme, writing interminable collections of phrases and clauses joined by *and*. Both problems can be corrected by using the syntactic options provided by the finer points of English grammar—the capabilities provided by subordinations and transformations. The trick is to put down a short base clause and then clarify it by adding subordinate elements. The base clause expresses the general idea, and the subordinations present specific details and examples. The following sentence illustrates the technique:

The linguist approaches language scientifically,
    recording speech,
    analyzing its structure, and
    formulating theories about it,
        to predict new utterances and
        to determine linguistic universals.

The phrases beginning with "recording," "analyzing," and "formulating" provide specific details, telling what it means to approach language scientifically. The phrases beginning with "to predict" and "to determine" clarify the phrase "formulating theories about it." The modifiers of the base clause are all expressed as participial phrases to show that they provide details on the same level of generality. The modifiers of "formulating theories about it" are on a lower level of generality, since they make a specific detail even more specific. Therefore, they are expressed by a different syntactic structure, in this case infinitive phrases. The existence of a variety of syntactic structures allows us to use a different one for each level of generality. This technique allows the writing of a long, detailed, complicated but readable sentence. The failure to use it causes the red pencil to note "faulty parallel-

---

[1] For a comprehensive treatment of this method of sentence writing see Bonniejean Christensen, *The Christensen Method: Text and Workbook* (New York: Harper & Row, 1979).

ism" in the margin of the paper. Here's a sentence with the same details, but with their semantic relationships obscured by failure to use parallel syntactic structures:

> The linguist approaches language scientifically,
> recording speech,
> the analysis of structure, and
> to formulate theories about it,
> so that he can predict new utterances and
> to determine linguistic universals.

Most of the time our ears will guide us in putting together properly subordinated sentences, especially if we have acquired reliable language intuitions by reading a lot. But a conscious knowledge of the syntactic equivalents is useful in correcting a sentence that doesn't work very well.

The existence of the different syntactic options also allows us to decide how many predications to put in the same sentence. The traditional definition, "A sentence is a group of words that expresses a complete thought," emphasizes the fact that we put clauses together because they are related semantically. We don't say, "It's raining in Northern Canada and next week there will be a demolition derby in Jacksonville, Florida." It's difficult, however, to know just which clauses to put together in a sentence, because most people's thoughts are somewhat blurred around the edges. In the European languages we are all most familiar with, the sentence is a very important level of analysis; but in the aboriginal languages of New Guinea, the clauses are combined into paragraph-like units. There's no clear distinction between the sentence and the paragraph. Even though our sentences are very separate units, they should flow into one another smoothly.

Needless to say, this careful matching of thought and syntactic form is unnecessary in the spoken language, since the hearer can interrupt with questions and the speaker can repeat or restate in another form anything that has been misunderstood. We do find these careful structures in formal addresses and other situations where the hearer is unable to "talk back." In order to use the full expressive potential of the language, the writer must have good control of these syntactic structures.

Basic Clause Types and Their Transformations

A number of years ago, linguists made an extensive effort to classify English clauses on the basis of how many and what kind of clause slots they had. In many cases, the classification depended almost wholly on whether the verbs were transitive or intransitive and what kind of complements could be combined with them. As we have already suggested, the relationship between complement and verb occupies a twilight zone between syntax and semantics, so that the classifications never work very well. However, these clause types are useful in showing us various ways that clause constituents can be moved around. So, the transitive-intransitive classifications are discussed briefly here and then again from a more semantic point of view in Chapter 6.[2] Here are the most common clause types and their transformations:

1. Linking verb, predicate noun or predicate adjective as complement:

    Predicate Noun: Mary is a *student*.
    Predicate Adjective: John is *handsome*.

    Sometimes a verbal or verbal phrase fills the complement slot:

    Three points are *to be remembered*. (Infinitive Phrase as Complement)

    Sometimes the linking verb has an adverbial word or a prepositional phrase expressing location in the complement slot, although most grammarians avoid calling these adverbials complements.

    My wife is *away*. (Adverb)
    The book is *on the table*. (Prepositional Phrase)

    Transformation: One available transformation of this clause type is sometimes called "there-insertion." "There" becomes the dummy subject, the true subject moves to the complement slot, and the complement, if any, apparently becomes an adjunct. Examples:

    There are three points to be remembered.
    There's a book on the table.

    Obviously not all clauses of this type can undergo the transformation.

2. Intransitive verb, followed by optional adverbial word or phrase. (Most grammars do not call the word or phrase a complement, although often it seems quite closely related to the verb.)

    No adverbial: The bird sings.
    Adverb adverbial: The arsonist ran *away*.
    Prepositional phrase adverbial: The ball rolled *under the table*.

    Notice that many intransitive verbs express some kind of motion. Others could easily become transitive with the addition of an obvious direct object, such as "The bird sings *a feeble little song*."

---

[2]You might try getting your instructor to let you skip this section and go on to "Problems with Passives." Students have so much trouble with the transitive-intransitive concept that I wonder whether it truly corresponds to anything in our intuitive language knowledge.

Transformation: The most common transformation is to begin the clause with the adverbial modifier. It's often used in children's books to make rather boring material sound more exciting:

Under the table rolled the ball.
Away ran the arsonist.

3. Transitive verb, one complement.
   Jim ate the *bread*.

Transformation: The passive transformation allows the direct object to appear at the beginning of the sentence as subject. The original subject is moved to the end of the sentence. A form of *be* plus past participle must be added to the verb phrase:

The bread was eaten (by Jim).

4. Transitive verb, two complements. These verbs all express some aspect of giving, showing, or telling. The two complements appear with the indirect object first, then the direct object.

           I.O.   D.O.
   Jim gave Bill/ a sandwich.
   Jim showed Bill/his new computer.
   Jim told Bill/ the news.

Transformations: In the passive transformation, either of the complements may become the subject. The other one remains in the complement slot:

Bill was given a sandwich by Jim.
A sandwich was given Bill by Jim.

Another common transformation is called *dative movement*. The indirect object, or benefactive, becomes a prepositional phrase:

Jim showed his new computer *to Bill*.

When dative movement is performed, we find that the verbs of this group fall into two sub-categories—those that require the preposition *to* for the benefactive and those that require *for*.

5. Transitive verb, two complements. These verbs express such actions as proving, electing, or making. One of the complements is a direct object, and the other is an object complement: that is, it completes the meaning of the verb and also describes the direct object. In this it's similar to a predicate noun or a predicate adjective:

                                       D.O.   O.C.
   Noun as object complement: Jim made Bill/his assistant manager.

                                                    D.O.   O.C.
Adjective as object complement: Jim made Bill/very happy.

Transformation: in the passive transformation, the direct object always becomes the subject and the object complement remains in the complement slot:

> Bill was made assistant manager by Jim.
> Bill was made very happy by Jim.

Problems with Passives

All three kinds of transitive verbs can undergo the passive transformation, rearranging the constituents so that a complement appears in the subject slot. In writing it's useful to know how to turn a passive into an active and vice-versa. Besides rearranging constituents, one must change the verb form. The verb contains some form of *be* as a structure word and a past participle *as the main verb*. Sometimes the past participle is the same as the past tense, but sometimes it isn't. Consider the following examples:

> The UFO *was seen* by a little boy. (be-auxiliary *was*, past participle *seen*)
> The cars *were washed* by members of the fraternity. (be-auxiliary *were*, past participle *washed*)

In the second example, the past participle is the same as the past tense form. Notice carefully: unless the verb phrase contains both a be-word and a past participle as the main verb, it cannot be passive. The following sentences do not contain passive verb phrases:

> The fraternity members *were washing* cars. (be-auxiliary but no past participle)
> A little boy *had seen* the UFO. (Past participle but no be-auxiliary)
> The fraternity members *had been* washing cars. (*Been* is both a be-auxiliary and a past participle, but it isn't the main verb.)

It's worthwhile to study these examples very carefully, because when asked to change the verb from passive to active, students commonly change the *tense* from past to present or the *aspect* to progressive, or make some other change that does not move the complement into the subject slot.

Furthermore, one of the most frequent red-pencil comments is "awkward passive" or "overuse of passive." Let's compare the characteristics of active and passive clauses to see what's involved in this criticism. An active clause arranges its constituents as follows: doer of action, verb naming the action, direct object—the person or thing affected by the action. This clause pattern leads to a clear awareness of the doer. It focuses on the separation between the doer, stated in the subject slot, and the process as a whole, stated in the other slots. The active clause is direct and blunt; it's peppy and vivid. Because it focuses so strongly on the doer, it places responsibility without equivocation. Therefore, wrongdoing children avoid it. "The window was broken" somehow sounds better to them than "We broke the window."

A passive clause, on the other hand, rearranges its constituents in this order: person or thing affected by the action, verb naming the action, and doer. The rules of syntax allow one to delete the doer, named in a prepositional phrase: "Bill was made assistant manager" is just as correct as "Bill was made assistant manager by Jim." This is useful, because in many instances the total process is more important than who or what did it. Oftentimes the doer is irrelevant, or obvious from the context. If someone was arrested, the police obviously were the doers; if someone was elected, the voters did it. Scientists naturally use the passive to report the results of their experiments, because a valid scientific procedure should have the same result no matter who does it. Omission of the doer often leads to a better fit between reality and the language which reports it. Consider this sentence:

> For many illnesses, an important interaction of mind and body has been discovered.

The active version, "For many illnesses, medical science has discovered an important interaction of mind and body," subtly distorts the situation by making an abstraction, medical science, into an actor. Discoveries are made by individuals and teams of scientists, not by "science."

If the passive is preferred in so many instances, why do writing teachers object to it? First, the omission of the doer can lead to actual dishonesty. To say "The funds have been spent" is dishonest when the real situation is that the mayor used the money for a vacation. Second, the association of the passive with scientific and other kinds of intellectual and formal writing makes it inappropriate in the casual, personal writing which many theme assignments call for. Even when the topic is academic and intellectual, a little informality makes the information easier to grasp. Finally, the list of verbs which can appear in passive clauses is not quite the same as the list of verbs which can appear in active clauses. Consider the following two sentences:

> Jerry had a hot fudge sundae. (active)
> A hot fudge sundae was had by Jerry. (passive)

Don't you agree that there's something a little peculiar about the second sentence? People commonly use *had* as a passive in the cliché, "A good time was had by all," but lovers of good style wince when they hear it.

Overuse of the passive is not wrong—that is, ungrammatical—but it is ungraceful. It's a fault of style rather than a violation of grammatical structure. Most writing becomes more effective when the writer increases the percentage of active clauses. The best way to learn to avoid awkward passives is to train your ear by constantly reading well-written English. But when "writing by ear" fails, you can ask yourself three questions:

1. Which leads to distortion of the facts—leaving out the doer or putting it in?
2. Is the overall impression I wish to create more formal, or more informal?
3. Is this verb one I should avoid putting into a passive clause?

These questions will usually resolve the problem and stave off the red-pencil blues.

Curing Red-Pencil Phobia

Now let's go back to our hapless student and the pock-marked theme with which we began, relating the cryptic red symbols to what we have learned about clause and sentence structures.

FRAG (short for *fragment*). This error occurs when a construction which should be incorporated into a larger clause is mistakenly punctuated as a complete sentence. For example:

Verbal phrase: Accomplishing your purposes with the least possible time and effort.

Correction: Through efficient planning you can have both achievement and free time, accomplishing your purposes with the least possible time and effort.

Subordinate clause: Even though the horses had been carefully groomed.

Correction: Even though the horses had been carefully groomed, they made a rather shabby appearance at the show.

Alternate correction: The horses made a rather shabby appearance at the show, even though they had been carefully groomed. (Notice the reversed positions of *horses* and *they*.)

Relative clause: That have a certain unmistakable social prestige.

Correction: He decided to work hard at learning the language usages that have a certain unmistakable social prestige.

Subject omitted: And introduced his fiancée to his parents.

Correction: He finally got up his courage and introduced his fiancée to his parents.

Alternate correction: And he introduced his fiancée to his parents. (Notice that a person who begins a sentence with *and* or *but* does not commit a fragment error as long as the necessary clause slots are filled.)

RO (short for *run-on sentence*). This error occurs when the writer fails to separate two closely-related clauses by standard punctuation and/or conjunctions. For example:

The laundry problem wasn't much different that April freshness eluded me.

Correction: The laundry problem wasn't much different. That April freshness eluded me. (A semicolon could be used after *different* instead of a period.)

Alternate correction: The laundry problem wasn't much different, since that April freshness eluded me.

CS (comma splice)[3] This error is just like the run-on except that the two clauses are separated by a comma:

The laundry problem wasn't much different, that April freshness eluded me.

Correction: same as for run-on.

SS (sentence sense). This notation covers a variety of errors, such as dangling participles, failure to put noun and pronoun in proper order, and failure to arrange the clause constituents in the best way. Example:

I have, for the past two years, done little of it except that I wrote a few checks here and there, which scares me.

Correction: Writing scares me, but I do a little of it: I've written several checks in the past two years.

Another try: Having written nothing but checks for the past two years, I'm scared of writing.

I must admit that neither of my corrections satisfies me. The first one, using coordinate clauses, builds up to a nice climax but has a choppy rhythm. The second one, using a participial phrase and a passive transformation, throws away the little joke about writing checks. In other words, everyone has trouble. Trying to fit simultaneous, complex, rather fuzzy thoughts into the neat linear structures of the written language is like trying to stuff a large and obstreperous cat into a small box. Most people need several tries—that is, revisions—before their work is passable, and even then professional writers need editors to polish and smooth their work further. That's why most composition teachers are frustrated editors and most editors are just frustrated. Although some knowledge of syntax can reduce the number of red pencilings, they can never be eliminated completely. They are in no way a slur on your intelligence or the validity of your thought, so don't let them give you the blues.

Exercises

1. Clause Slots

Fill the blank with an item of your choice.

1. _____ is more fun than anything else.
   subject

---

[3]In some composition texts the comma splice is called "comma fault." It's a perfectly correct way of punctuating in German, and many English writers are beginning to use it in informal writing.

2. The heroine of the soap opera _____ the other person.
                                               predicate

3. My personality is _____.
                     complement

4. _____, we decided to enroll for the class.
    adjunct

5. We plan _____ tomorrow.
               infinitive phrase as complement.

6. Nobody believed that _____.
                           noun clause as complement

2. *Clause Slots*

A. Identify the subject, predicate, complement(s) if any, and adjunct(s) if any in each of the following base clauses.

1. The winter season depresses many people.
2. The shortness of the day is a factor.
3. Also, the holidays are times of stress, at least for some people.
4. Those who work in mental health expect the yearly recurrence of "Christmas neurosis."
5. Some people will not admit that they are not experiencing joy.
6. They become withdrawn, thus complicating the problem further.
7. Withdrawing into oneself, as you might expect, hampers the natural recovery process.
8. As the days become longer, however, these people cheer up.

B. Rewrite specified sentences as follows:

1. Provide three other fillers for the subject slot of #1. Try to use something other than noun phrases. (See Fig. 10.)
2. Substitute two other verb-complement combinations in #4.
3. Suggest two other fillers for the adjunct slot in #7.

3. *Adjuncts*

A. Supply adjuncts in the introducer position for each of the following sentences, punctuating correctly. In the blank at left, state whether your introducer is a clause or a phrase.

Example:

phrase   *As a reminder of her war against excess flesh,* Janet has a large picture in her bathroom of St. George killing the dragon.

_____   1. _____
                            _____ West's team won the game handily.

_____   2. _____
                            _____ many people's conception of United States history was changed by *Roots*.

_____ 3. _____
_____ producers often include one
doubtful scene so that their film will receive a PG rather than
a G rating.
_____ 4. _____
_____ it is not surprising that electronic games have become big business.
_____ 5. _____
_____ at Christmastime the stores
are full of who-needs-it kitchen gadgets.

B. Rewrite each sentence with the adjunct in the medial or concluding position. Are there any of your sentences that definitely sound better when the adjunct is moved? Are there any sentences where moving the adjunct is impossible? Why?

4. Restrictive and Nonrestrictive Elements

State whether the italicized element is a post-modifier (restrictive) or an adjunct (nonrestrictive). If it's an adjunct, what punctuation should be added?
1. Food *that tastes the best* has the most calories.
2. Monster movies *which were very popular in the seventies* may be making a comeback.
3. Frontier Days *which includes one of the biggest rodeos in the United States* also provides an opportunity *for members of several Indian tribes to visit among themselves.*
4. Guiseppe Mozzarelli *who was known as the pizza king of Fourth Avenue* now sells Texas chili *having changed his name to Jose Martinez.*
5. A person *who can smile in the midst of disaster* has thought of someone to blame it on.
6. *Finding grammar difficult* she tried to have the requirement waived.

5. Coordinate and Subordinate

Rewrite the following coordinate clauses by subordinating one. Sometimes the new sentence will seem more effective, sometimes less effective, than the original.
1. Matt's parents wanted him to get an education, and they offered him free room and board in exchange for attendance at college.
2. "Star Trek" was not immediately successful in terms of huge audiences, and the network gradually withdrew support of it.
3. Love is as strong as death, and jealousy is as cruel as the grave.
4. He owns the only bat; therefore he can pitch if he wants to.

5. Marriage has become strictly optional with many couples, and the courts have recognized some non-marriages as being the legal equivalent.
6. Cats tend to maintain their independence, for they do not really need either human beings or other cats.
7. Dogs are social creatures, and they either live with human beings or run in wild packs.
8. They are the blindest people, for they refuse to see.
9. Monty Python has been acclaimed for satiric genius, but many people are displeased by the lack of respect for sacred institutions.
10. You photocopy valuable material for your term paper, and then you decide that it is worthless.

6. The Extraposition Transformation

A. Each of the following sentences contains an italicized noun clause or verbal phrase used as a noun. Rewrite the sentence using an extraposition. Example: *That the student had not prepared for the test* was obvious. Rewrite: It was obvious that the student had not prepared for the test.
1. *That the students were sleeping, playing cards, and reading newspapers instead of paying attention* did not bother the professor at all.
2. *Going to the mountains for a day of skiing* is time-consuming but worthwhile.
3. *To turn on the set after the evening meal* almost guarantees a wasted evening.
4. *How the veterinarian diagnosed the disease* was not the main issue.
5. *For the President to truly understand his power base* makes his leadership more effective.

B. Rearrange the following sentences so as to eliminate the extraposition. The noun clause or verbal phrase is italicized.
1. It was a major theme of Colonial literature *that the New World offered political hope.*
2. It is a great responsibility *being as perfect as I am.*
3. It is the purpose of safety programs *to educate the employees about potential hazards.*
4. It's irrelevant *exactly how the overalls got in Mrs. Murphy's chowder.*
5. It was a surprise *for the Fonz to develop an interest in classical ballet.*
6. It's human *to err,* but it requires a computer *to really foul things up.*

C. Which of the sentences in A and B sound better with extraposition? Which sound better without it? Can you see why?

7. Sentence Improvement

Combine each group of short, repetitive sentences into a single well-structured one.

Group 1. At the age of fourteen Franklin was sent to Groton. Groton is a boys' school in Groton, Massachusetts. Here at Groton is where Roosevelt began his fine education that brought him an excellent understanding of our language.

Group 2. From Groton, Franklin went to Harvard University where he completed his undergraduate work in three years. Roosevelt's study of English and American literature at Harvard was a main source of his rhetorical power.

Group 3. Roosevelt was elected senator in New York's senate and later was elected governor of New York. Roosevelt was appointed as Assistant Secretary of the Navy. This political experience and speech making experience prepared him for the most important job of his life. In 1932 Roosevelt was nominated and elected as president of the United States.

Group 4. Roosevelt's speech delivery had many fine phonetic qualities that shaped his audience persuasion. Roosevelt's widely praised voice quality and direct speaking manner are two main phonetic qualities attributed to his audience persuasion.

Group 5. Roosevelt's simple and clear literary style contributed to his audience persuasion. His literary style consisted of two talents. First, Roosevelt had the ability to use the force of empathy as his strongest emotional appeal. Second, Roosevelt had the ability to use words and phrases in a context that his audience understood.

8. Clause Types and Transformations

For each of the following examples, classify the clause type as linking, intransitive, or transitive with one or two complements. Then rewrite each sentence using one of the transformations appropriate to its clause type. Identifying the clause type may involve identifying the clause-level constituents of subject, verb, complement, and adjunct, or you may be able to do it just by looking at the meaning of the verb. Consider the book title as a single noun.

1. *The Elephant Who Liked to Smash Small Cars* is a children's book.
2. The elephant lived near a highway.
3. He watched the cars going by.
4. He smashed all the small cars on the highway.
5. One day an automobile dealer opened a car lot near the elephant's home.
6. He sold small cars.
7. The elephant smashed all the dealer's small cars.
8. The automobile dealer asked him to stop.
9. But the elephant refused, crossly.
10. So the automobile dealer bought a lot of big cars.
11. With one of them, he smashed the elephant.

12. He made the elephant completely flat.
13. Then the elephant promised the dealer not to smash the small cars any more.
14. This book was my child's all-time favorite.
15. But the librarian removed it from the reading room.
16. She considered it too violent.

9. *Active and Passive*

A. All the following sentences have passive verbs. Rewrite them as actives.
1. In the opening canto of the *Divine Comedy*, Dante is prevented from following the right path by three fierce animals.
2. He is rescued from this dilemma by Virgil.
3. He is guided through Hell and Purgatory by Virgil.
4. Various sins and their punishments are observed by Dante and Virgil.
5. At the top of Mount Purgatory, Dante is met by Beatrice, his first love.
6. He is guided from sphere to sphere to sphere in Heaven by Beatrice.
7. This great poem has been admired by people all over the civilized world.

B. All the following sentences have active verbs. Rewrite them as passives. You may wish to omit the subject of the active version.
1. Nuclear fission produced the first atomic explosions.
2. Scientists now trigger nuclear fusion with fission.
3. Great heat and pressure produce the fusion.
4. Technology can control nuclear reactions for peacetime purposes.
5. We hope to avoid nuclear shootouts.

C. Which of the sentences in A and B sound better as actives? Which sound better as passives? Why?

10. *Vietnamese Clause Structure*

Determine the meanings of the Vietnamese words. Then write a paragraph describing the clause structure of Vietnamese. In what order do subjects, verbs, and complements occur? Do you consider /kuʔŋ/ and xʌwɲ/ adjuncts, or would you consider them part of the verb phrase? How does Vietnamese differ from English in regard to which clause slots are required? How does the structure of the Vietnamese noun phrase differ from that of English?

(Phonemic tone is not indicated)

1. čɔ sem čim tɔ The dog sees the big bird.
2. čɔ tɔ xʌwŋ sem čɔ ñɔ The big dog does not see the little dog.
3. thʌy čim ñɔ Someone perceives the little bird.
4. čim kuʔŋ sem čɔ The bird also sees the dog.
5. čim kuʔŋ thʌy The bird also perceives.
6. xʌwŋ thʌy Someone does not perceive.
7. čɔ thʌy čim The dog perceives the bird.
8. sem Someone sees.
9. čim tɔ thʌy čɔ tɔ The big bird perceives the big dog.
10. čim ñɔ kuʔŋ thʌy čim tɔ The little bird also perceives the big bird.

6

I Mean ... You Know

In Ursula K. LeGuin's fantasy, *The Wizard of Earthsea*, part of the young wizard's training involves learning the "true names" of things in order to control them. This idea of a direct connection between the word and the thing is very old, and indeed it still exists. One thinks of tribal cultures in which people carefully keep their true names hidden from everyone except their most trusted friends, but even in twentieth century America there are people who refuse to name a possible disaster, lest by saying the words they bring it into being. Modern linguists, following in the footsteps of Ferdinand de Saussure (1857–1913), generally assert that the relationship between the name and the thing it signifies is completely arbitrary. They have observed, however, that words that sound alike are often similar in meaning. Consider the following: flip, flicker, fly, flow, flash, fleet, flap, and flare. All of these words begin with /fl/, and all of them suggest quick movement. This relationship between sound and meaning is called *phonesthesia*, or *sound symbolism*.

The existence of sound symbolism proves that the relationship between sound and meaning is not completely arbitrary on the word level. As we move into other levels, other questions arise. English clauses usually have subject-verb-object structures. Is the separation of the doer and the action a quality of "the real world," or is it merely a syntactic convention? In combining clauses, English speakers and writers try to maintain a correct "sequence of tenses" so that one is exceedingly conscious of the order in which events occurred. Again, is this a quality of the universe, of our perception of the universe, or mere convention? *Semantics* is the branch of linguistics that studies the relationship between language and reality. The same name is given to the component of language that organizes and structures concepts and meanings.

Both linguists and philosophers study semantics, but linguists study it in a special way, as one of the three components of language along with syntax and phonology. Both syntax and phonology have highly structured systems with some units subordinated to others. The semantic component of a language also has structure, but linguists are only beginning to understand it. Thus, the material in this chapter on semantics is less unified than the material on syntax and phonology.

The first thing to notice in our study of semantics, or the relationship between language and reality, is that language expresses our thoughts about our world rather than describing the world directly. If language described the physical world directly, then it would be impossible to apply the same word, *mouth*, to such completely different physical realities as the mouth of a person and the mouth of a river. This trick of language is possible only because a thinker has seen a resemblance between these two physical realities. Another proof that language does not directly reflect reality is our ability to understand words which do not refer to anything we can see in the physical world. To explain, we will need two technical terms, *referent* and *sense*. A *referent* is the object, action, state, or quality which a word designates. The lexical items "dog," "canine," "man's best friend," and "Spot" all have the same referent. *Sense* is meaning. The sense of "dog" involves four-footedness, hairiness, certain smells, and the ability to bark. A word can have sense without having a referent in the real world. Examples of such words include "dragon," "unicorn," "hobbit," as well as less poetic items such as "the king of the United States."

If language expresses thoughts about the world instead of expressing the world, what is the relationship between language and thought? The strongest view of this relationship is that language actually limits the concepts which can be formed. Benjamin Lee Whorf, an anthropologist-linguist of the 1930s, held this view. He argued that our physicists have had difficulty in formulating some concepts of modern physics because they were hampered by being speakers of Occidental languages. These languages, he claimed, forced speakers to conceptualize reality in terms of an artificial difference between actor and action; they also promoted a concentration on natural phenomena as linear, one-thing-after-another processes to the detriment of holistic thinking. Whorf maintained that the Hopi Indian language did not have these flaws and was therefore more compatible with modern physical science.

Whorf's theory was exciting to linguistic scientists, but they were never able to devise an experiment which would prove or disprove it completely. Several experiments were conducted on the terminology of color. English has words for about eleven "major" colors: black, white, red, green, yellow, blue, brown, purple, pink, orange, and gray. We have, of course, other terms, but they are variations of the major colors: crimson, cerise, scarlet, and maroon are all "kinds" of red. Russian has one more major color distinction—the distinction between light blue and dark blue, one which seems very natural when you think of the difficulty some small children have in grasping the fact that the indigo jeans and the sky are both "blue." The Hanunóo language of the Philippines has a less differentiated system of major colors: (ma)biru, which includes black and dark tints of other colors; (ma) lagti?, white and light tints of other colors; (ma) rara?, maroon, red, and orange; and (ma) latuy, light green, yellow and light brown.[1] Since presumably the physical laws governing light waves and the physiology of the eye are the same for all peoples, if the Hanunóo speakers were less able to differentiate subtle variations in color than English or Russian speakers, this would prove that language does affect thought in the Whorfian sense.

The practical difficulties in conducting such an experiment are enormous. Visualize the hapless researcher painfully learning the exotic language, trying to find informants whose minds have not been affected by learning an Occidental language for trading purposes, struggling to protect the color chips from changing through exposure to extreme weather conditions, trying to explain to the informants what information is wanted without suggesting answers to them—it's no wonder that the experiments, thus far, have been more or less inconclusive.

Even if Whorf's view that the semantic structure of a language restricts the thoughts of the speakers is correct, these restrictions cannot be absolute. If they were, it would be impossible to translate from one language to another. English has one word, *love*, where Greek has three: *agape* or goodwill, *philia* or friendship, and *eros* or sexual love. If the deficiency in English caused a deficiency in the ideas of English-speakers, then it would be impossible for them even to learn Greek. Despite the absurdity of such absolute restriction, our own experience teaches us that language does have some effect on thought. A person who takes botany and learns a lot of plant names finds, to his surprise and pleasure, that what was once an undifferentiated mass of greenery has taken on structure and individuality. He sees the plants more clearly because he knows what to call them. To a large extent, becoming knowledgeable in any branch of study is a matter of learning to speak its language. There's truth in the saying, "People go to law school to learn to talk like lawyers." And when we learn a new word, we feel that we have gained control over a small chunk of reality.

There is, however, one group of thinkers who assert that this feeling of control is illusory. A philosophy of life called General Semantics, promulgated by Alfred Korzybski and popularized in the U.S. by S. I. Hayakawa, asserts that a great deal of our frustration and mental illness is caused by trusting words too much. According to General Semantics, to call an object a chair builds up certain expectations, including the one that the object will

---

[1] Cited from H. C. Conklin, "Hanunóo Color Categories," *Southwestern Journal of Anthropology* (11: 339–44), Geoffrey Leech, *Semantics* (Harmondsworth, England: Penguin Books, 1974), p. 29.

support the weight of a human body. But chairs differ greatly in their solidity and state of repair. Korzybski recommended that we use index numbers to remind ourselves that the name is different from the thing, that chair $_{296}$ supports the sitter while chair $_{297}$ is likely to collapse. This philosophy is outside the province of linguistic semantics, which has to do with the structure of language rather than the formulation of a healthy attitude toward life. As Korzybski himself would say, (linguistic) semantics $_{1985}$ is not (General) Semantics $_{1933}$.

Like other branches of linguistics, semantics is concerned with describing the *competence* (linguistic knowledge and abilities) of the speaker. Linguists have found important semantic patterns on word, phrase, and sentence levels.

Semantics on the Word Level

One approach to analyzing the linguistic system on the word level involves the use of *semantic features*, or components of meaning. For example, "man," "woman," "boy," and "girl" all have the semantic features of +Animate and +Human. "Man" and "woman" share the semantic feature of +Adult, while "boy" and "girl" are −Adult. This approach, first used by anthropological linguists to analyze kinship terms, allows us to define relationships between synonyms and antonyms very precisely.

Synonyms are words that share a great many semantic features. "Fat" and "obese" are synonyms. Both have the semantic features of +Animate, and +Overweight, but "obese" has the additional feature of +Human, whereas "fat" can be either +Human or −Human. We say "a fat steer" or "a fat man," but we would not say "an obese steer." The fact that it sounds all right to say "an obese dog" does not disprove this distinction between "fat" and "obese," but rather shows that many people treat dogs as if they were human. Synonyms never have exactly the same lexical features. The old saying, "If you and I are exactly alike, then one of us is unnecessary" applies to synonyms. If two words seem to have exactly the same meaning, then differences between them will develop, or else one of them will drop out of the language.

A pair of antonyms shares all semantic features but one. A word may be put into several antonym pairs, depending on which feature is being contrasted. Thus "man" is the opposite of "woman" when the contrastive feature is ±Male, but the opposite of "boy" when the contrastive feature is ±Adult. It's an oddity of English that "short" has two common antonyms: "tall," applied to objects perpendicular to the earth's surface, and "long," applied to objects parallel to the earth's surface. Some words are not exactly antonyms, but they do contrast. We do not think of "red" and "green" as antonyms, yet the statements "That apple is all red" and "That apple is all green" cannot both be true of the same apple, for the two terms are *incom-*

patible. When there are only two incompatible terms, such as alive/dead, they are said to be *complementary*. When a sentence contains words with incompatible or complementary features, it is called an *anomalous* sentence. Children's books and folk songs often use anomalous sentences for humor. For example, "Oh Suzanna" contains the line, "The sun was so hot I froze to death." To some extent, one's judgment that a sentence is anomalous depends on cultural presuppositions. In times when monogamy was strictly observed, the sentence "My brother is an only child" would be anomalous. Now that step-relationships are so common, the sentence might be perfectly natural.

Antonyms such as tall/short, hot/cold, intelligent/stupid are *gradable;* that is, the meaning of the word is determined in relation to a norm. To call an insect "large" means that it's large for an insect. A large insect is many times smaller than a small dog. This principle is illustrated in the children's book *The Phantom Tollbooth*, where an average-sized man claims to be the world's smallest giant, the world's largest midget, the fattest thin man, and the thinnest fat man.[2] Gradable antonyms differ from complementary ones in that one of the complementary antonyms must apply, while this is not true of gradable antonyms. A thing must be either alive or dead (complementary), but it may be neither tall nor short (gradable), but just average.

Another peculiarity of antonyms is that one member of a pair may be *marked*, which implies that it's unusual, while the other member is *unmarked* or usual. The unmarked term is the one used to ask about gradability. We say, "How tall is he?" and not "How short is he?" "Tall" is the unmarked member of that pair. Whether a word is marked or not may depend on the situation. For example, we say "How cold is it?" when talking about a freezer and "How hot is it" when talking about an oven. In English, the pronoun *he* is supposed to be unmarked. If the instructions say "Every candidate must bring *his* own pencil," the candidates may be either men or both sexes. If the instruction is "Every candidate must bring *her* own pencil," the candidates are all women. (Our language—and society—seem to be undergoing change on this point.)

The study of synonyms and antonyms is important because they're part of our language competence. The lexical items that we know are not isolated bits of knowledge, but are patterned into semantic categories. Apparently our mental "filing system" puts these related words together. In addition to synonyms and antonyms, our language knowledge is organized by *taxonomic sets*. As we learn the meanings of words, we learn relationships like X is *part of* Y and A is *a kind of* B. The terms "chassis," "bumper," "hood," "transmission" are related in our minds because they're all parts of

---

[2]Example suggested by Victoria Fromkin and Robert Rodman in *An Introduction to Language*, 2nd ed. (New York: Holt, Rinehart and Winston, 1978), p. 173.

a car. "Copper," "iron," "aluminum" and "lead" are related because they're kinds of minerals. Of course, words often belong to more than one set. "Turkey" is related to "robin," "duck," and "gull" as a kind of bird, but to "pig," "sheep," and "chicken" as a kind of domestic animal. When lexical items are related in terms of general-specific categories, then the more general term is a *superordinate* and the more specific one a *hyponym*. "Athlete" is a superordinate with respect to "football player," "sprinter," and "swimmer." "Football player" is a superordinate for which "guard," "quarterback," and "end" are hyponyms. Taxonomic sets are determined by the needs of a particular culture or subculture. Eskimos and skiers, for example, have many hyponyms for the superordinate "snow." People less concerned with the weather may lack a well-developed set in this semantic area. One reason that learning a foreign language gives us a new view of life is that we learn different ways of classifying items into taxonomic sets.

One of the tasks of our elementary school years was learning to distinguish between various homonyms such as "bear" and "bare," "son" and "sun." Homonyms come about when, through phonetic change or some other accidental occurrence, two words happen to be pronounced alike. If people began to leave off the second syllable of "data" it might become a homonym of "date." Even now, such words as "find" and "fine" are homonyms in some dialects of English. We often distinguish between homonyms by spelling, but not always. "Bear" in "I saw a bear" and "bear" in "I bear my troubles bravely" are homonyms even though they are spelled the same way. They are derived from two completely different Indo-European roots.

Polysemy is the ability of a word to have quite different sets of semantic features in different situations. *Charged,* for example, has the semantic feature of +Physical in the sentence "The mechanic charged the battery," but −Physical in "The speaker charged the graduating class to create a better world order." *Child* has the semantic feature of −Adult in the context of determining the admission fee to an entertainment, but +Adult in the sentence "It's a child's duty to make wise decisions on behalf of a senile parent." In practice it's impossible to distinguish clearly between homonyms and polysemic words, although dictionary-makers try to do it by giving separate entries to homonyms.

The way semantic features change, especially in antonyms and polysemic words, shows us that the "meaning" is never an absolute, quantifiable attribute of a lexical item, but rather something produced by a relationship. Every word in a sentence modifies the meaning of every other word. The interpretation of speech or writing is a kind of guessing game in which the hearer chooses the most relevant meaning he can. "The pipes (*plumbing? tobacco? bagpipes?*) are out of order (*probably plumbing*) but the church (*oh!*) can't afford to have the organ repairman come." In such guessing games, context and our knowledge of what the speaker is likely to be talking about play a greater part than we realize. If the preceding sentence was spoken by a minister, the guesser might think first of organ pipes.

In communicating bits of meaning, giving clues to the guesser, different languages focus on different semantic features. Swahili, for example, focuses on the difference between animate and inanimate nouns by using animate prefixes with one and inanimate prefixes with the other. English focuses on number. For all but a few exceptions, it's impossible to use a noun in English without choosing between a singular form and a plural form. In English, a politician can be tactfully ambiguous in saying "We must cut down on spending for a while." Does this mean that the politicians will cut down, or that only the citizens will? This ambiguity is impossible in Desano, a tribal language of Colombia, which distinguishes between an exclusive *we* (speaker and his group, but not the hearers) and an inclusive *we* (speaker, hearers, and possibly others).

Semantics on the Phrase Level

The use of semantic features helps us recognize patterns of meaning when we compare single words with one another. Combining words into larger units presents a different problem. As we've already seen, the meaning of a word is affected by the sentence in which it appears, so that the meaning of a word group is something different from a simple addition of Word 1 Meaning + Word 2 Meaning + Word 3 Meaning. This difference is especially obvious when we consider *idioms*. An idiom is a set phrase whose meaning cannot be derived from the meanings of the individual words. Some examples of idioms are "to hit the road," "gave up the ghost," "passed away," "put up with," and "couldn't care less." Since the idiom has meaning as a whole, a word-by-word translation into another language produces a ludicrous result. The German equivalent of "couldn't care less" is, translated literally, "it makes me nothing out." To determine whether a phrase is an idiom or not, try to restate it in another syntactic form. For instance, "They hit the road" is meaningful; but the passive form "The road was hit by them" is impossible.

A group of words which usually appear together but which are not as "frozen" as an idiom is called a *collocation*. For example, we "make" a bed, a pizza, a deadline, a business deal, or a point in backgammon, but we "fix" hair, "reach" a goal, and "take" a trick in bridge. Often the major difference in synonyms is in the words with which they collocate. "Pretty" and "handsome" are synonyms, but they collocate with different nouns. Girls, women's clothes, wall decorations, and some animals are called "pretty"; men, men's clothes, large items of furniture (especially office furniture), and exceedingly expensive pieces of jewelry are called "handsome." Needless to say, collocations which "sound right" differ according to the individual's dialect, and it's often difficult to decide whether an expression should be classified as an idiom or a collocation.

Semantics on the Clause and Sentence Levels

One useful way to study semantic relationships on the clause or sentence level is by looking at *paraphrase* relationships. Two sentences are in paraphrase relationship if they say the same thing in slightly different words. Consider the following pair of sentences:
  A. The cloud formation was not unlike my memory of the Chicago skyline.
  B. The clouds produced a configuration like a city skyline—like Chicago, at least as I remembered it.

These two sentences have the same semantic content in that they have the same truth value. Both of them are logically incompatible with such statements as "I saw nothing in the cloud formation" and "I don't remember what the Chicago skyline looks like." They are analogous to synonyms; in fact, synonyms are sometimes called "lexical paraphrases." In studying paraphrases, linguists have concentrated on a special kind of paraphrase called the *transformation*. The transformation differs from the example cited above in that it contains the same meaningful words but arranges them according to a different syntactic pattern. For example:
  A. Jerry saw a cloud formation that looked like Chicago.
  B. A cloud formation that looked like Chicago was seen by Jerry.

If you've studied Chapter 5, you know that there are certain transformational relationships between clauses, and that they can be expressed by a syntactic formula: NP_1 + Active VP + NP_2 –> NP_2 + Passive VP + by NP_1. Although these sentences are arranged differently, they have the same semantic components: an action, an actor, and something acted on. The semantic function of each noun phrase is called its *role*.

In studying role patterns, linguists have come up with different numbers of roles and different names for them, varying from three to about eight. The number of roles listed depends on the analyst's judgment of what is needed to describe language accurately and understandably. The following roles are those most often cited:
  1. agent (or actor)—the doer of an action, usually animate. Example: *Scotty* repaired the Enterprise.
  2. instrument—the inanimate doer of an action, or the means by which an action is done. Example: *The key* opened the safe.
  3. patient—the receiver of an action, the one on whom the action is performed. Example: *The patient* was X-rayed to determine the location of the bullet.

4. experiencer—an animate being inwardly affected by an emotion, a sensation, or an intellectual insight. Since the role of experiencer has been particularly ignored by traditional syntactic analysis, let's look at several examples:
   A. *Dante* loved Beatrice.
   B. *The nurse* felt hot.
   C. *Mary* understands linguistics.

In Sentence A, Dante is not an agent, and in the story Beatrice is not a patient; she's completely unaware of his love for her. The love affects only Dante's inward being, so Dante is an experiencer. In Sentence B, the nurse is an experiencer rather than an agent. Contrast this sentence with "The nurse felt the child's forehead," in which the nurse is an agent. (Question: Is "felt" a polysemic word?) In Sentence C, Mary is an experiencer because she enjoys intellectual insight—although considering the amount of work involved, she could be excused for demanding agent status.

5. goal—the place to which someone or something arrives by traveling, or something achieved by an action. Examples: We reached *Denver* in the middle of the night (place). She wrote *a book* (something created). Jack scored *a touchdown* (both a place on the field and something created).

6. benefactive (or dative)—the one, usually animate, for whose benefit an action is performed. Example: The orchestra performed an encore for the enthusiastic *audience*. Some linguists do not include this role, because many benefactives can accept an alternate analysis of experiencer (the audience, after all, experiences the encore) or goal, as in "Jennifer passed a love note to *her boy friend*."

7. locative—location in space or time. Example: The orchestra performed in *Denver*.

8. source—the place or direction from which something comes. Example: I would rather buy local produce instead of vegetables from *California*.

9. possessive (or genitive)—something associated with something or someone else in a special way. This role overlaps with other roles, especially location and source, in subtle ways. To say "the manager's car" for example, may refer to the manager's private possession, or it may refer to a company car that the manager is using. To say "Kathy's children" may refer to the ones that came from her body in birth (source), or it may refer to the ones who are with her in the classroom as her pupils (location). Apparently, possession is a rather sensitive subject, and often the users of a language do not wish to be too specific about it.

We must emphasize that the roles are semantic, not syntactic. A good deal of confusion has arisen in the past through mixing the two. Because the subject of the sentence is so often the agent or actor, we have come to feel that subject and agent are the same thing; but as the passive transformation shows, sometimes the patient is the subject. Each of the semantic roles appears most frequently or normally in a particular syntactic slot. Agents and experiencers, for example, normally appear as subjects, while patients and goals normally appear as direct objects. The most normal syntactic position is *unmarked;* less normal positions are *marked* because they call attention to that part of the sentence. To restate an active sentence as a passive causes more attention to be focused on the patient because it appears as the subject rather than the usual direct object. Instruments, benefactives, locatives, and sources are most often expressed by prepositional phrases in English; other syntactic positions call special attention to them.

Consider the following pairs:
Instrument, unmarked: He opened the can with his scout knife.
Instrument, marked: *His scout knife* opened the can.
Benefactive, unmarked: She made lollipops for the children.
Benefactive, marked: *The children* had lollipops made for them.
Locative, unmarked: The accident happened in the kitchen.
Locative, marked: *The kitchen* was where the accident happened.

Languages differ greatly in the choice of semantic distinctions to be made in the syntax. The distinction between locative and goal, for example, is less obvious in English than in German.

Consider the following sentences:
He arrives in Reno. (goal)
He works in Reno. (locative)

In German, the goal is usually stated in the accusative case while the locative is stated in the dative case:[3]

Er kommt in *die* Stadt. (goal: He comes into the city.)
Er arbeitet in *der* Stadt. (locative: He works in the city.)

This distinction can be made in English by distinguishing between the prepositions *in* and *into:*
The child dived *into* the water. (goal)
The child played *in* the water. (locative)

When we have to make the distinction clear, we can, but our language doesn't force us to make the distinction automatically.

Placing the semantic role in its unmarked syntactic position is one way to de-emphasize it. Another way is to omit it completely. As is discussed in Chapter 5, one of the functions of the passive transformation is to allow the

---

[3]Case is a syntactic category closely connected with role. Charles Fillmore, who first proposed that roles be used to explain some aspects of sentences, called the roles *cases,* but it is better to separate the two clearly. Languages which have syntactic cases do not have a case for each role. The dative case, for example, is often used for instrument, experiencer, benefactive, and locative, and sometimes even for source and possessive.

deletion of the agent. In the sentence "The room felt hot," the placing of the locative in the subject position allows the deletion of the experiencer. The fit between the semantic roles and the syntactic patterns, like everything else in language, is inexact and subject to the vagaries of human cussedness. Both agent and patient can be expressed in an *of* phrase, so that "the love of parents" can mean either "Parents love their children" or "Children love their parents."

A language unit such as "the love of parents," which has two or more possible meanings, is called an *ambiguity*. Much of our present knowledge of clause-level semantics has been achieved through the analysis of ambiguities. Some ambiguities occur because individual lexical items are polysemic. "The bill is too long and complex" is ambiguous because it could refer to a bill presented to the legislature or a statement of payment due. Other ambiguities, such as "the love of parents" occur because two different semantic role relationships can be expressed by the same syntactic pattern. For another example, consider "The lamb is too hot to eat." This clause has two meanings depending on whether the subject slot contains an agent or a patient. (Notice that this particular ambiguity cannot occur when the lexical item for the food is different from the word for the live animal. "The steer is too hot to eat" and "The beef is too hot to eat" are not ambiguous.) Although the analysis of ambiguities is useful to the linguist in studying how language works, normal communication is not much hampered by them.

The Semantics of Combining Clauses

In addition to the structure of the lexicon and the role structure of clauses, linguists have studied the semantics of the way clauses are joined together. The simple fact that two clauses are combined implies that they are related in meaning, but the conjunction system is often imprecise in expressing the relationship. Here are some examples of various relationships:

Coupling—two facts are simply joined together: I made the salad *and* Gerry cooked the steaks.

Contrast—the joining of different statements: Robin flunked the test, *but* Stacy passed it.

Alternation—the joining of statements seen as alternatives: Maybe I will inherit some money to pay my bills, *or* maybe the world will come to an end.

Adversative—the second statement frustrates the expectation implied by the first: The students flunked the test, *but* the teacher did not lower their grade for the course.

Causative—Event A causes or perhaps only implies Event B: *Since* the students flunked the test, their final grades were low. (Notice that in a sense the causative relationship contrasts with the adversative relationship, since here normal expectation does come to pass.)

Paraphrase—the second clause repeats the idea of the first one in different words: Happy is the man who has many children, *and* blessed is he whose family grows.

There are also three important kinds of time relationships: the simple succession, in which one event happens followed by another event; the overlap relationship; and the simultaneous relationship.

Succession—one event completed before the other begins: He remodeled the house *and then* sold it for three times what he had paid for it.

Overlap—the second event begins before the first one ends: *While* the teacher was writing on the blackboard, three students sneaked out of the room.

Simultaneous—the two events overlap completely: *Just as* the conductor raised his baton, the concertmaster gave a fortissimo sneeze.

As in other semantic-syntactic relationships, there is great imprecision and chance of ambiguity. The conjunction *but*, for example, is commonly used to express both contrasts and adversatives. *While* can express both overlap and simultaneous time relationships. *And*, perhaps the most neutral conjunction, could be used without sounding awkward in almost all the sentences quoted above. An amusing example of the slipperiness of *and* is the complete misinterpretation of the old medical advice, "Feed a cold and starve a fever." People nowadays assume that the sentence expresses a contrast: if you have a cold, you should eat, but if you have a fever you should not eat. In the original meaning of the sentence, however, the *and* was almost certainly causative, because "starve" originally meant "die" and "a" might have been a phonologically reduced form of "of." Thus the original meaning warns against eating when you have a cold: "(If you) feed a cold, (then you will) starve (or die) a (of) fever."

The interpretation of conjoining words, like the interpretation of gradable antonyms, ambiguous sentences, and other language units with more than one meaning, must be decided on the basis of which meaning is relevant to the context. In "He chopped the vegetables and poured salad dressing on them," we interpret the *and* as a temporal succession rather than as a causative or a simple coupling, because we know that these are two successive steps in making a salad. In "She refused to pay the fine and the court sent her to jail," we immediately rule out the possibility that the *and* introduces a contrast between what she did and what the court did. One possible interpretation is temporal succession, but our knowledge of the justice system leads us to decide that the *and* in this sentence expresses cause-effect. Our use of context to determine the meaning of language depends on our knowledge. As the knowledge that "starve" was a synonym for "die" faded, the possibility of interpreting the *and* as a causative also faded. Any act of communication involves a subtle interaction between the speaker's world-view, the hearer's world-view, and the shared assumptions of their culture. That is, they share presuppositions.

Presupposition

One of the basic differences between the language of mathematics and natural language is that the former has only a few assumptions, and those few are stated explicitly, whereas natural language has many unstated, relatively unconscious, assumptions. The effort to put natural language into a form which could be accepted by a computer led to the analysis of *presupposition*, the unconscious assumptions which underlie all uses of language, even the simplest. The invitation to "have some more mashed potatoes" implies that the addressee has already had at least one serving; to say, "The professor gave the same test to the afternoon class" implies that there are at least two classes and that a test was given to a previous class, probably one meeting in the morning. (To say, "The professor gave the same test to the night class" implies that there is another class which meets in the daytime, but does not hint as to whether it meets in the morning or afternoon.) There's perhaps an additional implication that professors usually make up different tests for different classes. This implication becomes quite clear if we add the word *even:* "The professor even gave the same test to the afternoon class." "The Ph.D. candidate doesn't know French" presupposes a universe where some candidates do, and some don't have this knowledge; "The Ph.D. candidate doesn't even know French" casts aspersions on the candidate's background, because it presupposes that a knowledge of French is normal.

Normally presupposition serves us well, allowing us to communicate with an economical use of words. When the speaker says, "My wife got a new job last week," the hearer can grasp the idea without needing to have the speaker explain that he has a wife, that she previously worked outside the home, that she quit or lost her old job, etc. When the words "my wife" are spoken, the hearer automatically assumes that the other person has a wife. But sometimes presupposition is used to befuddle the hearer. The administrator who blandly says, "The committee will look into that" is relying on the commonly-understood rules of presupposition and hoping that nobody will ask whether the committee has in fact been appointed. "Have you stopped beating your wife?" is an unanswerable question because of its presupposition. Whether the man answers yes or no, he remains a wife-beater.

The conversation at the mad tea party in *Alice's Adventures in Wonderland* is mad precisely because the creatures violate the rules of presupposition. The Mad Hatter asks, "Why is a raven like a writing desk?" When Alice gives up trying to guess the riddle and asks for the answer the Hatter replies, "I haven't the slightest idea." Alice is annoyed, because the act of asking a riddle implies that it has an answer. When the March Hare invites Alice to have some wine, he implies that the wine exists, and she is quite puzzled to find none on the table. This presupposition is, of course, cultural. We can visualize a culture where "Have some wine" might be a socially accepted way of saying, "I like you very much, I wish you well, and if I had some wine I'd give it to you."

Speech Acts

In fact, there's quite a gap between what words, added one to another, might be expected to mean and what the speaker intends them to mean. In analyzing this facet of language, linguists have borrowed from logicians the term *speech acts*. When a person says something, he performs, simultaneously, a locutionary act and an illocutionary act. The *locutionary act* is the utterance of noises which can be interpreted as fulfilling the phonological and syntactic patterns of a particular language. The *illocutionary act* is the attempt by the speaker to accomplish some communicative purpose. If the wind moved a door so that the noise of the hinges shrieked "Help me, help me," this noise could be called a locutionary act, but there would be no illocutionary act because there was no intention of communicating. Locutionary and illocutionary acts can, of course, be written rather than uttered. If an archeologist tries to decipher markings on a cliffside, he does so because he believes that they constitute a message placed there by a human being with a communicative intention. He would not analyze them if he thought they had been made by running water. In describing the operations of tongue, lips, and breath—the phonological processes—we are concentrating on the locutionary act. So also when we describe syntactic ordering of words, phrases, and clauses. But in order to describe the function of language in life we must focus on the illocutionary act. The branch of linguistics which does this is called *pragmatics*. The list of speech act types differs with different analysts, but the following ones are commonly mentioned:

1. *Referential* (also called *informative* or *representative*)—The speaker intends to give information to the hearer. Example: This car received a new paint job last year.
2. *Directive*—The speaker intends to get a response from the hearer. Two common types of directives are commands, which call for an action from the hearer, and questions, which call for a reply from the hearer. (The terms *imperative* and *interrogative* refer to the syntactic form rather than communicative intent, though obviously the two are related.)
3. *Commissive*—The speaker undertakes a *commission*. That is, he promises or commits himself to do something. Example: I will answer that letter the first thing in the morning. (Notice that the modal "will" is the syntactic element which signals communicative intent in this particular sentence.)

4. *Performative* (sometimes called a *declaration*)—The speaker's act of speaking actually makes something a fact. Examples: A judge or minister says, "I now pronounce you man and wife." An umpire says, "You're out."

Performatives are curiously similar to the spells of the sorcerer in that they bring about the condition they speak of. They are limited in that the speaker must be a person with special authority; the occasion is a highly structured, ritualized one held at a certain time and place; and the hearers must recognize the occasion and accept the speaker's authority. When the speaker utters the proper words, what he says becomes fact. No matter what the position of the ball, if the umpire calls it a strike, a strike it is. But the illocutionary force of the speech is governed by the total situation. If a professional umpire is pitching in an informal sandlot game, he cannot call a particular pitch a strike. Similarly, if the minister says "I now pronounce you man and wife" at the wedding rehearsal, the couple are not yet married. Actually, he would avoid doing so, because of the reverence people feel for the words themselves.

5. *Expressive*—The speaker expresses a feeling, either real or customary, toward the hearer. Examples: "How do you do?" "You were laid off? That's terrible! I'm very sorry to hear it." "Congratulations!"

Determining what kind of illocutionary act is actually being used is far from simple. The speaker may not even know himself exactly what he intends to communicate. Furthermore, a locution which seems on the surface to be one kind of speech act may be an indirect way of communicating something entirely different. A parent who says "We have less than a quart of milk in the refrigerator" may be performing a referential (informative) act, or the speech may be a delicate hint that the teen-age son should volunteer to go to the store—a directive. When the professor says "The exam covers the material presented during the past four weeks," is the speech referential, or is it commissive—a promise to construct the test in a particular way? "Don't go yet" sounds like a directive, but it's more likely to be an expressive—a conventional, polite way to say that the guest's presence is appreciated. The host is probably hoping fervently that the guest will leave even as he says it. In fact, the more we analyze speech acts, the more we are inclined to agree with Sturtevant, who suggested that language originated through man's need to tell lies.[4]

More often than not, the syntactic pattern chosen for the locutionary act implies an illocutionary force quite different from the one actually intended. We would expect that the syntactic pattern of the imperative would

---

[4]Edgar H. Sturtevant, *An Introduction to Linguistic Science* (New Haven: Yale University Press, 1947), pp. 47–49.

be used for a directive: "Please go to the store for me." Instead we find the request being expressed as a question: "Could you go to the store for me?" In the culture of the ancient Hebrews, a referential speech act was often expressed as a question: "And the Ziphites came unto Saul at Gibeah saying, 'Doth not David hide himself in the hill of Hachilah, which is before Jeshimon?'" (I Sam. 26:1) A mother, naming her child (a declarative) may use the form associated with the representative or the commissive: "His name is Craig" or "I'm going to call him Craig."

In addition to saying one thing and meaning another, speakers often speak without meaning much of anything. The analysis of illocutionary acts implies a transaction between speaker and hearer. But often the importance of the transaction is secondary to the act of talking itself. Such a speech situation is known as "phatic communion." An example of phatic communion is this: A person has a flat tire, and another driver stops to help. Approaching, the would-be helper says, "Got a little problem?" He can see that the first person has a problem—that's why he stopped. Although he may seem to be asking a question (a directive illocutionary act), he is actually saying, in effect, "I'd like to be friends. This is what my voice sounds like. What does your voice sound like?" Almost all talk about the weather is phatic communion. The old complaint that everybody talks about the weather and nobody does anything about it completely misses the point. The seemingly futile talk allows two people to express a minimal friendliness while deciding from clues of voice and body language whether they want to share more substantive topics of conversation. The weather is the ideal topic for this purpose, because everyone knows something about it, and no one will be threatened by the possibility of embarrassment.

As we look over the patterns of meaning on the various levels of lexicon, clause and sentence, and speech acts, we find a certain amount of "slippage." Language certainly does not express meaning exactly. The process of communication requires cooperation between speaker and hearer. Both must understand the subtleties of choice—of one synonym rather than another, of focus on one conjunction rather than another, of one illocutionary act rather than another. The hearer must be willing to help as the speaker says, "I mean . . . you know."

Exercises

1. Sound Symbolism

Here are some groups of words that share one or more sounds. What sound(s) do they share? Do you see a common meaning in the words? Can you think of other words that share the sound symbolism?
1. snort, sniff, snuff, snout, snot, snorkel, snoot, snob
2. toil, moil, roil, coil, soil

3. strong, strict, straight, stress, strenuous, strive, stroke
4. creep, crawl, crinkly, cramp, cracker, crank, crock
5. bud, bulb, bulk, bull, bump, bundle, burden, Bertha

2. Synonyms

In each of the following instances a student looked up the word in a cheap dictionary, found the definition here given, and used the word in a sentence. How do the term and the definition differ in semantic features or in collocational restrictions? What synonym of the term would be correct?
1. competent—adequate but not exceptional
    The Thanksgiving turkey was competent until five extra guests arrived unexpectedly.
2. tranquil—free from commotion or tumult
    The automatic carwash finished its cycle and became tranquil.
3. transgress—violate
    She transgressed the teacher's instructions by analyzing a modern poem instead of one from the Romantic Period.
4. pregnant—carrying a child
    The fireman climbed the ladder, entered the burning building, and came down pregnant.
5. vision—sight
    After many days at sea, Columbus had a vision of the new world.
6. radical—thoroughgoing or extreme
    The doctor gave the youngster a radical checkup before okaying him to play football.

3. Polysemy

Write three sentences for each of the following polysemic words demonstrating three of the different meanings the word may have.
1. strike
2. drive
3. green
4. spring
5. people

4. Taxonomic Sets

If you've studied Chapter 5, you know that mature, rhythmic writing is frequently done in this pattern: first there is a short base clause; to it, free modifiers expressing details, examples, or parts of the idea are added. The modifiers that are on the same level of generality and that belong to the same classification are expressed in the same type of grammatical construction. In other words, the modifiers belong to *taxonomic sets,* and the syntax reflects this semantic relationship.

For each of the following sentences, write a brief comment on the specific semantic relationships between modifiers and item modified.

Example: Because of her depression, she procrastinated with all her housework, letting the dishes pile up in the sink, the ironing mold in the basket, and the leftovers spoil in the refrigerator.

Comment: The modifier contains three examples of undone housework.

1. We know, thanks to the memory stores in the brain,
    that whatever message comes in it must consist of
        a string of phonemes belonging to a certain inventory,
    that the morphemes are to be found in the list we carry in our heads,
    that the words are card-indexed in our dictionary and
    that the sentence formation will be based on routines we are familiar with.

    —*Dennis Fry*

2. People who respect themselves are willing to accept the risk
    that the Indians will be hostile,
    that the venture will go bankrupt,
    that the liaison may not turn out to be one in which
        every day is a holiday because you're married to me.

    —*Joan Didion*

3. [Football players] are easily read emblematically as embodiments of heroic qualities such as
    "strength,"
    "confidence,"
    "perfection," etc.—
        clichés really, but forceful enough when represented by the play of
            a Dick Butkus,
            a Johnny Unitas or a
            Bart Starr.

    —*Murray Ross*

4. To be or not to be,
    that is the question:
        whether 'tis nobler in the mind
            to suffer the slings and arrows of outrageous fortune,
            or to take arms against a sea of troubles,
                and by opposing end them.

    —*William Shakespeare*

5. There are many urgent special problems which the population is raising—
>how to provide the increasing numbers of human beings
>>with their basic quotas of
>>>food and shelter,
>>>raw materials and energy,
>>>health and education,
>>with opportunities
>>>for adventure and meditation,
>>>for contact
>>>>with nature and
>>>>with art,
>>>for useful work and fruitful leisure;
>how to prevent frustration
>>exploding into violence or
>>subsiding into apathy;
>how to avoid
>>unplanned chaos on the one hand and
>>unorganized authoritarianism on the other.

—*Julian Huxley*

5. Roles

A. Consider each of the italicized nouns and decide by guessing which role it fills. Then write two paraphrases of the sentence, each time putting a different noun role in the subject slot. Comment briefly on the differences in meaning (implication or emphasis) between the original sentence and the two paraphrases.

1. *Lizzie Borden* killed her *parents* with an *axe*.
2. The *children* heard this gruesome *story* at *bedtime*.
3. *Carl* cooks *eggs* for his *wife* for *breakfast*.
4. Because *he* prefers natural foods, the *microwave* never cooks his eggs; instead, *they* cook on a natural electric *burner*.
5. The *sheriff* arrested the *car thief* and put him in *jail*.
6. The *door* opened; the *ghost* floated into the *room* and sat on the large *amplifier*.

B. In *The Hobbit*, Bilbo told the trolls who had caught him, "Please don't cook me, kind sirs! I am a good cook myself, and cook better than I cook." Explain the change of roles in "I cook better than I cook."

C. Analyze a portion of a short story to determine which semantic role occurs most often in the subject slot. You may find an interesting key to the style and tone of the story. In particular, compare the analysis of a relatively low-key passage with that of the climax.

6. Roles and Direct Objects

One reason that syntactic analysis is confusing is our habit of defining the structures in terms of semantic relationships. For example, the direct object is often defined as "the receiver of the action" (patient). Study the following sentences and decide what the semantic relationships between the verb and two nouns are in each case. Is the direct object ever the patient—"the receiver of the action"?
1. Stacy ran the vacuum cleaner.
2. Stacy ran the marathon.
3. Stacy ran the babysitter ragged.
4. Stacy ran more than twenty-six miles.
5. Stacy ran the candy concession.

7. Kinds of Possessives

"Possessive" is a cover term for a number of poorly-defined semantic relationships. For example, we say "my hand" and also "my hat." The first is an *inalienable* possession, since it's permanently attached to the individual; the second is an *alienable* possession. In the following exercise, explain precisely what the speaker means when he/she speaks of possessing the house.
1. We can have the committee meeting at *my* house.
   (The speaker lives in a duplex and is a renter.)
2. *My* house has a mansard roof.
   (The bank holds a mortgage of 80% of the purchase price.)
3. *My* house was judged the most energy-efficient.
   (The speaker is an architect.)
4. *My* house has never been bothered by the police.
   (The speaker is a madam.)
5. Everyone was relieved when I moved out of *my* house and into an apartment. (The speaker is an adult child.)

8. Interclausal Relations

In the following story, the clauses are joined by imprecise conjunctions, usually *and*. Decide, in each case, what is the relationship between the two clauses. Then rewrite the paragraph, striving for smoother flow and more precisely-stated relationships.

I couldn't get a job last fall *and* I came to college. My girl friend went to a business school in our home town *and* I chose a small liberal arts college in Ohio. We stayed in touch *and* wrote letters *and* ran up huge phone bills. We couldn't take the separation any longer, *and* we got married during spring break. We are living in the same place now *and* things are easier. I dropped out of school *and* next fall we will go to business school together. We will have complementary majors *and* we will graduate eventually. We plan to open our own business *and* work together in it *and* become parents. Economic conditions are poor now, *and* it is a long road.

Writing for Insight and Review—
Adjusting to the Audience

Although the standard definition of semantics says that it deals with the relationship between language units and the real world, it's more accurate to say that it's not the real world, but rather someone's concept of the real world, that is involved. All of us have different concepts according to our different experiences. For one person, the word "dog" would be primarily a hyponym of the word "pet," and it would inhabit a world of Disney cartoons, advertisements for dog food, and methods of training animals to stay off the furniture. Another person, though marginally aware of the dog's function as a pet, would think primarily of dogs in the context of hunting, of guarding the out-buildings against trespassers, of bringing the milk cows in from the pasture. Still another person might be most aware of the dog as a source of danger. When introducing your own dog to one of these persons, you would try to use language including their presuppositions. To the first person you might say, "It's o.k. to give him a snack. He's not on a diet yet." This bit of conversation implies the presupposition that pet owners often have to make a special effort to keep their animal's weight normal. To the third person you might say, "He won't bite you." Thus automatically you would adjust your language to your audience.

This adjustment, which seems so natural in speech, seems to render the beginning writer tongue-tied (hand-tied?), and the simple advice to remember the audience begins to look like a faintly dishonest magic trick. Actually, it's a matter of being aware of the other person's presuppositions, of his taxonomies, of those items which are normal, and therefore unmarked, in his view.

To develop some awareness of the adjustment process, try one or more of the following exercises:

1. Describe a wedding—first for a member of your peer group, and then for your maiden aunt, whose ideas of wedding procedures date back to the fifties.
2. Describe an American football game—first for your father, and then for your Australian or South American friend who is more familiar with soccer.
3. Explain your faith—first to someone who holds a similar but not identical belief, and then to someone who has a completely different religion, or no religion at all.
4. Explain your decision to live with your boy or girl friend—first to your shrink or counselor, then to a foreign fellow student who is looking forward to an arranged marriage.
5. Write a brief description of the federal government—first for your political science teacher, then for someone who is used to the parliamentary system.

7

Taking Bigger Bites

Until very recently, people took it for granted that the business of linguistics was to describe the bugs and imps of language—sounds, morphemes, and individual words. The absolute upper limits of linguistic analysis was the sentence. But as the linguists strove for greater precision in describing language, they had to attempt to analyze larger units, paragraphs and discourses, as well. Rhetoricians had been studying these larger units for centuries. Their interest was strictly practical: what discourse rules produce effective speaking and writing? They formulated their rules by observing what effective communicators did and generalizing from their observations in an intuitive, impressionistic way. They worked entirely in the Greek and Roman tradition and virtually ignored non-Indo-European languages. It was in the 1960s that the linguists began to establish scientifically what the rhetoricians already knew impressionistically, working primarily with languages outside the Indo-European tradition. This linguistic approach to larger units of language is called *discourse grammar* or *text linguistics*.

A discourse is any unit of language that is complete with regard to the situation in which it occurs. It contains at least two, and usually more, sentences. A conversation, for example, is a discourse. It begins when people greet one another, and ends when they say goodbye, or perhaps just stop talking. A political speech is a discourse. So is a riddle, or a joke, or a novel, or a poem. Just as on the sentence level one clause may be inserted into another, so also one discourse may be inserted into another. Thus a political speech or a conversation may contain several jokes. A novel will probably contain numerous conversations. For all the discourse types, there are discourse-level slots and fillers.

We know intuitively what a discourse is. Just as we have internalized the lexicon and syntax of our language, we have learned how to deal with a larger context. We know that a conversation begins with a greeting formula such as "hello" and ends with "bye-bye" or "have a nice day." We know that questions normally require an answer. We know that the second sentence in a paragraph will be related to the first one in some reasonable way. In dealing with discourses we use phonological, syntactic, and semantic clues. When a lecturer is winding down, he normally provides such phonological clues as these: slower pronunciation, lower overall pitch, lower volume. Syntactic clues include the use of pronouns, consistency in verb forms, and the use of conjunctions. Semantic clues include unity of subject, logical relationships, and repetition of lexical items or synonyms for them.

To say that these things are intuitive, of course, simply means that we have learned them so completely that we've forgotten we know them. One thing that makes conversation with young children so disconcerting is their imperfect mastery of discourse procedures. For example, a kindergartner whose mother was a dedicated dieter responded to an introduction with "I'm glad to meet you. And how much do you weigh?" At present, this isn't the proper way to initiate a conversation in our culture, although it may become proper if people continue to be so concerned about their weight. I'm told that in some African languages the polite expression would have been "Have you eaten today?"

The rules of oral discourse are mastered late in the child's language development; the rules for written discourse are mastered even later, if at all. We internalize the rules of oral discourse by listening to thousands of hours of the stuff; we fail to internalize the rules of written discourse because we never have such constant exposure to it. We try to shortcut the process by memorizing rules, but memorization doesn't work for discourse any better than it does for spelling or sentence structure. Nevertheless, the sense of discourse unity is part of our language competence, and even an introductory study of discourse grammar often significantly improves a person's writing skills by increasing his awareness of the tools of language structure. Thus, discourse grammar is more immediately practical than many other aspects of linguistics. But, as with these other aspects, our primary purpose is to survey the field—to present knowledge for the sake of knowledge. First we will look briefly at the basic oral discourse, the dialogue. Then we will consider monologues, which can be oral but in our culture are often written.

Dialogues

The dialogue involves two speakers each speaking in turn. A pair of turns, one for each speaker, constitutes an *utterance-response pair*, an *exchange*, a *transaction*, or an *adjacency pair* (different linguists' terms for the same thing). One speaker produces an utterance and the other speaker responds to it. The utterance may be a question, a proposal for some sort of action, or

an informative remark. The response normally fits the utterance. It's an answer to the question, an assent or dissent to the proposal, or an evaluation of the information. For example:
1. Question-Answer
   Utterance: Where are you going?
   Response: To the library.
2. Proposal-Assent (or Dissent)
   Utterance: Let's go to the library.
   Response: O.K.
   or I can't—I'm expecting a phone call.
3. Remark-Evaluation
   Utterance: I'm going to the library now.
   Response: That shows will power.

Notice that we can't specify the class of fillers for discourse-level slots as precisely as we specify the class of fillers for sentence-or clause-level slots. Instead of saying "I'm going to the library," the first speaker could change the syntax by making a cleft sentence: "Where I'm going now is to the library" or add to the semantic content by saying, "I'm going to the library now to finish the research on my term paper." Although we can't list all the fillers for a slot, we can recognize that some fillers are ungrammatical—that they break the normal structure of discourse. For example, a textbook for teaching English as a foreign language might provide the following model dialogue:
Utterance: Where are you going?
Response: I am going to the library.

This response is not normal as the answer to a question; the normal response is "To the library." The full clause form normally occurs in the utterance slot, and the reduced clause, sometimes called a minor sentence, in the response slot. A similar error occurs when teachers ask questions and require the students to "answer in complete sentences." On a test the teacher may ask, "What is the capital of Maine?" The student correctly answers, "Augusta." This one word is a complete sentence if the exchange between student and teacher is a dialogue. But what the teacher means by "complete sentence" is "a complete sentence in expository written English." A good deal of educational friction could be avoided if the teacher would either accept the dialogue form of response as correct or else compose a question that doesn't sound like the first part of a dialogue unit.

In some circumstances the responder may use a *skewed* response instead of the normal one. For example:
Utterance: Where are you going?
Response: What do you want to know for?

By answering a question with another question, the responder gets control of the conversation, thus forcing the other person to become the responder.

Another skewed response involves changing the subject as a means of control:

Linus: On Halloween the Great Pumpkin brings toys to all good little girls and boys.
Lucy: I had a quarter, but I lost it.

Psychologists have measured the degree of dominance of one person over another by observing the number of times that the dominant member proposes a new topic instead of supplying a normal, unskewed response.

When more than two people are involved, the rules governing utterance-response pairs become more complicated. The conversationalists realize that only one person at a time should talk, so they time their participation to avoid both rude interruptions and uncomfortable silences. In some cultures there's a recognized order of participation, such as by seniority, but in the United States such a system is not usually operative, so that a listener who wishes to become a speaker must watch carefully for the opportunity. Change of speakers normally occurs at the end of a syntactic group, so that the would-be speaker must anticipate the end of the speaker's sentence and be ready to jump in. The speaker's turn is one sentence long unless he indicates that he needs a longer space to tell a joke or story. Some speakers manage to keep the floor by avoiding anything that sounds like the end of a sentence. (The nontechnical term for such a person is *a bore.*)

In addition to the rule that the speaker's turn is one sentence long is the rule that the speaker can choose the next speaker, either by addressing a remark specifically to that person or by looking in his or her direction. The speaker cannot, however, designate more than one following speaker. If two people begin to take a turn simultaneously, the one who is younger or less respected normally yields. If the two are equal in status, the more dominant or outgoing person keeps the floor.

Another rule is that the new speaker's contribution must be tied into the previous contribution by topic. If a speaker says, "I went surfing yesterday," the new speaker responds with a remark logically related: where the new speaker went surfing, what he did yesterday, something about surfing (or another sport, if necessary), or (using time as a topic) what will happen tomorrow. If the first speaker tells a joke about a mother-in-law, it will seem more interesting if the new speaker's joke is also about mothers-in-law, or at least about women. But lacking a joke on a truly relevant topic, the new speaker still ties in his contribution by saying, "That reminds me of the one about . . ."

The rules of dialogue may be summarized as follows: make sense, take turns, be relevant. In addition, members of some cultures must know how to take part in a stylized form of dialogue, the verbal duel. Among ghetto blacks, for example, sociolinguists have observed a stylized dialogue called

"playing the dozens." The two participants trade insults about their respective mothers. Here's a brief sample:
B: Yeah, Constance (A's mother) was real good to me last Thursday.
A: I heard Virginia's (B's mother) lost her titty in a poker game.
B: 'Least my mother ain't no cake, everybody got a piece.'[1]

Another example comes from the West Indies, where the original calypso was an insult contest which required the use of rhyme.[2] In some cultures, the duel takes the form of riddling speech. Finnegan reports the following exchange from Southern Africa, where the "bird riddle" is favored:
Challenger: What bird do you know?
Proposer: I know the white necked raven.
Challenger: What about him?
Proposer: He is a missionary.
Challenger: Why so?
Proposer: Because he wears a white collar and a black cassock and is always looking for dead bodies to bury.[3]

Verbal duelling in a Semitic culture is seen in the Bible, in the story of how Sampson expressed his hostility toward the young men of Philistia by posing a riddle for them (Judges 14:12–18).

Monologues

A monologue is any discourse that is complete without the participation of a second person. In our culture, oral monologues include lectures, campaign speeches, sermons, and pep talks. In addition, we have a large variety of written monologues, such as textbooks, newspaper editorials, recipes, and contracts. Some of our discourse types combine monologue and dialogue—novels, short stories, and biographies, for example.

Written discourses differ from oral discourses in their semantic and syntactic features. The difference seems to be made necessary by the differing mediums of communication—marks on paper rather than modifications in the air stream. Literacy workers report that when a language community which previously had only oral discourses attains literacy, the people don't simply transfer their oral discourses to written form, but rather develop new discourse procedures for the written medium. They seem to have a well-defined, intuitive sense of what a written discourse should be.

In our own culture, the basic difference between oral and written dis-

---
[1] Cited from Roger D. Abrahams, "Playing the Dozens," *Journal of American Folklore* 75:209–220 in Fernando Peñalosa, *Introduction to the Sociology of Language* (Rowley, MA: Newbury House, 1981) p. 150.
[2] Peter Farb, *Word Play: What Happens When People Talk* (New York: Bantam Books, 1975), p. 123.
[3] Farb, p. 115.

course is made even more complex by differences between the different kinds of oral and written mediums. The story of a disaster as presented orally on the radio differs in structure from the story of the same disaster as presented orally on television. The radio talk show is different from the television talk show, the made-for-television film from the theater film. Intonation patterns, grammatical patterns, and lexical choices are subtly different. In looking at written discourses, we find that the information about the disaster will be structured differently for the weekly news magazine than for the daily newspaper. Information about black holes will be presented one way in a textbook, another way in a trade book, and still a third way in the *Scientific American*. These differences in structure will be manifested in certain grammatical patterns and lexical choices, but also in paragraph structures, punctuation, and the use of typographical devices such as headings and different styles of type.

Any study of these subtle differences in medium would be complicated by the fact that we constantly transfer material from one medium to another. The interview or panel discussion is printed in a magazine or book; the made-for-theater film is bought for television; books such as Tolkien's *Lord of the Rings* are recorded on cassettes. Linguists who work with discourse are not able to handle this kind of subtle detail as yet. Most of their work thus far has been on relatively brief conversations, jokes, and folk tales in oral discourse, and on written discourses such as short stories. In dealing with the latter, their work begins to overlap with that of the literary critic.

Classifying Monologues

Traditional textbooks of English composition list four types of writing: narration, description, exposition, and argumentation. This is a common-sense division based on purpose: to tell a story, to describe a place or thing, to explain something, or to persuade the reader to do something. Linguists prefer to classify monologues on the basis of observable features of syntax, such as verb tense. They also get clues from the use of certain lexical items such as "meanwhile" or "therefore." When classified on this linguistic basis, there are still four basic types, but only narrative is the same in both classifications.

Narrative. Since the most natural way to tell a story is in chronological order, one way to recognize a narrative discourse is by time words: "one day," "the next week," "after that," "at last," and "meanwhile, back at the ranch." These time words signal the division of the narrative into incidents and scenes, if there are more than one. Another feature of the English narrative is the use of past tense, although the teller sometimes uses present tense (traditionally called "historical present") in an informal situation. That is, instead of saying "Clark Kent *stepped* into the phone booth and *became* Superman," the narrator will use the historical present and say, "Clark Kent *steps* into the phone booth and *becomes* Superman." Sometimes a narrator who has been using past tense will switch to historical present at the high point of the story. A third linguistic feature of narratives is the presence of personal pronouns, either first person (I or we) or third person (he, she, they)—naturally enough, since stories are about people.

Other languages have similar markers for narrative monologue. In Manobo, a language of the Philippines, *hane* (meaning "behold") alerts the reader to a rapid change of scene or introduces a new speaker. Another lexical item is *engkey pe' be te*, which introduces a surprising event. Manobo also has the possibility of using pronouns in an unusual way. In the story of Ukap, a folk hero, the moment of greatest danger is marked by a shift from third to second person. Instead of calling Ukap "he," the narrator uses "you."[4] Verb forms are likely to be important markers of narrative. In Biblical Hebrew, for example, the *waw*-consecutive, a verb form beginning with a morpheme meaning *and*, is used in narrative.[5]

Procedural. As the chart (Fig. 11) shows, procedural discourse is like narrative in the importance of chronological order. Its purpose is to tell how to do something, so naturally it uses a large number of time words. The pronoun orientation is normally second person, "you," although the pronoun is sometimes deleted. The speaker or writer may say "Soak one cup of garbanzo beans" rather than "First you soak one cup of garbanzo beans." In English, we also have the option of getting rid of the personal pronoun by using passive verb forms: "First the garbanzo beans are soaked." The choice of verb tense for procedural monologues is normally present or future. In Kotia Oriya, a language of India, it's possible to use infinitive verb forms throughout the procedure, so that both verb tense and pronoun are eliminated.[6]

English composition textbooks do not pay much attention to procedural discourse, although sometimes you see references to "the description of a process" as a writing assignment. In our culture the procedural discourse is usually quite informal, so that academic analysis is not considered necessary. The "process paper" is more likely to have the linguistic features of the explanatory monologue rather than the procedural one.

Explanatory. The purpose of the explanatory monologue is to convey information, to explain or describe something. It's the most impersonal of the genres. Unlike the narrative and procedural monologues, it has no particular time orientation. If the description concerns something that existed in the past, then the speaker sometimes chooses past tense. But more often he or she chooses a present tense which does not really refer to the present

---

[4]Reported by Hazel Wrigglesworth in Robert E. Longacre, *Philippine Languages: Discourse, Paragraph & Sentence Structure* (Santa Ana, CA: The Summer Institute of Linguistics, 1968), pp. 4–5, 11–12.

[5]Longacre, personal communication.

[6]Uwe Gustaffson, "Procedural Discourse in Kotia Oriya," in *Papers on Discourse*, ed. Joseph E. Grimes (Dallas: The Summer Institute of Linguistics, 1978), p. 283.

KINDS OF MONOLOGUES

Observable Linguistic Features	Discourse Genre			
	Narrative	Procedural	Explanatory	Hortatory
Time sequence?	yes	yes	no	no
Most common tense	past	future present	present	future
Pronoun orientation	3rd, 1st	2nd, Ø	3rd, Ø	2nd
Semantic units	Incidents, scenes	Steps	Logical Themes	Points
Discourse unit signals	time words, character name	time words	sentence adverbs, lexical dominance	sentence adverbs, lexical dominance

Fig. 11

time, but rather to a general, timeless state. Thus a lecturer may say, "In translating *The Divine Comedy* Sayers is careful to . . ." even though the translator is dead and her carefulness is long past. In Koiné Greek, this timeless state is expressed by the aorist (simple past) rather than the present tense.

The choice of pronoun for an explanatory monologue is as nearly neutral as the language allows. If the language permits subjectless clauses (as English does not), the discourse may include a large number of them. Otherwise the pronoun is likely to be "it," "we" (including both speaker and hearers), or, in very informal discourse, "you," as in, "When you're a politician, your main purpose is to get elected again." Since time orientation isn't crucial, the number of time words is small. Instead of organization by time periods, the explanatory discourse is organized by themes or topics according to the writer's understanding of the subject. In discussing language, for example, one linguist might use the topics of phonology, syntax, and lexis; another might use syntactics (including both phonology and grammar), semantics, and pragmatics. These parts of the subject then become paragraphs or paragraph clusters.

Hortatory. The purpose of the hortatory monologue is to exhort, to give advice and warnings urging someone to do or not do something. It's not quite the same as the argumentative essay of the English composition textbook, because the formal academic argument uses the linguistic features of the explanatory discourse. Instead of telling someone directly what to do, we're taught to explain the facts in such a way that the reader will be persuaded to do what we advocate. The hortatory monologue speaks directly to the reader or hearer. In fact, the use of second person pronouns ("you") is the chief distinguishing feature. Sometimes the speaker will soften the tone of the persuasion by identifying himself with his audience, so that he chooses the "inclusive we": "Let us be very careful to protect the beautiful natural environment which we have inherited." Or he may soften his tone even more by using the "exclusive we." That is, he will state what "we" (meaning his own group) do and hope that his hearers will take it as an example to be followed. "As a family we decided to stop buying expensive junk food and to give the money we save to the poor."

One common hortatory pattern is the contrast: not x, but y. Another is the action-consequence pair: "If you smoke, you will become vulnerable to many diseases." Thus the lexical markers of hortatory discourse include such words as "if," "since," "because," and the ominous "or else."

Since the hortatory monologue is oriented toward future action, it normally uses the future verb, or, in English, the unmarked or "present" verb. Like the explanatory monologue, the hortatory discourse is not oriented toward relating an action by dividing it into time frames. Instead, the divisions of the discourse—paragraphs and paragraph clusters—are signaled by such sentence adverbs as "therefore" and "furthermore" in English, or *pigoya* "all right" in Fore, a language of New Guinea.[7] (You may have noticed that some Americans say "O.K." between major points of an informal explanatory or hortatory speech.)

The four monologue types just described represent the most normal, most obvious fulfillment of the four purposes. But in all aspects of language use, one of the most normal things human beings do is to depart from what is normal. In syntax we may take a word that is normally a noun, like *book*, and use it as a verb, saying "Now I'm going to book it." In dialogue we may take an informational utterance, like "I'm going to the library," and use it as a delicately-hinted request, so that it implies "Will you go with me?" So also one type of monologue may be used to fulfill the purpose of another. And almost always, the narrative is the basic kind of monologue. The other three types are presented in narrative form, not the other way around. A speaker who wishes to persuade a listener to beware of trusting the wrong people may adopt the technique of telling a story, and the result is "Little Red Riding Hood." Instead of straight directions on how to improve productivity, the procedure can be presented as a narrative, "How Marvin Salesman Doubled His Productivity." Instead of an explanation of the tourist attractions of Hawaii, the material may be presented as the narrative of someone's trip there (usually complete with slides). Furthermore, discourse types are often combined. An explanation may end with a persuasion—a call to change the

---

[7] Robert E. Longacre, *Hierarchy and Universality of Discourse Constituents in New Guinea Languages: Discussion* (Washington: Georgetown University Press, 1972), pp. 146–7.

situation which has been explained. The steps of a procedure may be halted while the speaker explains the advantages of a particular material or tool. In oral discourse, such a change is often signaled by changing the intonation pattern. In written discourse, it may be signaled by a typographical device such as using a different size of print.

The combinations of the various dialogues, conversations, and monologues allow human beings to create an almost infinite variety of discourse forms.

Recognizing Discourses

The general classifications of dialogues and monologues are applicable to all cultures, all discourse mediums. Within these groups we can recognize many specific discourse types. A writer or speaker who chooses to produce a specific type of discourse simultaneously takes care of a number of smaller choices, particularly in regard to the number of parts the discourse will have, verb forms, phonological features like rhyme, and vocabulary items. The reader or hearer responds to these choices by recognizing what kind of discourse it is, what the communicator is trying to accomplish. Let's look at a few easily-recognized discourses and their signals. You'll be able to add many more to the list.

The *fairy tale* conventionally begins with "once upon a time" and ends with "and they all lived happily ever after." It has three major discourse divisions: the introduction of the problem, which is often experienced by the youngest son or daughter, an account of how the problem is solved with the help of courage, luck, and magical aids, and the conclusion, in which everything is set right and the hero or heroine makes a good marriage.

The *recipe* has three discourse-level slots: the list of ingredients, the steps in preparing them, and final comments on the appearance of the finished product, what to serve it with, or possible substitutions of ingredients.

The brief discourses we describe as *jokes* actually belong to several different types. One type is the utterance-response pair, commonly known as the two-liner. The straight man makes a remark or asks a question, and the comic delivers the punch line. Other jokes are brief narrative discourses consisting of some sort of opening phrase (necessary to alert the audience that a joke is coming up), the main plot, and the punch line. More often than not, the main plot is divided into three parts. If it's a traveling salesman joke, the salesman makes three attempts upon a lady's virtue. If it's a clergyman joke, three faiths are represented. A specialized narrative joke is the shaggy dog story, in which the plot development is much longer than normal—four or five slots instead of three. Then the punch line is an elaborate pun.

Another simple discourse is the *limerick*. Its usual discourse-level slots are introduction of a character, a line describing the character, what happened, and the result. The limerick has lexical, syntactic, and phonological markers. The opening words, "There once was a . . ." provide a lexical marker. A syntactic marker is the adjective phrase or clause which follows the name of the character. And the phonological markers are almost too familiar to need mention: the rhyming pattern and the specified number of stressed syllables per line. In oral discourse, the division of the limerick into lines is accomplished by pauses and intonation contours; in writing, the line division is a feature of typography.

Television has given us many new kinds of discourses. The evening news, for example, proceeds in an orderly fashion, beginning with political events and other disasters, then the weather report, an optional editorial or human interest feature, and finally the sports. Each anchorman or woman develops an individual way of signaling "the end," a phrase as predictable as the "amen" at the end of a prayer.

The commercials also proceed according to a predictable fashion. One kind divides neatly into two major discourse slots—problem and solution. First there is a brief drama presenting the problem—the children who won't brush with fluoride toothpaste, the visitors who notice that the house smells bad, the lawnmower that won't start. Then the pitchman appears with the solution—a product to buy. Sometimes, less believably, a character in the drama acts as pitchman, pulling a can of the preferred lawnmower fuel out of her handbag. Another kind of commercial begins with a gee-whiz statement about the product. Then the speaker, pretending that he or she has just noticed you watching, says "Hi. I'm so-and-so." Then follows a discussion of the virtues of the product. There are three discourse-level slots—the attention-getter, the greeting, and the pitch—with an optional fourth slot, the get-yours-today conclusion.

Each of the discourse types mentioned above can be recognized by objective features. For the fairy tale, we pointed out standard opening and closing phrases. For the written recipe, there's usually a typographical separation of parts, with the list of ingredients appearing by itself and the final comments headed by a caption in boldfaced type. For the television commercial, the change from one part to another may be signaled by nonlinguistic features like music or a different camera shot as well as grammatical and lexical items. There's an almost infinite variety of discourse patterns, and it's fun to recognize the features which characterize each one. For academic purposes, however, it's important to recognize an underlying narrative pattern, the quest story, and an underlying explanatory pattern, the oration.

The Quest Story

In the early 1950s, a content analysis was made of about 200 Russian folk tales. A remarkable consistency of plot structures was found. If the different plot elements are designated by letters of the alphabet, then a rather lengthy story can be symbolized by a formula not much more complicated than the ones for the English noun phrase or verb phrase. This "morphology" or "grammar" of the folk tale is as follows:

1. Introduction. The story opens on a fairly stable situation. The hero and his family are described. Then something happens to disturb the stability. Sometimes an elder—a parent or other guardian of the community—dies. Sometimes there are warnings or threats of danger.
2. Separation. Because of the new instability in the situation, the hero is forced to leave home.
3. Initiation. The hero is involved in meeting conflict and surviving it. Conflicts are of two basic types: the battle and the road of trials. In a battle the hero proves his worth by aggressively overcoming a villain; on the road of trials, the proof comes in the patient endurance of hardships. In J. R. R. Tolkien's *The Lord of the Rings*, both types of initiation are used. Frodo and Sam experience the road of trials while the other two hobbits, Merry and Pippin, are tested in battles.
4. Return. After becoming wiser and more worthy through suffering, the hero returns home. Often he finds that a false hero has taken his place and must be ousted. Once this is done, stability is restored. He receives a reward, often a marriage.
5. Conclusion. This is a brief passage rounding off the story, such as, "That's how Jason won the Golden Fleece."

There are countless variations on this structure. In our urbanized culture, a favorite pattern for a story has been Boy Meets Girl, Boy Loses Girl, Boy Wins Girl. The first stage is the original happy, stable situation. The second is the Separation and Initiation, and the third is the Return. Another variation is to have more than one struggle, more than one hero or villain. In Shakespeare's comedies, for example, there are usually two boy-meets-girl stories, one from the upper class and one involving servants.

Expository and persuasive discourses also tend to have five major parts. The first part, instead of introducing the characters in a story, is designed to introduce the author or speaker and to set up a relationship, a bond of shared information, with the readers or hearers. The second part, which is analogous to the Separation, presents a problem—a situation which needs to be changed in the persuasive discourse, a lack of understanding which needs to be explained in the expository discourse. Next comes the road of trials, a careful tracing of various aspects of the problem, which finally leads to the conviction that the author's answer to the problem is the only, or at least the strongest, one available. Linguist Joseph E. Grimes comments, "In a considerable amount of scientific writing the hero, the author, slays a dragon, ignorance or the bumbling of former investigators, by means of a helper, a second order differential equation, and thus rescues the victim, his branch of science."[8] (The reward, a raise in salary or a promotion, occurs outside the linguistic text.)

The Oration

The classical oration has six parts, but one of those is sometimes optional, so that the overall structure is about the same as the quest story. Indeed, our nonfiction discourses usually resemble the oration in structure.
1. Exordium—the speaker (or writer) tries to establish himself as a trustworthy person, one whom the audience will like.
2. Narratio—the speaker introduces the problem, narrating the relevant background information.
3. Divisio—the speaker summarizes the points he plans to make.
4. Confirmatio—the speaker develops his points.
5. Confutatio—the speaker refutes the opinions of his opponents. May be omitted; may also precede #4.
6. Peroratio—the speaker asks for a decision, for agreement from his hearers.

This is just a general outline, a norm to be departed from whenever the situation warrants it. The exordium is omitted in an article for a scientific journal, since the audience of scientists will be interested only in data and results, not the personality of the writer. If the speech or essay is quite short, the divisio may well be omitted.

At this point a skeptic might object that if you factor out everything that makes discourses unique and individual, then naturally what is left will be the same for everything. Nevertheless, this overall pattern for dividing the discourse into parts has helped linguists get a handle on narrative structures in many languages. It even provides a starting point for analysis when the sort of story favored by a non-Western culture is quite different. For example, in Papua New Guinea, there's a family of plots in which Boy meets Girl, Boy and Girl elope, Boy and Girl decide to seek reconciliation with their families, return to their village and are killed. In that culture, the boy is not the hero but the villain, since he's the one who introduced instability into the society.[9]

One composition teacher, who was disturbed by the "illogical" and "repetitious" essays his Chinese students produced, solved his problem by learning about their traditional formal discourse, the Eight-legged Essay. Although the writing of such an essay is no longer used as a civil service exami-

---
[8]Joseph E. Grimes, *The Thread of Discourse* (The Hague and Paris: Mouton, 1975), pp. 43–44.
[9]Grimes, pp. 244–45.

nation as it was in ancient China, the tradition is still very much alive. Here are the parts:

The Topic—often a quotation or question
1. The Breaking Open—announces the aspect of the topic that the writer will discuss.
2. Accepting the Title—gives supporting evidence for #1. The sentences are parallel in form to #1.
3. Embarking—elaborates the point; demonstrates the scholarship of the author by quoting from a traditional source.
4. Introductory Corollary—author's main point, most elaborately stated. Parallel in form to #3.
5. First Middle Leg—Restates main point as a rhetorical question (an opinion expressed as a question rather than a statement).
6. Second Middle Leg—Answers the question of #5, maintains a structure parallel to #5. May introduce information that seems somewhat irrelevant by Western standards.
7. First Final Leg—Expands on the information in #6.
8. Tying the Knot—Conclusion. Maintains structure parallel to #7. Ends in an exclamation, an expression of strong feeling.[10]

With only this brief summary, we can see that the essay form traditionally favored in China is repetitious and illogical according to our ideas. Because the Chinese writer is attempting to make his point very indirectly, almost every paragraph is likely to end with a rhetorical question. The meat of the discourse, the main point, is found in #4, while Western writers usually try to build up to a climax just before the conclusion.

Analyzing Discourse Features

Traditional composition books urge us to work for unity, emphasis, and coherence. Text linguists are now analyzing the linguistic behaviors that produce these desirable qualities, basing their observations on texts from many languages. Unity of text seems to be achieved primarily by the use of lexical linkage, emphasis by exercising certain syntactic options, and coherence by the occurrence of pronouns and other kinds of anaphora. Let's look at these behaviors in written English.

Lexical Linkage. In determining whether a collection of sentences is a discourse or not, our first and most important clue is unity of subject. A discourse without a single, easily-grasped topic (according to our culture's standards of relevance) is boring and ineffective. Because the discourse has unity of subject, it also has a certain unity of lexicon. Consider the following example:

---

[10]Robert B. Kaplan, *The Anatomy of Rhetoric: Prolegomena to a Functional Theory of Rhetoric* (Philadelphia: The Center for Curriculum Development, 1972), pp. 48–59.

Well, you can see at once how *ideas* go to work, *organizing* the world into *understandable patterns* such as everyday life and typical Monday mornings when it is time to put on a clean shirt again. You need an *organizing idea* in mind in order to see two angry strangers as a happily married couple. Similarly, it requires an *idea* to transform a bunch of black lines and dots on a page into a newspaper of meaningful words and pictures.

In the same way, you must have an *idea* in mind before you can even hear *music*. You must have an *idea* of a *musical pitch* in order to distinguish *tones* from the other noises in the world. And then you need a further *idea* of *music* so as to *organize* oncoming single *tones* into an *understandable pattern* known as a *melody*. [11]

These two paragraphs, part of the same discourse, repeat several lexical items: *idea*, *organize*, and *understandable pattern*. The second paragraph has an additional lexical item, *music*, and some related words (in this case aspects of music), *tone*, *pitch*, and *melody*.

Notice that the natural unity of lexicon, derived from unity of subject, has been heightened by an artistic use of *lexical linkage*. A word or phrase from a preceding sentence is repeated in the first part of the next sentence. In our example, the three sentences of the second paragraph repeat "have an idea" and its variant "you need a further idea." Some languages of the world are highly repetitive, to such an extent that the first clause of each sentence always summarizes the content of the preceding sentence. Although writers of English are not happy with that amount of repetition, they still have to struggle with maintaining a good balance between *old information* (what is understood by general agreement or available in a previous part of the discourse) and *new information*, which is more or less unpredictable. Lexical linkage is a means of leading the reader gently from one point to another.

Some composition students have been taught not to repeat words and phrases, so they go through the thesaurus and carefully replace the repeated words with synonyms. Although this does not destroy the lexical linkage, since a synonym can also be a carrier of old information, it does erase some clues to easy interpretation. It seldom results in an improvement of style.

Emphasis and Change of Focus. In order to produce an easily understood text, the writer must emphasize some points and de-emphasize others. Every language has means, mostly syntactic, of calling special attention to one part of a discourse. One available means is to place a noun in a syntactic position that is unusual for its semantic role. For instance, we can change "He was killed in a car wreck" to "A car wreck killed him." (See Chapter 7, marked and unmarked roles.) Another means is *topicalization*, often by

---

[11] Ward Cannel and Fred Marx, *How to Play the Piano Despite Years of Lessons* (Paterson, NJ: Crown & Bridge, 1976), p. 15.

changing the expected word order of the sentence. For instance, "Joe ate the party food before the guests came" can be changed to "*It was Joe* who ate the party food," thus emphasizing Joe. Or the important information can be repeated at the beginning or end of the sentence: "He ate the party food, did Joe," at the end or "That sucker, I could wring his neck" at the beginning. Finally, the complement can be front-shifted: "A great pitcher, we haven't got." In Tamang, a language of India, fronting is used, but there are also a number of morphemes—affixes, enclitics, and particles—which are used to show topicalization.[12]

There are many other ways to emphasize some part of a text. The following ways are common to many languages:

1. a shift in *verb tense*, often from past to present;
2. a shift in *pronouns*, so that third person is replaced by second or first;
3. a change of *pace*, so that a story which has previously favored long sentences will suddenly show a high percentage of short, choppy ones;
4. a change of *focus*, so that the name of the character who has been the subject of a series of sentences will be replaced by the name of another character as subject. (In nonfiction, of course, this last point will apply to a change of topic rather than of character.)

Analysis of focus is particularly useful to the literary critic. Often a story writer tells us how to feel about the story by his choice of focus. In the following paragraph, Bud is the character in focus as he takes over driving the family car for the first time:

Bud walked out of the patrol building with the precious document in *his* hand. "Move over, Dad," *he* said cheerfully, opening the car door. *He* started the motor, put the car in gear, and backed as carefully as he could. As *he* pulled out into the street, the waiting members of *his* driver education class watched. *He* gave them a jaunty wave, and they cheered as *he* drove off into the sunset, *an adult* at last.

Since Bud is the active one, the paragraph begins with his name, and all but one of the pronouns refer to him. This second paragraph focuses on Bud's father. It's more difficult to focus on him, since he is relatively passive. The author does it by repeating his name and telling what he experienced. Notice also the verbs. In the first paragraph, Bud *walked*. In the second paragraph, he *came*. That is, he moved toward the character who is in focus. As you read the paragraph, notice what is done to de-emphasize Bud's actions in getting the car to move:

Ron hadn't been waiting long when *his* son came out of the patrol building with the driver's license in hand. "Move over, *Dad*," he com-

---

[12]Doreen Taylor, "Topicalisation in Tamang Narrative," in *Papers on Discourse*, ed. Joseph E. Grimes (Dallas: The Summer Institute of Linguistics, 1978), pp. 149–56.

manded, opening the car door. As the motor began to turn over, *Ron* tensed his muscles. As the car backed, *he* automatically looked over *his* shoulder. The car pulled into the street. *Ron* heard *his* son's driver ed class cheering, saw the jaunty wave in response. *He* told *himself* to relax.

Besides using names and pronouns to show focus, there is, in every language, a set of directional verbs such as *go-come, bring-take*. Then there are the deictics, or pointing words. Bud would refer to the license as *this* license; his father would call it *that* license. Analysis of one or more of these features often enables a literary critic to give solid evidence for his reactions to a literary work.

Cohesion and Anaphora. Cohesion refers specifically to the way clauses and sentences are pasted together. Consider the following sentence:

Then he got to the store and found that he didn't have any money.

Standing alone, this sentence makes no sense because we don't know what *then* and *he* refer to. (So much for the traditional definition of a sentence as a group of words that expresses a complete thought. This is a sentence, but not a complete thought.) Let's add the sentence it needs:

James planned to buy some much-needed deodorant. Then he got to the store and found that he didn't have any money.

Notice that the change to the pronoun is not optional, but mandatory, as this unacceptable version shows:

James planned to buy some much-needed deodorant. Then James got to the store and found that James didn't have any money.

If you had a set of sentences on cards and dropped them, you'd be able to put them in the right order by paying attention to the occurrence of pronouns and to sentence adverbs like *then*. This process of referring back to previous sentences is called *anaphora*. Pronouns provide our most important means of referring back, but we also have pro-verbs, pro-adverbs, and pro-determiners. Consider the following examples:

When the bells started ringing for the New Year, Bill kissed his date and Joe *did* too.

When I ate at The Place, my food was cold and stale. I won't go *there* again.

The City Council is talking of raising taxes again. *This* is ridiculous.

One way to become aware of the importance of anaphora and other devices of cohesion is to reverse sentences or clauses and see what changes you have to make. In the first example quoted, notice that reversing the two sentences requires a change in verb tense as well as pronouns:

James got to the store and found that he didn't have any money.
He had planned to buy some much-needed deodorant.

In the example using *this*, reversal requires a change to *it*, a shift in the verb tense, and the combining of the two sentences:
It is ridiculous *that* the City Council *should talk* of raising taxes again.

When sentences are switched in this way, their emphasis is slightly different, but the meaning (that is, the truth value) remains the same. A skilled writer may try several arrangements of clauses before finding the one that produces exactly the desired effect.

A Linguistic Approach to Paragraphing

Some people believe that the grouping of sentences into paragraphs is strictly a typographical device, something to make the written material look attractive on the page. They point out that the newspaper, with its narrow columns, favors short paragraphs, often single-sentence ones, while books with their different format favor longer paragraphs. However, experiments in "the psychological reality of the paragraph" have suggested that just as the knowledge of what constitutes a sentence is part of the native speaker's knowledge of language, so also is the knowledge of what constitutes a paragraph. This knowledge is not part of the earliest mastery of the language— that acquired by age five—but it is something which develops as the language-user matures. Part of the psychological reality of the paragraph comes from the previously-mentioned syntactic devices of cohesion. Researchers found that if they replaced the content words of the discourse but retained syntactic markers, including the markers of cohesion, people could group sentences into paragraphs with remarkable consistency. The syntactic markers of paragraph units are powerful communication devices.

Of course, the experiments also allowed people to use the signals of lexical linkage. If the nonsense word for *world* was *gorness*, it remained *gorness* throughout the discourse. In many discourses, a paragraph could be defined as a span of lexical dominance. Thus, in the segment previously quoted, *idea* was the dominant word in the first paragraph; then *music* was added to it in the second paragraph.

A paragraph is also a unit of semantic relationship. In narratives, paragraph breaks occur when there is a change of focus from one character to another. There are also breaks when the scene of the action changes or when the action enters a new stage. (By convention we put each person's speech in a separate paragraph in a short story or novel. This has nothing to do with the linguistic analysis of discourse.) In non-narratives, paragraph breaks occur when the writer moves from one aspect of his topic to another. In the beginning of this chapter, for example, the first paragraph introduces the subject. The second defines discourses. The third discusses intuitive knowledge of discourses. In each paragraph the writer moves from a general statement to more specific information or examples. This process is diagrammed in Fig. 12.

PARAGRAPH COHESION

1 We *know intuitively* what a *discourse* is.
2 Just as we *have internalized* . . .
    we *have learned* how to *deal with a larger context*
3a We *know* that a *conversation* begins
3a We *know* that *questions* . . . *answer*
3a We *know* that . . . *paragraph*
3b In *dealing with discourses*
    we use *phonological, syntactic, semantic* clues.
4 When a lecturer . . . such *phonological* clues
    5 slower pronunciation
    5 lower overall pitch
    5 lower volume
4 *Syntactic* clues include
    5 use of pronouns
    5 consistency in verb forms
    5 use of conjunctions
4 *Semantic* clues include
    5 unity of subject
    5 logical relationships
    5 repetition of lexical items

Semantic relationships:
    know intuitively = have internalized = have learned = know
    deal with a larger context = dealing with discourses
    genus—discourse; species—conversation, question-answer, paragraph

Note: If shorter paragraphs were desired, a new paragraph would logically begin with 3b.

Fig. 12

Why, then, the variation of paragraph length in different types of reading materials? In part, it's due to differences in communicative situation. Just as sentences in conversations tend to be shorter than sentences in very formal speeches, so also the lengths of paragraphs vary. In making the paragraphs long or short, however, the writer or editor maintains certain semantic patterns of discourse. If the paragraph in Fig. 12 were divided into two shorter ones, the division would come after Sentence 5, because Sentence 6 returns to a higher level of generality. If it were divided into three, the divisions would probably come after Sentence 2, and Sentence 5, so as to keep the three sentences beginning "we know" together.

Occasionally paragraphs are presented in inverted order, from specific to general. This tends to be an emphatic order, just as inverted sentence order is emphatic (Remember "A great pitcher, we haven't got"?). It isn't used often, and I don't think there's an inverted paragraph in this chapter.

Another type of paragraph, more common than the inverted one, is simply an enlarged version of the utterance-response pair. The first part of it asks a question or makes a proposal, and the second part responds. The question or proposal represents what the reader would say in an actual conversation and the answer represents what the writer would respond. The paragraph beginning "Some people believe" is of this type.

Short poems tend to be structured much like paragraphs. This resemblance in structure is particularly easy to see in the sonnet. Two major kinds of sonnets are the Petrarchan (Italian) and the Shakespearean (English). These kinds are usually defined by their differing rhyme patterns, but the rhyme pattern merely reflects the difference in paragraph structure. The Petrarchan sonnet is an utterance-response pair. The first eight lines, or *octave*, ask a question, make a proposal, or set forth a problem. The last six lines, or *sestet*, provide the response. The Shakespearean sonnet is an inverted explanatory paragraph. There are three four-line units, and each one sets forth a specific point—three examples of a situation, three comparisons, or three related problems. These are resolved by a general statement in the final two lines of the poem.

Although sonnet-paragraphs are complete discourses, other paragraphs are not. Skillful writers avoid creating paragraphs that are too separate from each other. Instead of presenting a succession of ideas like a collection of slides, the paragraphs should flow into one another like the frames of a film. The most commonly used linguistic device for achieving this flow is lexical linkage, the repetition of a key word or the restatement of the point of the preceding paragraph. If you'll check the last few paragraphs of this discussion, you'll find that the word "paragraph" appears in every first sentence.

All this discussion of the linguistic features of discourse should not lead to a rigid adherence to the patterns which have been described. Just as people do not pronounce words precisely, just as they do not make sentences that can be easily analyzed, so also they do not conform exactly to the patterns of paragraphs, monologues, and conversations. These rules of discourse are norms which, like phonology and syntax, are part of our intuitive knowledge of language.

Exercises

1. Narrative Structures in Jokes.

A. Consider the following four jokes. Find two discourse-level slots in each one. Which one has a structure different from the other three?

1. from *Reader's Digest*, Oct. 1974, p. 163: (orig. from *Kiwanis Magazine*)

    "Who was that gorgeous curly-haired blonde I saw you with last night?" somebody asked the middle-aged man.

    "That was no gorgeous blonde," the man grumped. "That was my son-in-law."

2. from *Reader's Digest*, Oct. 1974, p. 48: (contrib. by D. Case)
   One bright, sunny day, I was driving to Salt Lake City to give a lecture to a high-school science class. My small foreign car was piled high with displays and animals, including cages of mice and bowls of fish. In addition, due to a short circuit, my windshield wipers had spontaneously started and could not be turned off. I was late and driving a little erratically and too fast.
   The policeman who pulled me over took a long look at the car and its contents, then exploded, "My God, lady, are you expecting The Flood?"

3. From *Reader's Digest*, Sept. 1974, p. 85: (contrib. by Rev. H.V. Buchholz)
   After I accepted a call to serve a parish in northern Minnesota, it was determined that the local water supply and my digestive tract just wouldn't agree unless a water softener and a charcoal filter were installed in the parsonage water system. The governing body of the parish voted to have the units installed.
   When reading the minutes at the following meeting, the secretary, with tongue in cheek, reported the action: "Moved, seconded and carried that the trustees of the congregation take care of the pastor's drinking problem."

4. from *Reader's Digest*, Oct. 1974, p. 164: (orig. from *Catholic Digest*)
   One day, instead of the usual hamburgers, ham or fish, the school cafeteria served bologna and peanut-butter sandwiches as the entrée. After lunch a satisfied first-grader marching out the door complimented the manager of the school kitchen. "Finally," he said, "we got a home-cooked meal."

   (All reprinted by permission)

B. 1. What two major discourse units can you see in the three jokes which are alike in structure?
   2. What two major discourse units can you see in the joke which is the different one?

2. Clause Reversal

The following story is printed with each main clause numbered separately. Rewrite the story, reversing each pair of clauses. That is, instead of reading 1, 2, 3 the story will read 2, 1, 4, 3 etc. Make whatever changes in pronouns, verb tenses, connecting words, etc. that are needed for smooth flow. Underline all these changes.

Example: *The vampire* was very hungry *when he* came out of his coffin.
1. The vampire came out of his coffin.
2. He was very hungry.

3. He needed to find a young maiden in a billowy white gown,
4. but maidens of today seem to sleep in old T-shirts and cutoffs, or sometimes only a dab of perfume.
5. Anyway, unless they are very young,
6. they are not maidens in the technical sense.
7. Our fanged friend decided to find a housewife instead.
8. One who had read *The Total Woman* might own a billowy white gown.
9. She would be sitting at the piano in it,
10. waiting for her husband to come home.
11. She would expect him to kiss her on the back of the neck.
12. Then he would press his hungry lips on hers.
13. It would be a surprise
14. when the vampire opened the door instead.
15. He would pretend to be a vacuum cleaner salesman.
16. He licked his lips in anticipation.
17. But when he sneaked into the room,
18. he found the housewife ready for him.
19. A gold cross nestled in her cleavage.
20. The sight of it nauseated him.
21. He advanced toward her anyway,
22. one hand covering his eyes.
23. She quickly removed her spike heels.
24. She used them to give him the old one-two.
25. As he floundered on the carpet in pain,
26. she took a miniature pearl-handled pistol out of her lace hand-bag.
27. She shot him with a silver bullet no bigger than a B-B.
28. The vampire began to fade away, more glad than sorry.
29. He realized that the vampire business isn't what it used to be.
30. And neither are women in white gowns.

3. Paragraph Signals

The following theme has been "cooked up" to demonstrate the linguistic signals of paragraph cohesion. Go through the sentences and mark the following features:
1. the times indicated by verb tenses and other time words
2. pronoun orientations
3. lexical linkages

After you've examined the features, determine how many paragraphs the theme should contain. Where do natural divisions occur?

Compare your results with those of other members of the class. When you disagree, is it merely a matter of the placement of a transitional sentence? What kinds of paragraphs do you find—utterance-response, general-to-specific, etc.?

1. Is the dog man's best friend? 2. Not any more. 3. Only yesterday a six-year-old child making his way home from school was attacked and seriously injured by a pack of free-running dogs. 4. Two months ago a friend of mine, riding his bicycle past a certain residence, was bitten by an over-zealous watch dog. 5. And last year one of the blind students on our campus was seriously endangered when her seeing-eye dog was attacked by loose dogs. 6. At worst, the dog is a vicious enemy in today's society; but at best he is nothing better than a ceaseless nuisance. 7. In the daytime you can't take a carefree walk in the park or even stroll around your own neighborhood. 8. One relaxed moment, one instant of ceaseless vigilance, and you step in a pile of dog dung. 9. At night the howling of dogs keeps you awake, and at all times the barking of nervous, bored, penned-up family pets adds to the quota of noise pollution which you have to put up with. 10. There are, of course, many valid reasons for keeping a dog. 11. In our over-civilized, over-urbanized society, many people experience loneliness and alienation. 12. The dog provides them with a love object and contributes to their mental health. 13. In some cases, the dog provides a substitute child for people who are too immature to be parents. 14. People who are trying to lose weight can feed the leftovers to the dog and let him get fat instead of themselves. 15. Some small dogs are as good as cats in catching rats and mice. 16. And occasionally (very occasionally) a dog actually discourages a burglar. 17. Even so, it is high time for us to consider whether we can continue to tolerate dogs in urbanized areas. 18. We have laws against keeping livestock in the city, and lots of dogs are as big and smelly as a sheep or goat. 19. Furthermore, we should start thinking about whether it is moral to spend such a large amount of our resources on food for useless dogs when so many people are starving. 20. We are not doing the dogs any favor by keeping them as pets. 21. Dogs, like us, need a purpose in life. 22. They need to have a job—hunting, sheep-herding, pulling a sled. 23. They need something to do with their time. 24. Since we cannot give them purposeful lives in the city, we should not have them at all.

4. Scrambled Paragraphs

By paying attention to semantic and syntactic signals, restore each of the following paragraphs to the proper order. In each case, the first sentence of the paragraph is given first. All the paragraphs occur in Chapter 8 (pp. 174, 176, 177, 182 and 183) so that you can check your arrangement. If you find that your arrangement is better than the original, drop me a line.

1. There are three kinds of local exceptions to the overall dialect pattern, variations which occur when a small area differs noticeably from the area surrounding it.

A. It's a focal area when a major city develops speech patterns of its own and these patterns spread to the surrounding area.

B. It's a relic area when an isolated group retains old-fashioned speech patterns while the area surrounding it changes.

C. The area is a speech island if it occurred because a whole group of people migrated to a new location and settled together, bringing their speech patterns with them.

D. The focal area is usually in the process of expanding; speech islands and relic areas are often in the process of disappearing.

E. These are named according to the cause of the difference.

2. Related to geographic mobility as a leveling factor is industrialization.

A. However, other vocabulary differences are arising in the naming of features or urban life, differences which linguists are only now beginning to record.

B. Industrialization has also brought about increased urbanization.

C. This urbanization has caused the loss of many dialectal vocabulary items having to do with farming and nature.

D. Throughout the colonial period, 95% of the people lived in rural areas; now the figure is 30% or less.

E. When a new industry is developed, people from many regions move in to take advantage of the new jobs, so that different speech patterns come into contact with each other.

3. There are some difficulties in vocabulary study, however.

A. Another difficulty is that informants will usually know two terms for the same thing—the local one and a more national one.

B. Finally, in an area where two vocabulary items are competing, people often claim to perceive a difference in meaning between the two.

C. New questionnaires are being developed to show regional differences with regard to modern vocabulary—words for limited-access roads, for carbonated drinks, for calling a taxi—but obviously these are not strictly comparable to the old.

D. For example, babies in Northern dialect areas "creep" while babies in Southern areas "crawl."

E. The oldest studies were heavily biased toward rural speech, and some of the test items used to determine dialect areas refer to farm tools or customs no longer in existence.

F. When taking a "test" they are likely to offer the national term as being more correct or prestigious.

G. In many Midland areas both terms are used, but people will say that "creeping" is what the baby does at first, and "crawling" is the relatively skilled hands-and-knees locomotion.

4. At present, there's simply not enough evidence to decide between the anglicist and creolist theories.

   A. But the exact relationship of BEV to other dialects of English remains controversial.

   B. Other research has shown that many words common in the South such as *goober* (peanut), *gumbo* (okra), *jigger* (chigger), *cooter* (tortoise) and *tote* (carry) come from words in African languages.

   C. The anglicist-creolist controversy had a good effect in that it caused researchers to look at Black English Vernacular more carefully than they had done before.

   D. The evidence from before the 20th century is derived from dialect novels and poetry, descriptions of speech by untrained observers, and sheer guesswork.

   E. The intense study of ghetto culture amassed enough evidence to kill the deficiency theory of language difference among linguists, though it remains alive and well in many classrooms.

   F. The research of the 20th century, largely financed by government grants, has been hampered by the fact that data was collected within the context of a very sensitive social problem.

5. Authors sometimes increase the realism of their fictional characters by portraying their dialectal peculiarities.

   A. If the dialect writing differs too much from normal writing it will be hard to read, thus frustrating the main purpose of literature, the purpose of entertainment.

   B. He or she is concerned with creating an effect, not providing a scientific report of someone's idiolect.

   C. The attempt to indicate dialect in the standard written language presents many problems.

   D. The skillfull author will make no attempt to represent all the linguistic features of the dialect, or even the most frequent features, but will include only enough items of vocabulary, grammar, and pronunciation to create the desired effect.

   E. The author must give us enough samples of the fictional character's deviation from standard speech to create the illusion of reality.

5 Paragraph Coherence

Given the assignment of writing a one-paragraph character sketch of a classmate, one freshman turned in the following collection of sentences. Supply the paragraph with a topic sentence. Then rewrite it so as to create lexical and semantic unity:

Today, T—stands six feet tall, has hazel eyes, and light brown hair. He is shy and introverted to a degree. He is somewhat sensitive, but he does not use it as a handicap. "Sensitive people have a hard time going through life, and they need special crutches to help them get by," he said. T— is also very competitive and hates to lose. He believes health is a state of mind. "Proper motivations to keep you busy are all that you need to keep from getting sick," he said. T— inherits quite a temper from his Irish mother. When ired, he will argue about anything and loves to frustrate his opponent with trivialities.

6. Pronouns and Other Devices for Syntactic Unity

This paragraph from a theme about Franklin Roosevelt has unity of content, but a Dick-and-Jane style because it uses the awkward "first," "second," and "third" instead of gaining coherence through pronouns and other syntactic methods. Rewrite it for smoothness and then list the syntactic devices you used:

The preparation of Roosevelt's speeches went through many stages. First, Roosevelt consulted a wide range of sources for information needed in his speech. Second, Roosevelt would assemble the source material and write out a rough draft. Third, Roosevelt would always ask for advice from a small advisory group to questions about structure, grammar, etc. Roosevelt, however, had the final say in his speech writing. The last stage in Roosevelt's speech preparation was the writing and re-writing of drafts to cut down the wordiness, correct sentence structure errors, and correct errors in usage. The ultimate product of combined efforts invariably yielded addresses identifiable as peculiarly Rooseveltian!

Writing for Insight and Review: Analogy

Joseph E. Grimes asserts a resemblance between the quest story and the scientific article. Such a comparison between two dissimilar things is called an *analogy*. John Donne's comparison of his marriage relationship to a compass—you, the woman are the fixed foot; I, the man, am the traveling foot—in "A Valediction, Forbidding Mourning" is a famous analogy. Some linguists assert that this ability to see similarity in unlike things is the basis of our ability to use language, that human beings are born to speak because they are born to perceive patterns.

Whether this idea is true or not, we know that the analogy is a powerful tool in explanatory, persuasive, and sometimes procedural writing.
1. The analogy catches the reader's attention. The child in the poetry workshop who wrote, "Death is like an orange bikini" certainly brought the class to life. Everyone wanted to hear the next line.
2. The analogy makes abstract ideas easy to follow by enabling the reader to visualize them. Instead of such abstract terms as "superego," "id," and "neurosis," the Transactional Analysis psychologists use such terms as "Parent," "Child," and "Game." Another school of psycholo-

gy uses a hydraulic analogy to describe the human mind, speaking of dammed-up emotions, of pressure, and flow. Although such visualization of abstract concepts can lead to distortion, it's a beginning, something to build on. The alternative may be making no attempt to understand the difficult concept.
3. The analogy is useful in persuasive writing because its very vividness gives the reader a tool with which to convince himself. In this respect an analogy is like a slogan—it stands for a whole complex of reasons and emotions.
4. For anyone who is working on a very difficult problem—a scientist, sociologist, engineer, or philosopher—the analogy may actually suggest a new line of research, an answer that otherwise might never have been found.

To further your understanding of analogy, try one of these writing projects:

A. It's common to use the analogy of a tennis game in visualizing the dynamics of a dialogue. Take a passage of dialogue from a work of fiction and identify each bit of conversation as a specific tennis play. Or, you might find a passage of conversation that you felt was not like tennis at all, but more like football or baseball.

B. Do some research in the history of science and write a report on a famous discovery that came about through the use of analogy.

C. Write a review of a book, short story, or film in which you compare the work to a quest story.

8

It Takes All Kinds

No other shock is quite like the one that comes when an acquaintance says, laughing, "You talk funny." Most of us tend to feel that the way we talk is right, and that anyone who differs from us talks funny. It's reported that many Southerners reacted to the election of Jimmy Carter by saying, "Well, at last we have a President who talks without an accent." If we can rise above this linguistic self-centeredness, however, we find that variety in language gives us a glimpse into human social groups and our own humanness. The old saying, "It takes all kinds to make a world" expresses the attitude of tolerance necessary to enjoy the study of language variety.

The ordinary person applies the term "dialect" to the kind of language used by uneducated people in odd corners of the world. For the linguist, *dialect* is a technical term designating the degree to which one set of speech patterns differs from another. When two people speak so differently that they cannot understand each other, we say that they speak *different languages*. When two people notice differences in each other's speech but are still able to understand each other, we say that they speak *different dialects* of the same language. In practice, this test of *mutual intelligibility* does not provide a hard-and-fast classification. Many nonlinguistic factors affect intelligibility: the mental flexibility of the speakers, the strength of their desire to communicate, the similarity of their cultural backgrounds. To give an extreme example, an American racist might find it virtually impossible to understand the Black dialect of American English, while two doctors, speakers of Hungarian and German, might communicate pretty well as they struggled to help the victims of a plane crash. The doctors' common medical education and common purpose is in strong contrast with the racist's lack of interest in the black's point of view.

Because mutual intelligibility is so variable, linguists arbitrarily designate languages according to national boundaries. We speak of Danish,

Swedish, and Norwegian as languages because they are three separate political units, but they are just about as mutually intelligible as Sicilian and Tuscan, two dialects of Italian. On the other hand, we think of Mandarin and Cantonese as dialects of Chinese, even though they are not mutually intelligible. But whether a language pattern is a "language" or a "dialect" is not, for the linguist, a value judgment; he or she is looking for interesting information wherever it may be found.

One area of interest is the *regional dialect*, the speech habits of the people in a particular geographic area. This sort of study is called *dialect geography*, or, more recently, *areal linguistics*. Dialect geographers plot the regional dialects by establishing isoglosses. An *isogloss* is a line separating two areas with respect to a single dialect item, whether it's a pronunciation, a grammatical construction, or the use of one vocabulary item rather than another.

With regard to pronunciation for example, there is a distinction between people who say "greasy" with an /s/ and people who say it with a /z/. The isogloss enclosing the z-speakers runs from the southwestern corner of Connecticut, north of New Jersey, and across northern Pennsylvania. The isogloss enclosing the s-speakers is harder to describe in words, but it includes most of Connecticut, most of upstate New York, parts of Pennsylvania, and the areas north of those states. Between the s-speakers and the z-speakers there is a strip of territory where both pronunciations are found. This is called a *transition area*. When a number of isoglosses occur together, an *isogloss bundle* is formed. Patterns begin to emerge, and the dialect geographer is able to delineate and name dialect areas. The names of regional dialects change as new studies correct previous information. A linguist may propose a new name because he perceives two dialects where other linguists had perceived one, or vice versa.

The first great achievement in dialect geography for the United States was the *Linguistic Atlas of New England*, published between 1939 and 1943. Field workers under the direction of Hans Kurath collected the information, and what resulted was six huge volumes of detailed maps. Originally funded as a government project during the Depression, this work was intended as a pilot project for a complete linguistic atlas of the United States. World War II intervened, and the whole project has never been completed. One additional atlas has been published—the *Linguistic Atlas of the Upper Midwest*, edited by Harold B. Allen. Field work has been completed for the following other areas: the Middle and South Atlantic States, the North Central States, the Gulf States, Oklahoma, and California and Nevada.

One result of all this research has been to change the names of American regional dialects. Dialectologists no longer speak of "General American." Instead, they find three major dialect areas: Northern, Midland, and Southern. Eastern New England forms an additional area, with speech patterns quite different from those of other Northern regions. The Midland areas are further classified as North Midland and South Midland, depending on whether the speech patterns have received influence from Northern or Southern areas. (See Fig. 13.)

Within these major dialect boundaries there are many smaller areas. The Southern dialect of East Texas is different from that of Mississippi or Tidewater Virginia, the New England dialect of coastal Maine differs from that of Wisconsin. The number of dialect boundaries which can be drawn is endless. Even such a small area as the island of Martha's Vineyard shows a division into two dialect patterns.[1]

There are three kinds of local exceptions to the overall dialect pattern, variations which occur when a small area differs noticeably from the area surrounding it. These are named according to the cause of the difference. The area is a *speech island* if it occurred because a whole group of people migrated to a new location and settled together, bringing their speech patterns with them. It's a *relic area* when an isolated group retains old-fashioned speech patterns while the area surrounding it changes. It's a *focal area* when a major city develops speech patterns of its own and these patterns spread to the surrounding area. The focal area is usually in the process of expanding; speech islands and relic areas are often in the process of disappearing.

In addition to regional dialects there are *social dialects*, speech varieties correlated with social class, age, sex, occupation, religion, and recreational preferences. The speech of each individual is a composite of the regional characteristics plus all these other factors. One individual's version of the language is called an *idiolect*. When a linguist is studying dialect, he must try to determine which speech characteristics are common to the group and which ones are peculiar to the individual, for the idiolect is not properly the subject of dialect study. Social dialects are discussed in Chapter 9.

Leveling

The United States has a great variety of speech patterns, but compared with the rest of the world, it's remarkable for its uniformity of language rather than its variety. Great Britain, with a land area about the size of Oregon, has many more dialects of English than the United States. Furthermore, British dialects are more distinct from one another than American dialects, which have undergone a great deal of *leveling*.

Probably the greatest single leveling factor in the United States is *geographic mobility*. The most distinct regional dialects are found in the East, particularly in the thirteen original states. As the settlers moved westward, they came into contact with people from other dialect areas. Each group tended to adopt some of the practices of the other and to drop their more conspicuous differences. As a result, people west of the Appalachians speak

---

[1] William Labov, "The Recent History of Some Dialect Markers on the Island of Martha's Vineyard, Massachusetts," in *Studies in Linguistics in Honor of Raven I. McDavid, Jr.* (University, AL: The University of Alabama Press, 1972).

Fig. 13

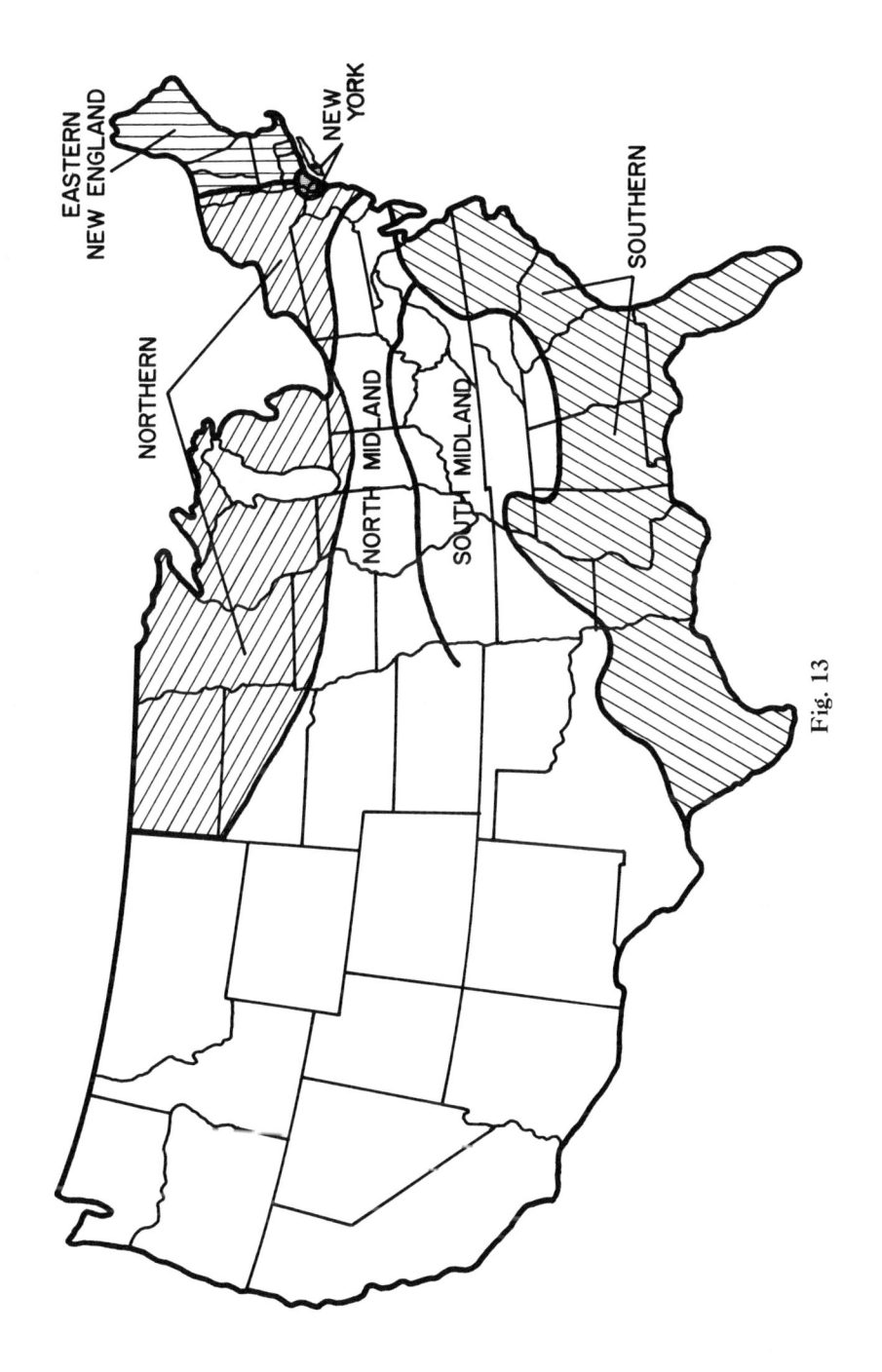

mixed dialects. Further west, there is even more mixing, resulting in a greater degree of leveling.

Related to geographic mobility as a leveling factor is *industrialization*. When a new industry is developed, people from many regions move in to take advantage of the new jobs, so that different speech patterns come into contact with each other. Industrialization has also brought about increased *urbanization*. Throughout the colonial period, 95% of the people lived in rural areas; now the figure is 30% or less.[2] This urbanization has caused the loss of many dialectal vocabulary items having to do with farming and nature. However, other vocabulary differences are arising in the naming of features of urban life, differences which linguists are only now beginning to record.

In the twentieth century, our increased dependence on the electronic media has undoubtedly contributed to the leveling of dialects. In pronunciation, radio and television speakers shift away from their native dialect toward a more neutral "broadcast English." In grammar, they try to use the structures more common in written English and thus contribute to the loss of dialectal peculiarities. In vocabulary, media speakers contribute to uniformity by introducing new words simultaneously all over the country. These new words probably contribute to the displacement of old dialectal expressions. On the other hand, the media may have broadened people's tolerance of language different from their own by exposing them to a wide variety of speakers—international figures who speak English as a second language, comedians with exaggerated idiolects, singers who use the dialects associated with rock or country western music. We can only guess about the effects of the media on dialects, because it would be almost impossible to design a study to collect objective, indisputable facts.

Dialect Pronunciations

Although it takes a well-trained linguistics student to perceive the many pronunciation characteristics of the speech varieties, there are a few features that the beginner can observe. The most obvious difference is between r-pronouncing and r-less dialects. The Eastern New England and Southern dialects are r-less; the Northern and Midland dialects are r-pronouncing. The western third of the United States, where dialect lines are not well established, is also an r-pronouncing area. The two r-less areas can be distinguished on the basis of the presence or absence of the *intrusive-r*, which is present in the Eastern New England dialect and absent in the Southern dialect. The term *intrusive-r* refers to the habit of adding an *r* when one word ends with a vowel and the next word begins with a vowel. The speaker who has this feature says "idea-r-of" and "sofa-r-is."

Another obvious pronunciation feature concerns the word "greasy."

---

[2]"United States of America," *Encyclopaedia Britannica* (Helen Hemingway Benton, 1979).

The Northern dialect pronounces it with an /s/, the Midland and Southern with a /z/. However, North Midland speakers are apt to use /s/, and many Midland speakers vary between the two sounds. Those who do often use the /s/ when the word has its basic meaning, as in "a greasy pan" and /z/ in a metaphorical meaning, as in "a greasy-looking loiterer." Another well-known feature is the pronunciation of the three words Mary-merry-marry. A Northern speaker pronounces all three alike: /mɛr i/. A Midland speaker pronounces "Mary" and "merry" alike, but uses the /æ/ sound in "marry." New England and Southern speakers pronounce all three differently, using /aɪ/ as the vowel in "Mary."

This analysis is, of course, an oversimplification. There are many local variations, and the patterns are also complicated by social dialects. For example, New York City is basically an r-less dialect, but r-pronouncing is considered prestigious by some speakers in some contexts. Likewise, the use of the intrusive-r is associated with low status by some New Yorkers.

Vocabulary

The various regions show numerous differences in vocabulary. Northerners say "stone" while Southerners say "rock." Northerners say "pail" while Southerners say "bucket." Northern housewives "make" dinner while Midland and Southern ones "fix" dinner. The procedure of locating vocabulary items on the map is called *word geography*. The knowledge of word geography is more detailed than the knowledge of pronunciation, because vocabulary can be obtained by sending out questionnaires, while pronunciations can only be obtained by time-consuming personal interviews. Differences in vocabulary can show that two parts of a state were settled by different speech groups even after pronunciations have leveled out. Vocabulary also reflects foreign influences more than pronunciation does.

There are some difficulties in vocabulary study, however. The oldest studies were heavily biased toward rural speech, and some of the test items used to determine dialect areas refer to farm tools or customs no longer in existence. New questionnaires are being developed to show regional differences with regard to modern vocabulary—words for limited-access roads, for carbonated drinks, for calling a taxi—but obviously these are not strictly comparable to the old. Another difficulty is that informants will usually know two terms for the same thing— the local one and a more national one. When taking a "test" they are likely to offer the national term as being more correct or prestigious. Finally, in an area where two vocabulary items are competing, people often claim to perceive a difference in meaning between the two. For example, babies in Northern dialect areas "creep" while babies in Southern areas "crawl." In many Midland areas both terms are used, but people will say that "creeping" is what the baby does at first, and "crawling" is the relatively skilled hands-and-knees locomotion.

Grammar

Dialectal variations in grammar include such items as past tense and past participle verb forms, choice of prepositions, and the choice of pronouns. For example, the use of "dove" as the past tense of "dive" is characteristic of Northern speech. Someone who is nauseated is "sick *at* his stomach" in Southern dialect areas, but "sick *to* his stomach" in Northern dialect. The Southern and South Midland "you-all" as a plural pronoun is well-known, as is the Northern plural "youse."

Regional variations in grammar are of two kinds: those found at all educational levels, and those associated with relatively uneducated people. To distinguish such variations, dialect informants have traditionally been divided into three educational levels: Group I with an eighth grade education or less and no travel outside the region; Group II with at least some high school; and Group III with some college and travel. The results thus obtained are not entirely accurate, of course, since other factors than education may govern responses. In some groups, men may avoid so-called correct grammar in order to seem more manly. Some grammatical constructions are more closely associated with an ethnic group than a region. And some are dependent on context. For example, a speaker from the Southwest would be likely to describe a film projector as "broken" but a horse as "broke."

Dialect Locations and Settlement History

The people who settled the United States were not concerned with leaving records to facilitate the study of dialect patterns; they had many more urgent issues on their minds. The evidence that's available to linguists is scanty and capable of many interpretations. The following sketch of dialect locations and settlement history, based on one commonly-held theory, thus contains many disputable statements.

Eastern New England was probably settled by people from the southeastern counties of England. Its speech patterns are like those of the Coastal South because both areas were settled by speakers of the same English dialect. The very earliest settlers in New England and Virginia, who came in the early 1600s, must have pronounced their r's, because the people of southeastern England were still pronouncing r's at that time. R-dropping was apparently an innovation of 18th century London speech. Since southeastern England was the cultural and political center of the country, the new pronunciation spread more rapidly there than in other areas. Both Eastern New England and the Coastal South maintained cultural and commercial contact with England, so that the speakers in these areas began to drop their r's along with the English.

The Eastern New England dialect did not spread westward as much as some others because the people were oriented toward England and the sea. Sometimes, however, whole communities would move together to a new location farther west, and thus a speech island of Eastern New England dialect would be formed. When gold was discovered in California, New Englanders sailed all the way around the tip of South America and up the western coast to California. For this reason Eastern New England dialect features are found today in old, well-established families of California.

The *Midland* dialect has a complicated origin and settlement history, but its basis is the speech of people other than those from southeastern England. First the Middle Atlantic states were settled by three groups: the Quakers, who probably came mostly from non-southeastern areas of England; the Scotch-Irish, also non-southeastern; and the Germans, popularly called "Pennsylvania Dutch." Beginning in Pennsylvania, New York, New Jersey, and parts of Delaware and Maryland, the Midland dialects spread into the highlands of Virginia and the Carolinas and westward along the easiest transportation routes. The Wilderness Road was opened by Daniel Boone from Virginia to Central Kentucky before the Revolutionary War. Later the Cumberland (or National) Road from Cumberland, Maryland, to Vandalia, Missouri, provided a path for Midland speech. The Midland dialect divided into North Midland and South Midland as its speakers were influenced by the neighboring Northern and Southern speech. In the 19th century, the Oregon Trail and the Santa Fe Trail, both originating in Missouri, provided paths further westward for Midland dialect features.

The *Northern* dialect, like the Midland, has as its basis the speech of settlers from parts of England other than the southeastern, and especially the Scotch-Irish. Settling first in Western New England, these people moved westward along the Mohawk Trail and the Erie Canal. They pushed into the Northwest Territory, especially around the Great Lakes, and then westward as far as North Dakota. Settlers from other parts of the United States, especially those from Eastern New England and Midland-speaking areas, affected Northern speech to some extent. Enclaves of settlers from various European countries contributed vocabulary items to various localities within the Northern dialect area.

The *Southern* dialect has as its basis the speech of settlers from the southeastern part of England. Its earliest locations were in Tidewater Virginia and the coastal areas of North and South Carolina. From there it spread into Florida and eastern Georgia. The highlands of Virginia and the Carolinas, which were mostly settled by the Scotch-Irish, spoke a basically Midland dialect, although they regarded Southern speech as prestigious and adopted many of its features.

The spread of Southern dialect was limited because the Southerners tended to grow tobacco, and later cotton, for export, so that good transportation by water was necessary. Southern dialect spread through the Gulf States as far as East Texas and northward along the Mississippi River. The Midland speakers, on the other hand, tended to live on small subsistence farms. Because their kind of farming required less land, less availability of transportation, and a smaller capital investment, their dialect spread faster and into more different areas. They were often able to establish their small farms in Southern-speaking areas, so that Georgia and the non-Seaboard Southern states show their influence. Much of what the general public calls "Southern dialect" is not Southern at all, but South Midland.

Further West As different parts of the West were opened up, settlers poured in from points eastward. Information about dialect in these states is scanty, and what there is concentrates on vocabulary. In the first half of the 20th century, when most of the dialect studies were done, many Western states were still sparsely settled and lacking in highways, so that vocabulary study by mail was more feasible than the more complete work which can be done by interview.

In general, the Western States show a large percentage of Northern and Midland vocabulary items, but a very small number of Southern items. Some of the words that give a distinctive flavor to Western vocabulary, such as *range, corral, mesa,* and *butte,* designate objects that simply aren't found further east. Some are ordinary words used with a special meaning. In the Rocky Mountain States, *park* sometimes means "a large treeless, grassy valley surrounded by mountains," and *hole* may mean "a remote valley enclosed by mountains." Many Western words are derived from Spanish, such as *plaza* for "town square" and (more recently) "shopping center." Speech patterns follow railroad lines, the trails of cattle drives, and rivers. In the Pacific Northwest, Midland words occur with greater frequency along the Columbia and Snake rivers.

More complete information about the vocabulary patterns of the whole United States has been gathered, but lack of money has prevented its publication. In the 1950s and 1960s extensive, systematic field work has done for the *Dictionary of American Regional English* under the direction of Frederic G. Cassidy. Specially trained field workers were sent to 1,002 communities from Florida to Alaska. The communities were chosen according to a careful analysis of demographics: areas with a larger population and a longer settlement history were represented by more communities. Informants were chosen with careful attention to age, sex, and education.

The field workers lived in vans fitted out for camping (called Logomobiles) while they took their informants through a carefully-developed questionnaire of 1,847 items. This vocabulary data has been computerized, and the audio tapes obtained at the same time are available for scholarly analysis.

At present, of course, this information is not accessible to the ordinary person. But if you're interested in learning more about speech varieties, try Carroll E. Reed, *Dialects of American English*. It emphasizes areas west of the Appalachian Mountains to some extent. You might also browse in the scholarly journal, *American Speech*, which reports on new developments.

More Recent Developments

The 20th century has brought other important dialect movements. The economic depression and crop failures of the 1930s caused many Midland speakers, especially South Midlanders, to move to California. *The Grapes of Wrath* by John Steinbeck provides a vivid account of this movement. In the 1940s and 1950s, large numbers of South Midlanders moved to the urban North seeking jobs in industries, especially to Detroit (which they pronounced /dí trɔɪt/) and Akron. Television coverage of a 1979 labor dispute in Akron showed the results of this movement: the workers interviewed on the program spoke South Midland, while the executives spoke a Northern dialect. During this period blacks from the Deep South also sought jobs in the urban North, especially New York and Chicago. In the 1960s and 1970s there has been a countermovement as more and more Northern industries have found it profitable to open plants in the Sun Belt—the South and Southwest.

Black English Vernacular

In recent years some linguists have begun to question the validity of the geographic approach to dialect study. The weaknesses of this approach are most obvious when one considers the problems raised by the dialect sometimes called Black English Vernacular, the language of many non-middle-class blacks. As these speakers moved out of the South into the industrialized Northern cities, it began to seem that race was a more important predictor of speech patterns than geography. Concentrated study of BEV has produced more questions than answers. Here are some of the questions:
1. Exactly how does BEV differ from the dialects spoken by non-blacks? One phonological feature of BEV is r-dropping, but as we have seen, it's also a feature of non-black Southern English, some South Midland varieties, Eastern New England, and New York City. Another is the raising of /ɛ/ to /ɪ/, so that *pen* and *pin* become near-homonyms, also a feature of Southern and South Midland varieties. Another is the simplification of consonant clusters at the ends of words, so that *pass* and *past* (or *passed*) are homonyms. Again, this feature is found in the casual speech of almost all ethnic groups. In syntax, BEV has such features as double subjects, as in "*John he* told me about it"; double negatives, such as "I *ain't* studying *no* boy friends"; lack of possessive inflection as in "he hat" instead of "his hat"; and verb phrases like: "I *done ate* it," "He *be working*," and "I *might could* go." Again, some of these features are found among uneducated speakers of all ethnic groups.
2. Is BEV a "deficient" or inferior language? Much of the motivation for studying BEV came from the problems teachers had in teaching black children to read. Because the children spoke very little in the classroom, many teachers believed that their language development was

deficient. It was also thought that the child who pronounced "walk" and "walked" alike did not understand the difference between present time and past time.

Evidence against the deficiency theory came when researchers began to use anthropological methods to study the whole ghetto culture. They found that far from being deficient in language, the children spoke very fluently within their own groups, using a number of subtle speech styles for different situations. They also found that the "unusual" verb forms were used systematically to make certain tense-aspect distinctions which can be made only by paraphrase in standard English: for instance, among many BEV speakers there's a distinction between "He sick," a temporary condition, and "He be sick," a protracted condition. There's also a distinction between the recent past, "I done tasted it," and the more remote past, "I been tasted it."[3] Thus, from one point of view it is Standard English, not BEV, that is deficient.

3. What's the origin of BEV? How the linguist answers this question greatly influences the answer to the two previous questions.

One theory says that the blacks learned their English from the whites with whom they were in contact when they came to the United States as slaves. Their lack of social interaction with the whites caused them to retain certain features of rural British dialects long after the whites had given up these features. This is the *anglicist* theory. It leads to minimizing the differences between BEV and other nonstandard dialects.

The other theory looks to the African origins of blacks for an explanation of BEV. The Portuguese began to trade with the blacks of West Africa in the 15th century. In such a *language contact* situation, the people involved resort to communicating in a *pidgin*, a kind of miniature language with a small vocabulary and simplified grammatical rules. This West African Portuguese pidgin apparently retained syntactic features of the West African tribal languages while using a Portuguese vocabulary. As other nations developed trade relationships, pidgins of French, Dutch, and English also arose. These differed in vocabulary but had much the same syntactic structures, because in each case the structure was derived from the structures of the West African tribal languages. When the blacks were enslaved, they had to communicate with each other—and their masters—in pidgin. Their children learned this pidgin as their native tongue, and the resulting English *creole* (A

---

[3]Ralph W. Fasold and Walt Wolfram, "Some Linguistic Features of Negro Dialect," in R.W. Fasold and R.W. Shuy, *Teaching Standard English in the Inner City* (Washington: Center for Applied Linguistics, 1970). Cited from *Black American English*, ed. Paul Stoller (New York: Dell, 1975), pp. 49–83.

creole is a pidgin which becomes the first language of some speakers.) is the basis of present-day BEV. This is the *creolist* theory. It leads to maximizing the differences between Black English and other dialects. It was very well accepted in the 1960s, and educational methods were modified on the basis of it. Drills were constructed so that the students could practice translating back and forth between Standard English and BEV. Primers were written in BEV, on the theory that the child should learn to read in his own language before tackling the standard language. These methods were largely ineffective, because the standard language was not part of the child's culture and daily life. As one sociolinguist vividly expressed it, "The teacher was saying, 'Don't talk like those hoods who sit in the back row and beat people up for their lunch money; instead, talk like the kid in the front row who gets beat up.'" During the 1980s the movement to drop such programs gained momentum.

At present, there's simply not enough evidence to decide between the anglicist and creolist theories. The evidence from before the 20th century is derived from dialect novels and poetry, descriptions of speech by untrained observers, and sheer guesswork. The research of the 20th century, largely financed by government grants, has been hampered by the fact that data was collected within the context of a very sensitive social problem. The anglicist-creolist controversy had a good effect in that it caused researchers to look at Black English Vernacular more carefully than they had done before. The intense study of ghetto culture amassed enough evidence to kill the theory that BEV was deficient for linguists, though it remains alive and well in many classrooms. Other research has shown that many words common in the South, such as *goober* (peanut), *gumbo* (okra), *jigger* (chigger), *cooter* (tortoise) and *tote* (carry) come from words in African languages. But the exact relationship of BEV to other dialects of English remains controversial.

Textbook descriptions of BEV are not always accurate because, like other American dialects, it's undergoing a certain amount of leveling. As blacks join the mainstream of economic and political activity they also join the mainstream speech community. In the other direction, non-black young people imitate the BEV speech of performers and athletes whom they admire. The musical traditions adopted from black culture reinforce this process. If certain songs are to produce the desired effect, they must be sung with the simplification of consonant clusters and the stress patterns of BEV pronunciation. Just how far this leveling process will go, no one can predict.

Dialects in Literature

Authors sometimes increase the realism of their fictional characters by portraying their dialectal peculiarities. The attempt to indicate dialect in the standard written language presents many problems. If the dialect writing differs too much from normal writing it will be hard to read, thus frustrating the main purpose of literature, the purpose of entertainment. The author must give us enough samples of the fictional character's deviation from standard speech to create the *illusion* of reality. He or she is concerned with creating an effect, not providing a scientific report of someone's idiolect. The skillful author will make no attempt to represent all the linguistic features of the dialect, or even the most frequent features, but will include only enough items of vocabulary, grammar, and pronunciation to create the desired effect.

When including dialect features, the author must allow for the needs of the reader. Local expressions and names for things must be introduced so that their meaning is clear from the context or else translated unobtrusively. The author's use of dialectal vocabulary for effect is similar to the use of foreign vocabulary. In giving a foreign flavor to a character's speech, the author has him use obvious expressions such as "Guten Morgen" and "Danke," expressions that the foreigner is likely to replace first with English equivalents. So also the dialect writer uses obvious expressions like "Howdy" and "Thanky ma'am" rather than little-known dialectal vocabulary.

Such nonstandard grammatical items as double negatives, wrong verb forms, and double subjects are likely to be used to produce the effect of a regional dialect, even though these things are characteristic of uneducated people everywhere. On the other hand, the educated characters in a story often use standard grammar. For example, an educated Southerner may be quoted as saying "you," even though all the people in his area, educated and uneducated alike, say "you-all." Included with these stereotypes, however, will be some accurate reportage of dialectal variants, depending on how good an ear for dialect the author has.

The attempt to represent variant pronunciations with our standard nonphonetic alphabet presents many problems. Careless authors, and those who are more interested in comic effect than realism often use *eye dialect*, nonstandard phonetic spelling. For instance, the character who is supposedly "speaking a dialect" will say "peepul" and "wimmin." The spelling suggests that he is using a nonstandard pronunciation, but everyone uses that same pronunciation. Other authors may record variant pronunciations quite accurately, but the catch is that the reader must know how to interpret the nonstandard spelling. The phonetic spelling chosen by the author will depend upon his own dialect, which he considers to be normal and therefore represents by standard spelling. For example, James Russell Lowell, who spoke an Eastern New England r-dropping dialect, would normally pronounce the word "sauce" as /sɔs/. He indicated a deviant pronunciation by the spelling "sarse." This meant, not that the character pronounced an /r/ in the word, but rather that it was pronounced /sas/. An author speaking a Midland r-pronouncing dialect, whose normal pronunciation was also /sɔs/, would indicate the same deviant pronunciation by "sahs" rather than "sarse." A Colorado author would indicate the /sas/ pronunciation by "sauce" and the /sɔs/ pronunciation by "sawse." By the same principle, Joel Chandler Harris's "Brer Rabbit" is not /brɛr/, but /brə/. As a speaker of an r-dropping dialect, Harris used the "r" to show vowel quality. Thus, one must know what the author regards as normal pronunciation in order to interpret his nonstandard spellings correctly.

And so the situation will remain, since authors and readers seem equally unwilling to learn and use the International Phonetic Alphabet. Besides, the use of IPA would give an undesirable effect of scientific reportage to what is supposed to be entertainment. The author of the dialect story is merely trying to show us, in his own artistic medium, that it takes all kinds of people to make a world.

Exercises

1.

Interview a number of informants to determine their dialectal preferences. Table 1 provides a list of words and the dialectal location of the various pronunciations. Table 2 provides a list of definitions and the vocabulary items preferred in various locations. Since the vocabulary tests consist to a great extent of rural terms, you may have more luck with the pronunciations. Find out from your informants their approximate age, length of time in present location, other places of residence, and locations of parents and grandparents.

The pronunciation guide is adapted from David DeCamp, "The Pronunciation of English in San Francisco" in *A Various Language: Perspectives on American Dialects*, Ed. Juanita V. Williamson and Virginia M. Burke (Holt, Rinehart and Winston, 1971).

2.

The following vocabulary items have been found useful in studying dialectal differences in urban communities. Interview people of both sexes over a range of educational levels and of various ages to determine how much variation there is in your area. In class discussion you may wish to share methods of gathering accurate responses and the difficulties you encounter. You may also wish to check your results against those reported by Lee Pederson in "An Approach to Urban Word Geography," *American Speech* 46 (1971), 73–86. If your results seem significant, the class might want to prepare a report for a local journal, or even a national one like *American Speech*. The starred items have not been surveyed extensively, so that your results from them are likely to be publishable.

  I. Geographical terms—places in your city. This will include airports, shopping centers, the center of the city, industrial areas.
 II. Topographical terms
     A. names of streams or rivers
     B. directional designations within the city
     C. grass strip between sidewalk and curb
     D. vacant lot
     E. limited access highway
     F. service area on limited access highway
     G. exit from limited access highway
     H. a limited access road in the residential section
     I. painted center line on a highway
     J. neighborhood street
     K. wide street in the city or a suburb
 VI. Buildings
     A. the largest, most showy building in town
     B. small neighborhood food store
         1. grocery store
         2. delicatessen
         3. *convenience store
     C. large neighborhood food store
     D. *a very tall building
     E. shabby hotel
     F. house of prostitution
VIII. Implements, tools, and containers: various artifacts
     A. electric frying pan
     B. vacuum cleaner
     C. vacuum bag
     D. kitchen garbage can
     E. galvanized steel garbage can
     F. large garbage box in parking lot or alley
     G. rubber band
     H. small paper clip
     I. drinking fountain
     J. fire hydrant
 IX. Vehicles and Parts
     A. emergency vehicles
     B. police vehicles
     C. instrument panel of car
     D. utility compartment in dash

Key Words	Eastern New England	Northern	North Midland	South Midland	Southern
1. hoarse, mourning, porch	o	ɔ	ɔ	o	o
2. Mary, dairy	e	ɛ	ɛ	ɛ	e
3. married, barrel, carried	æ	ɛ	ɛ/æ	ɛ/æ	æ
4. hogs, log, fog	ɔ	ɑ	ɑ	ɔ	ɑ
5. put it on	ɔ	ɑ	ɔ	ɔ	ɔ
6. greasy	s	s	s	z	z
7. calf, dance	ɑ	æ	æ	æ	a/æ
8. due, Tuesday	u	yu/u	u	yu̞	yu
9. bulge	ʊ	ʊ	ʊ	ʊ	ʊ
10. crop, God	ɔ	ɑ	ɑ	ɑ	ɔ
11. wash	wɑš	wɑš, wɔš	wɔšr	wɔšr	wɔšr
12. Mrs.	mɪsɪz, -əz	mɪsɪz, -əz	mɪsɪz, -əz	mɪz, mɪzɪz, -əz mɪsɪz	mɪz mɪzɪz mɪzəz

Table 1

Definition	E. New Engl.	Northern	N. Midland	S. Midland	Southern	Other
1. container	pail	pail	pail	bucket	bucket	
2. garbage	swill	swill	slop	slop	slop	
3. small stream	brook	brook (rare in Inland North)	run	branch	branch	-kill (NY, proper names only)
4. earthworm	angleworm	angleworm fishworm	fishworm	redworm fishworm	fish(ing) worm	dew worm (Canada)
5. cottage cheese	sour-milk cheese	Dutch cheese	smearcase	clabber cheese	clabber cheese	pot cheese (NYC)
6. dragon fly		(devil's) darning needle sewing bug	snake feeder	snake doctor	mosquito hawk snake doctor	
7. paper sack	bag	bag	poke, sack	poke, sack	sack	toot (E. Pa.)
8. string beans			green beans	green beans	snap beans	
9. haycock	haystack (general in Atlantic Coast states)	haycock, barrack (Hudson Valley)		hay shocks	hay shocks	hay doodle (W. Pa.)
10. cow's noise	low	moo	bawl	bawl	low	

Table 2

XV. Food and Cooking
  A. light, glazed doughnut made with yeast
  B. *frosted doughnut made with baking powder
  C. rectangular frosted doughnut
  D. twisted sugared doughnut
  E. *spiral-shaped frosted doughnut
  F. *a large sandwich on a long bun with several kinds of meat and cheese
  G. *coffee with cream
  H. *a carbonated drink with ice cream in it

Writing for Insight and Review: the Report

The report is supposed to present facts in the briefest, simplest way possible. Because it's directed at an audience who needs the information and is vitally interested in it, there's no need for an elaborate introduction to get the reader's attention. In fact, a catchy, clever introduction is a waste of time. Neither is there any need for an elaborate writing style, for a report is supposed to be as objective, as impersonal as possible. Facts are facts, and the writer's style is more or less irrelevant to the presentation of them. Nevertheless, the report is not necessarily the easiest kind of writing to do. Sometimes nothing is more complex than writing simply.

The biggest pitfall in report writing comes from the writer's reaction to the length of the material. When a person has been researching a topic for weeks, it's disappointing to find that the results will fit on one or two typewritten pages. His first thought is to stretch it out a bit—to choose wordier sentence structures, to add unnecessary details and examples. But a sophisticated reader—one familiar with the field of knowledge—will realize the solid work that underlies the brief report. He will appreciate the writer's sophistication in presenting only the relevant material. To make the report longer than it needs to be is an insult to such a reader's intelligence.

Another pitfall comes from the writer's effort to be objective. When trying to distance himself from the material he often introduces unnecessary, awkward passives and pretentious, overly-formal vocabulary. But the reader of a report, whether it's academic, business, or professional, is a busy person who is grateful for something simple and easy to read. The objectivity, the sense of distance, should come about because the writer lets the facts speak for themselves, not from inflated langauge. Casual, easy-going language will not detract from the seriousness of the report as long as the writer does not become slangy.

On the other hand, the writer should avoid chattiness. Phrases like "I found this interesting," and "I was amazed to learn" are completely out of place. So are anecdotes about how hard the material was to find. A simple list of sources consulted is sufficient. If the person or group for whom the report is being done wants conclusions or recommendations, these should be stated simply, without any overt attempt to convince the reader that they should be adopted.

One aid to producing an effective report is a visual display. Charts, graphs, and diagrams present information briefly and clearly. Even when visual displays are not needed, the reader will appreciate it if the writer organizes the facts well. To do so, the writer needs to think carefully about the most logical classifications of the facts, and also how to arrange them in paragraphs so that comparisons and contrasts can be made quickly. Often headings for individual paragraphs and sections help.

The exercises in this chapter are brief research projects in dialect. If these exercises are assigned to you, present your findings in brief, simply-written reports. Try to make your facts completely accurate, and do not guess at items you neglected to find out. Here are other topics for reports:

A. Where did the settlers of your home town come from? What speech characteristics does their origin imply? Do they seem to have the speech habits they are "supposed" to have?

B. Analyze the dialect in a particular work of fiction, applying the principles you have learned in this chapter.

C. Survey a small group of people by asking them the following questions. Report the results.
   1. Has your contact with speakers of different dialects caused you to drop or add any language habits that you're aware of?
   2. Which dialects strike you as most humorous? What performers do you associate with these dialects?
   3. Are you aware of any prejudices against certain dialects? If so, what are they? Did you learn your prejudice from your family or pick it up after you were on your own?
   4. Is there a manner of speech that you particularly admire? If so, who uses it? What efforts do you make to copy it, if you do?

D. Instead of reporting the dialect opinions of others, write a report giving your own answers to the questions in C. Try to analyze your opinions as objectively as you would if they belonged to someone else.

9

The Trouble with English

Psychiatrists, clergymen, and English teachers have one thing in common: they all try to conceal their occupation when attending a party. Why? Because the usual response to each one, when he says "I'm a psychiatrist (pastor, English teacher)" is invariably, "Oh, my, I'll have to watch what I say." Ordinary people feel that they cannot be themselves with these professionals whose job it is to guard public standards. The psychiatrist is the guardian of sanity, the clergyman of morals, the English teacher of grammar. The English teacher acquired this guardian role by default, because neither England nor the United States has ever had an *academy*, a group of scholars who say which words, pronunciations, and grammatical constructions belong to the standard dialect. In countries where there is an academy, its decisions are then enforced throughout the educational and communications systems. Even without an academy, the English, from the 18th century on, had a fairly clear idea of what Standard English was and who spoke it. Enforcement was informal and sporadic, depending upon the opinions of editors, lexicographers, and literary figures. In the United States, with its democratic principles, rough-and-ready frontier life, and general ferment of society, enforcement was even more informal and sporadic, usually resting squarely on the shoulders of the English teacher.

In this chapter we'll examine Standard English and the trouble it causes us. We will pay special attention to when and why the standards became so important, where they come from now, and what they contribute to social organization. We'll try to separate the myths about Standard English from the truth, hoping that "the truth will set you free" from worry and self-consciousness in this regard.

Worry about whether one is using Standard English is a relatively modern thing. In "merrie olde England" lords talked like lords and serfs like serfs, automatically. Nobody spent much time reading. Even university students went from term to term without cracking a book, not, like their modern counterparts, out of laziness, but because they had no books. Books were expensive, all copied by hand and representing a year's wages for an ordinary worker. Most of them were in Latin, and those who wrote in English did so for the benefit of the uneducated, mostly nuns and upper class lay people. Priests were supposed to know Latin, but often they didn't. Most people received information orally—by speeches, songs, sermons and by hearing books read aloud—and visually, through pictures and stained glass windows.

Vocabulary

All of this changed when William Caxton brought the technology of printing to England. Previously there had been more books in Latin and French than in English. The availability of printing encouraged the production of books in English. Because the cost per book goes down when more books are printed, and because the number of people who could use the Latin alphabet to read their own language exceeded the number who were fluent in Latin, it made economic sense to print books in English. It also made sense to produce books which could be used all over the country, and not just by the speakers of a local dialect. In this famous passage from Caxton's translation of the *Aeneid*, we see Caxton pondering the need for a more standardized vocabulary:

And certainly our language now used varieth far from that which was used and spoken when I was born; for we English men been born under the domination of the moon, which is never steadfast, but ever wavering, waxing one season and waneth and decreaseth another season. And that common English that is spoken in one shire varieth from another in so much, that in my days happened that certain merchants were in a ship in Thames, for to have sailed over the sea into Zealand; and for lack of wind they tarried at foreland, and went to land for to refresh them. And one of them, named Sheffeld, a mercer, came into an house, and axed for meat; and specially he axed after eggs. And the good wife answered, that she could speak no French. And the merchant was angry, for he also could speak no French, but would have had eggs, and she understood him not. And then at last another said that he would have eyren. Then the good wife said that she understood him well. Lo, what should a man in these days now write, egges or eyren. Certainly it is hard to please every man by cause of diversity and change of language.

Spelling

In reproducing this passage from Caxton we have normalized the spelling and punctuation according to modern conventions. In the original, the word "axed" is spelled "axed" in one place and "axyd" in another. Sometimes the word "and" is spelled out and sometimes the ampersand (&) is used. There was nothing unusual about this variation at the time; printers were quite casual in their approach to spelling at first. They often used extra silent e's and double letters to *justify* the line (that is, to give the line an even margin on the right side). Even the spelling of proper names varied. Shakespeare is said to have spelled his own name in different ways. On the other hand, some authors were quite picky about spelling. In *The Faerie Queene*, Edmund Spenser added many silent letters to words to create an archaic "Chaucerian" effect. He also varied the spellings of final words in poetic lines to increase the reader's awareness of the rhyme scheme. John Milton tried to distinguish the use of pronouns as stressed or unstressed by spelling "he" and "she" as "hee" and "shee" when they were stressed.

But the desire to see the same word always spelled the same way is strong. Even the scribes making manuscript books had continued to use traditional spellings after pronunciations changed, and as the increased availability of books brought about increased literacy, the force toward standardization of spelling became stronger. Various scholars tried to introduce more logical, more phonetic methods of spelling, but they were defeated because the force of custom was too strong. Richard Mulcaster in *The First Part of the Elementarie* (1582) was the most successful in standardization largely because he used the "cat obedience principle": if you command a cat to do what it is intending to do anyway, it will obey you. Mulcaster believed strongly that it was more important for a spelling to be accepted by most people than for it to be logical.

Even so, many words had not achieved standardized spellings by the time Samuel Johnson's *Dictionary* was published in 1755. Johnson decided, for example, to list both "soap" and "sope" in his dictionary, feeling that both spellings were equally valid. Some variant spellings he decided on the basis of etymology, spelling "enchant" with an *e* because it had been borrowed into English from French and spelling the related "incantation" with an *i* because it had come into English directly from Latin.

Johnson did not invent the practice of etymological spelling, but merely carried on the tradition of his learned predecessors. Another etymological spelling practice that has continued to plague learners is that of spelling a verbal noun "ence" if it came from one class of Latin verbs and "ance" if it came from another. Thus, we have to remember that it is depend*ence* but attend*ance*. Such an unnecessary complication becomes even more maddening when the etymological spelling is based on a mistaken etymology. For example, a silent *s* was added to "island" because it was thought to be derived from Latin *insula*. Its origin isn't Latin at all; it really came from Old English *iglond*. Likewise, the phonetic spellings "dette" and "doute" of Chaucer's day were changed to reflect the Latin words "debit" and "dubitum," even though English acquired these words from French rather than Latin.

The silent b's in "debt" and "doubt" are merely a nuisance. In other cases, spelling has actually changed the pronunciation of words. "Parfit," which Chaucer spelled as it was pronounced, had come into the language from French. ("Parfait" is another form of the same word.) But the learned etymologizers respelled it as "perfect" because it had ultimately been derived from the Latin "perfacio." Now we all pronounce the extra /k/, for this *spelling pronunciation* has become standard.

Pronunciation

The popularity of Johnson's Dictionary contributed substantially to making the vocabulary and spelling more uniform throughout England. The search for uniformity in these areas had begun very early, in medieval times, and had been of utmost importance during the Renaissance, so that Johnson's Dictionary was the culmination of many years of thought by many people. The search for uniformity in pronunciation and grammar, however, did not become urgent until the 18th century.

In the time of Chaucer, gentlefolk spoke regional dialects without being self-conscious about them. The major dialects were Northern, West Midland, East Midland, Kentish, and Southern. Important literature was produced in each of these dialects, but Chaucer's works are the only ones that we can read today without great difficulty. Chaucer used the London dialect, which was primarily East Midland with a few Southern and Kentish features. Because London was the center of business, government, and later printing, its dialect became dominant; but for two more centuries people of outlying regions felt little pressure to conform to London pronunciation when they came to town.

The situation changed in the 18th century. The unification of the British Isles allowed unprecedented numbers of the Scots and the Irish to seek their fortunes in London. The Industrial Revolution allowed many members of the middle class to become rich. Naturally enough, the people already established defended their territory against the newcomers; and like birds, they recognized the interlopers by the way they sounded. As long as a person had no hope of rising in the social structure, it didn't matter how he talked; but people who became prosperous wanted to talk properly so that they could have the social status that befitted their economic success. Whether this is the reason or not, it's notable that the first dictionaries to record pronunciation were published during the 18th century, and that the first and best-known pronouncing dictionaries were produced by a Scotsman, James Buchanan, and an Irishman, Thomas Sheridan.

In the 19th and early 20th centuries, the upper class, and those who aspired to it, were educated in boarding schools where they could learn RP (Received Pronunciation) if they did not already use it. For the men, RP was reinforced by further education at Oxford or Cambridge. Proper pronunciation was the key to social advancement, and parents often made great financial sacrifices to send their children to schools where they could acquire it. Although the avoidance of some pronunciation errors, such as wrongly dropping or inserting h's, was taught to the lower and middle classes in state-supported schools, the instruction was not sufficient to allow the person to move to a higher status. It is this situation which Shaw satirized in *Pygmalion* ("My Fair Lady") written in 1916. In the preface Shaw complains, "It is impossible for an Englishman to open his mouth without making some other Englishman despise him." As an Irishman, Shaw may have experienced some of the discrimination which Eliza Doolittle overcomes by learning to use RP.

Today the use of pronunciation to express one's identity is still important in England, but there are some new developments. Members of the lower class, even when they become prosperous, may try to retain their regional and class dialect. Their attitude is, "I'm working class, and I'm proud of it." The monopoly on education which Oxford and Cambridge formerly enjoyed has been broken by the regional red-brick universities (so called because they lack the stone and ivy of the older institutions), and it's now possible to become highly educated without a lengthy exposure to RP. In fact, business and professional people, instead of trying to acquire RP, often feel now that it would be "putting on airs" to do so. At the same time that many people are trying to retain some individuality in speech, the media, including American films and international news broadcasts, are exposing people to more varieties of English and are leveling speech differences.

Grammar

The rise of printing in the 15th century did not immediately bring about a concern for the standardization of grammar; two more centuries elapsed before it became important. Shakespeare, writing in the 16th century, uses many constructions that are ungrammatical by modern standards. When the standardization of grammar did become important, in the 17th and 18th centuries, it was motivated partly by social mobility, but also by additional factors. First, there was the rise of scientific research. The scientists felt that the traditional rules of Latin rhetoric hampered the communication of research results. The Royal Society, officially recognized in 1660, specified that experiments were to be reported in the plainest possible language.

Second, there was an interest among philosophers in the problem of the relationship between language and thought, leading to much speculation about the origin of language and about universal principles of grammar. Many thinkers believed language had developed from simple forms to a peak of perfection in Classical Latin and Greek and had then begun to degenerate. At the same time, to an extent we find impossible to imagine today, men were schooled in Latin and Greek rather than their native tongue.

Thus, we find John Dryden, poet and essayist, solving his grammatical problems by first expressing his thought in Latin and then translating to English. And why not? After all, his knowledge of Latin grammar was technical and conscious, while his knowledge of English grammar was only the unconscious, practical knowledge we all acquire as children.

Although there were earlier grammars of English, the best-known one, *A Short Introduction to English Grammar* by Robert Lowth, was published in 1762. These 18th century grammars were not what a modern linguist would call a grammar, since they were not descriptions of how the English language works. A linguistic grammar will list the phonemes of a language, the rules for combining them into syllables, and the way the sounds change under certain conditions. It will tell into what categories the words and morphemes of the language may be classified; by what formulas these categories may be combined into phrases, clauses, and sentences; and what transformations may occur. It will tell which semantic categories, such as animate-inanimate, masculine-feminine, past-present, and factual vs. nonfactual, are communicated by syntactic means. It will state the large regularities of language structure, such as English clauses normally favor an SVO word order; there are several classes of questions, including one group that begins with an auxiliary and another that begins with a wh-word; if a modal occurs, it is the first word of the verb phrase.

Instead of describing how the English language works, these early grammars listed the part of speech categories of Latin and tried to apply them to English. For example, because Latin had six tenses in the indicative (present, imperfect, future, perfect, pluperfect, and future perfect), six tenses were listed for English, even though English has only two tense inflections (present and past) and all the rest of its distinctions in verbs are made by auxiliaries. Instead of stating the large regularities of the language, these grammars ignored all the things that no native speaker ever gets wrong to concentrate on marginal issues. One question they discussed at some length was whether there should be a distinction between the past and the past participle. In weak (or regular) verbs there was no doubt; they said "walked" and "have walked" just as we do today. Many excellent writers did the same with strong verbs: "He would have spoke" (Milton, *Paradise Lost*, X. 517), "you have swam" (Shakespeare, *As You Like It*, IV, i, 38), "will have stole it" (Swift, *Tale of A Tub*, Sect. ix). These constructions were denounced as "corruptions" and "absurdities."[1] The grammarians apparently never thought that it might be absurd to suppose that the most skillful artists in the language didn't know how to use it properly.

There are several reasons the grammarians were so authoritarian and

---

[1] Quoted from Robert Lowth, *A Short Introduction to English Grammar*, 2nd ed. (London, 1764), p. 106, in Charlton Laird and Robert M. Gorrell, *English as Language: Backgrounds, Development, Usage* (New York: Harcourt, Brace & World, 1961), p. 205.

rigid in their rulings. Some of them, at least, were reacting against the exuberance of the written language during the preceding centuries. Although the period from the reign of Elizabeth I to the Restoration (roughly 1560–1660) had been the Golden Age of English literature, a lot of slag had been produced along with the gold. The quality most admired in this period was "copie," or fullness of thought and imagery; but often the copiousness of lush imagery degenerated into wordy, complicated sentences of unclear meaning. The 18th century grammarians, like the literary artists of their time, admired "perspicuity" instead. They wanted language to be so clear that one could "look through" it and immediately grasp the thought. Today we look back to the poetry and prose of the Golden Age and admire it just because it is ambiguous. The possibility of more than one meaning stimulates our imagination and seems to us more in tune with the complexity of human existence. But in the 18th century both grammarians and artists hoped to make language so clear that nobody could misunderstand it. This goal was reinforced by the philosophers of the time, who were seeking to set up clear laws of thought and to get away from the confusion of badly used language.

Finally, the search for rigid rules in grammar was motivated by the same reasons that people desired correct pronunciation—to help them achieve upward mobility. There's only one way to be sure of using the grammar considered correct among people of high status: to live among such people, to read their books, and thus to learn correct grammar by association. This way, of course, is impossible for those who lack the status but hope to acquire it. Their only recourse is to study the grammar book. Unfortunately, the writers of the grammar books were philosophically committed to a simplicity and clarity that never occurs in natural language. In instances where usage was divided, they tried to determine which was the more logical; where two usages were almost equally logical, so that a reasonable person could not see a dime's worth of difference in them, they still strongly advocated the one that was a penny's worth better; where no problem existed, they often created one by bringing in rules from Latin. As George Bernard Shaw has cynically observed, the religious prophet is likely to be believed if he tells people that what they have always done is a sin; if he tells them that something they thought was a sin is really all right, he will not be accepted. To put it another way, errors sell grammar books.

The grammarians were probably motivated by conviction rather than a cynical desire for sales. At any rate, they succeeded in making grammar a moral issue, in making people feel guilty and unsure in their use of language. They succeeded in bringing back the separate past participle for verbs like speak-spoke-spoken and swim-swam-swum. They succeeded in establishing a distinction between "each other" (two) and "one another" (three or more). They succeeded in destroying the double negative. Chaucer had written "He never said no bad things in no way to no person"; the grammarians argued that only one negative could be used in a sentence because the second one would cancel the first and make the sentence positive. (I'm quite incapable of applying this grammatical algebra to Chaucer's sentence.) Today the double negative is so out of favor that it is used only by illiterate people, or as a joke. The grammarians' greatest success was in establishing two completely unnecessary rules which, ironically enough, are all most people remember from eight or more years of required English classes: never end a sentence with a preposition and never split an infinitive. The first rule causes people to write awkward sentences like "The student should choose a competent, sympathetic counselor with whom to talk." Sometimes, in the effort to write a "correct" sentence—correct according to this artificial rule—they absent-mindedly put the preposition in both places and come up with a monstrosity like "The students involved in the problem are the ones with whom the administration should consult with." The second rule causes actual confusion and change of meaning, as this example from Fowler shows: The author wrote "When the record of this campaign *comes dispassionately to be written*" when he meant "comes to be dispassionately written."[2] The phrase avoiding the split infinitive is absurd, implying that the record will calmly present itself before someone in order to get itself written. Let us state once and for all that neither the preposition rule nor the infinitive rule has ever been followed consistently by skillful English writers.

The Standardization of American English

The first settlers to North America spoke Elizabethan English, which, as we have seen, was in the process of developing and expanding its national vocabulary. Many, but not all, questions of spelling had been decided, and grammatical constructions were much freer than they became later. For a long time the colonists were concerned with more urgent problems than correct English, but once independence was achieved the same sort of national pride that motivated the English lexicographers and grammarians was the order of the day. In vocabulary the Americans developed a few "Americanisms"—words borrowed from Indian languages and from settlers of other nationalities—but in general words were not an issue. Spelling was. Noah Webster, America's first dictionary-maker, financed the publication of his dictionary by the sale of his enormously popular blue-backed speller. Spelling was a large part of the curriculum in early American schools: it could be taught by relatively unqualified teachers, it was enormously time-consuming, and it required nothing in the way of library or laboratory equipment.

---

[2]H. W. Fowler, *A Dictionary of Modern English Usage*, 1st ed. (Oxford: The Clarendon Press, 1926), pp. 416, 417, in Leonard F. Dean and Kenneth G. Wilson, eds., *Essays on Language and Usage*, 2nd ed. (New York: Oxford University Press, 1963), pp. 301–302.

Even more than in England, correct spelling became the mark of an educated person.

Writing after Johnson had produced his *Dictionary*, Webster tried to simplify American spelling. The first edition of his dictionary advocated such spellings as *bred, giv, bilt, frend, speek, dawter, tuf,* and *obleek*. Obviously, none of these simplified spellings survived to become standard, although Webster did succeed in establishing a few of his preferences: *check* instead of *cheque, color* instead of *colour, plow* instead of *plough*. His simplified spellings of *theater* for *theatre* and *dialog* for *dialogue* are seen often, but are not universally accepted.

The American preoccupation with spelling actually led to some pronunciations different from those of the English. It was customary for students to spell out the words syllable by syllable: "e-x, ex; t-r-a, tra; extra; o-r, or; extraor" and so on through such a lengthy word as "extraordinary." As a result of this training, Americans were especially conscious of the syllable structure of long words and were more likely to pronounce every syllable clearly instead of running them together as the English did. These spelling pronunciations were more prevalent in the North than in the South, where the public schools were less influential. To this day, an educated Northerner is more likely to say /laɪ' brɛr i/, while his Southern counterpart will say /laɪ' bri/. To this day also the spelling of a word is regarded as its true form, and students who have trouble with spelling are advised not to use "sloppy" pronunciations. The teacher may say "Danny, don't say *ol' knight*, say *old knight*. Can't you see the *d*? You must learn to pronounce words the way they are written."[3] If Danny took her advice seriously, he would also pronounce the *k* and the *gh*. He doesn't, of course.

In England, the failure of the spelling system to accurately reflect the pronunciation allowed the setting up of a national speech, so that people who wished to raise their status had to learn to conform to the standard. In the United States, such a national standard was never established. Instead, there were educated and less educated versions of each regional dialect. In Webster's day and for a long time afterward the Boston-New Haven area was regarded as the intellectual center of the country, and the dictionaries gave precedence to New England pronunciations until well into the 20th century, but people in other areas were likely to ignore the pronunciations recommended in the dictionary, except for words they had never heard pronounced. Certainly, little or no social stigma was attached to the failure to use New England pronunciations.

In spite of Webster's patriotism, he considered England's English superior to that of America in many ways. After all, in his view the pronunciation of New England was superior to that of the rest of the United States

---

[3]L. M. Myers, *The Roots of Modern English*, 1st ed. (Boston: Little, Brown, 1966), p. 6.

precisely because it was closer to English pronunciation, and he looked to England for standards of grammatical usage also. He wrote the first American grammar as well as the first dictionary, and later grammarians followed in his footsteps. Like the grammars produced in England, the American grammars contained lists of parts of speech based on Latin categories plus a number of rules concerning marginal issues of correctness. Lindley Murray, a Philadelphia lawyer, produced in 1795 what was to be for many years the most popular textbook of grammar. Murray's grammar contained the infamous rule against ending a sentence with a preposition, defending it with the rather sensible argument that the rhetorically emphatic last word in the sentence should be a strong content word rather than a particle. Later, the rule was presented to students on etymological grounds: since "preposition" means "before-place," a preposition must not be the last word in the sentence.

Many other such rules were based on etymology. For example, "different from" was preferred to "different than" because "different" came from the Latin *de* + *fero*, and *de* means "from." Other rules were based on logic, like the one against double negatives and the rule against comparing "absolute" adjectives. A person should not say "most perfect," it was argued, because a thing is either perfect or it's not; if it can be improved in any way, it is not perfect. The same reasoning forbade such expressions as "most unique" and "roundest." Finally, some rules were based on analogy with Latin grammar. Since the subject of a gerund was in the genitive case in Latin, the possessive inflection should be attached to the noun preceding the gerund in English.

As Bolinger points out, there seems to be no pattern determining the expressions chosen to be forbidden. The books tell us to avoid "the reason is because" but say nothing about other combinations that are identical in syntactic construction: the time is when, the place is where, the question is why. Much teacherly energy is spent on the subtle difference between "I only had five dollars" and "I had only five dollars," but none on the similar uses of "even," "also," and "just."[4]

Probably the Oscar for the most useless rule of grammar should go to the one governing the use of shall and will. The rule, first stated in a grammar book by John Wallis in 1653, is that with first person pronouns (I and we) one uses "shall" to express simple futurity and "will" to express determination. For second and third person pronouns and for nouns the rule is reversed: "will" expresses simple future and "shall" expresses determination. Philologists differ in their opinions about whether this rule was ever part of the natural, internalized grammar of English speakers; the evidence is not clear. Rightly or wrongly, it came to be considered an important fea-

---

[4]Dwight Bolinger, *Aspects of Language*, 2nd ed. (New York: Harcourt Brace Jovanovich, 1968 and 1975), p. 572.

ture of the prestigious London dialect. Henry Bradley, in writing about *shall* in the *Oxford English Dictionary*, said that the wrong use of these two modals was the mark of "Scottish, Irish, or provincial, or extra-British idiom."[5] Dorothy L. Sayers defends the shall-will distinction as the very essence of Englishness in an outburst of linguistic chauvinism:

> It is well, then, to know what we mean and to learn how to say it in English. And by English I mean English, and not any other tongue. In a day when the British Broadcasting Corporation imports its language committee from Ireland and Scotland, and when Fleet Street swarms with Scots, Irish and Americans, it is well to remember that all these persons are foreigners; . . . that they speak our language as foreigners; and that while [we may] enjoy their sing-song speech and their quaint foreign barbarisms, to imitate these things is childishness and folly . . . .Let us take as our example that famous distinction which we English alone in all the world know how to make: the distinction between "shall" and "will."[6]

According to Webster, the proper use of the shall-will distinction was also a mark of the New England dialect's superiority to other American speech varieties. Even if he, Bradley, and Sayers are correct in asserting that the shall-will distinction is a mark of the most prestigious variety of English, one may still question the amount of classroom time spent on trying to create the usage in people who do not have it naturally. I remember writing the "correct" forms in the blanks of pages and pages of workbooks. When I pointed out to my sixth-grade teacher that the distinction did not exist in conversation, since both "shall" and "will" were contracted to '*ll*, I was promoted to standing on tiptoe at the blackboard with my nose in a circle instead of filling out workbook pages.

The Case for Standard English

Despite such misuse of teacherly authority, there is a case to be made for "proper" English. Standardization of vocabulary, spelling, pronunciation, and syntactic constructions are all helpful in various areas for users of the language.

It's perhaps easiest to see the advantages of standardization in vocabulary. In the example quoted from Caxton, people from different regions of England actually could not understand each other because they used different terms for the same thing. Many of us have had a similar experience: we have found that it's useless to ask for a "rest room" in Windsor, England, or for a "tonic" in Windsor, Colorado. If we expect to be helped, we must ask

---

[5]J. J. Lamberts, *A Short Introduction to English Usage* (New York: McGraw Hill, 1972), p. 243.
[6]Dorothy L. Sayers, "The English Language," in *Unpopular Opinions* (London: Victor Gollancz, 1946), p. 92.

for a "W.C." in one case and a "pop" in the other. Of course, people sometimes use nonstandard vocabulary precisely because they do not wish to be understood. They wish to confine their communication to a small in-group. The slang of teenagers is perhaps the most obvious example of such vocabulary, but various adult communities do the same thing. One obstacle to solving the problems of our society is that the various branches of science and technology have such different vocabularies that people often can't understand each other, so that one group may spend large amounts of money finding out something that has long been known in another group.

A traditional formulation of good writing style recommends that the vocabulary be *national, reputable,* and *current. National* vocabulary avoids *regionalisms*—such as "tonic"—and *jargon*—the language of an in-group such as teenagers, linguists, or computer technicians. *Reputable* vocabulary avoids the language (sometimes called *argot*) of subcultures such as gangsters, carnival workers, or rock musicians. *Current* vocabulary avoids terms that are obsolete: outmoded slang words like "swell" or "groovy," poetic terms like "e'en" and "wend," and archaisms like "by scent and by slot." Avoidance of these words in books is eminently sensible. When authors invest perhaps five years in writing a book and publishers invest thousands of dollars in producing it, they naturally want to make it as permanent in value as possible. These vocabulary guidelines enable them to do so.

Spelling

Standardization of spelling, too, has its advantages, as anyone knows who has ever tried to find a person's name in the phone book without knowing whether it's spelled "Meyer," "Myer," "Mayer," or "Maier." Learning English spelling is admittedly tedious, but if standard spellings are not maintained, much of the literature and information of the past will become inaccessible to future readers, and the use of all alphabetically-arranged reference tools such as card catalogs, encyclopedias, dictionaries, bibliographies, and abstracts will become even more difficult than it is now. The good reader learns to recognize words partly by their visual configurations, without stopping to look at individual letters or syllables. If spelling were less standard, people would be forced to read more slowly.

But standardization and rigid adherence have their disadvantages. Thorsten Veblen exaggerates only a little when he denounces correct spelling as an instance of "archaism and waste" whose only purpose is to identify members of the leisure class able to afford such conspicuous consumption:

> English orthography satisfies all the requirements of the canons of reputability under the law of conspicuous waste. It is archaic, cumbrous, and ineffective; its acquisition consumes much time and effort; failure to acquire it is easy of detection. Therefore it is the first and readiest

test of reputability in learning, and conformity to its ritual is indispensable to a blameless scholastic life.[7]

In arguments, those who disagree with a person are always ready to defend their own position by criticizing the other person's spelling. Often, if they can find a misspelled word, they feel free to disregard the other person's whole chain of thought, no matter how logical it may be. This attitude is ridiculous, for traditional spelling is becoming more and more difficult as the gap between spelling and pronunciation widens because of natural phonetic shifts.

Grammar

As for standardization of grammatical usages, here we have an unavoidable conflict between the need for comfortable individuality and the need for good communication. Writing lacks many of the communication tools of speech—intonation, gesture, facial expression. Precise syntactic constructions and small distinctions in word meanings help to make up for these deficiencies. A speaker can indicate the difference between simple futurity and determination by his presence and tone of voice; a writer cannot. The shall-will distinction could help the writer to make up for the lack of voice. But if this distinction is unknown to the reader, it's useless to the writer. It's always difficult to tell just when a distinction is unknown. Certainly the distinction between the subject form *ye* and the object form *you* is no longer made. The distinction between *shall* and *will* is probably lost. But the distinction between *imply* and *infer*, between *disinterested* and *uninterested* is understood by some people but not by others, and those who understand look down on those who do not.

When a language item such as the imply-infer distinction is in the process of change, listing the "error" in a handbook and marking it wrong on student papers rarely prevents the change. By the time such an expression is listed in handbooks as an error, it has already become so common that eliminating it is impossible. Purists thundered against *hopefully* a few years ago, but in vain. Their efforts to outlaw the use of *contact* as a verb also failed. On the other hand, some mistakes such as *ain't* never become acceptable, no matter how common they are.

The "correctness" problem became acutely obvious in 1961, when *Webster's Third New International Dictionary, Unabridged* appeared. Its new editorial policy of avoiding status labels such as *colloquial, slang, cant, facetious,* and *substandard* caused a public outcry. The dictionary was called a "calamity," "a scandal and a disaster" that would "accelerate the deteriora-

---

[7]Thorstein Veblen, *The Theory of the Leisure Class* (New York: Macmillan, 1915), pp. 398–400.

tion" of the language. Defenders of the dictionary pointed out, in vain, that the dictionary's job is not to approve or disapprove various usages, but merely to report them; that the status of a particular word or expression depends partly on the context in which it appears; and that such comments on grammatical constructions as "used by speakers and writers on all educational levels though disapproved by some grammarians" is more accurate than to label the construction "illiterate." *The New York Times* advised readers to keep their Second Internationals from 1934, since the 1961 dictionary had betrayed the public trust. The issue of the *Times* containing this advice also contained 172 separate words, phrases, and constructions either not listed in or condemned by the Second International.[8]

To such explanations of language change the public replies, in effect, "Don't confuse me with facts—my mind is made up." People continue to regard all changes in language as corruptions, looking to the dictionary and the English teacher to keep these corruptions from happening and to deny their existence when they happen anyway. Of course, as the use of English becomes more and more worldwide, and as the number of English-speaking cultures and subcultures multiplies, it becomes less and less possible to define a universal standard.

Many English teachers would like to drop the sport of error-hunting and spend all their class time on literature, hoping that students would absorb "good" English by osmosis, but they are painfully aware that this policy leaves them vulnerable to accusations of laziness and incompetence from the community, who wish children to suffer as they suffered. Anyway, it's doubtful that one hour in the English classroom, whether spent on literature or grammar drills, can counteract the hours spent elsewhere.

What shall we do? Language must not change so fast that the books five or ten years old become unreadable; ludicrous as it seems, the old-fashioned emphasis on "grammar" performs a useful service by promoting conservatism in language. But with knowledge increasing so fast in all directions there is less and less classroom time available for teaching this somewhat artificial, conservative dialect of English.

Not Standard, but Standards

With less time available, the English class needs to expand the knowledge it offers. Traditional classroom English presents a misleading, oversimplified view of language. It implies that there's only one correct version of English, that this one correct version should be used all the time, and that anyone who does not do so is ignorant or "sloppy." Nothing could be further from the truth. There are at least five versions of spoken English, all equally correct, all serving to define a particular *register*, or usage context.

---

[8]Bergen Evans, "But What's a Dictionary For?" *The Atlantic Monthly* (May, 1962). In Dean and Wilson, p. 102.

The *oratorical* register is used for ritualistic, solemn speeches—the ones that become part of our literary heritage when well done. Such speeches use rather old, "poetic" words; many sentences are structured according to special rhetorical patterns; and they are delivered in a special tone of voice. Lincoln's "Gettysburg Address" and Martin Luther King, Jr.'s "I Have a Dream" are famous examples of such speeches.

The *formal* register is used primarily to convey information to nonparticipating listeners. Its lexicon consists of "current, reputable, and national" terms, along with the technical terms common to the subject at hand. Sentences are structured carefully, but according to the ordinary SVO patterns and without special rhetorical inversions. Although the speaker does not use a ritualistic, solemn tone, he or she pronounces words fully, carefully, and somewhat crisply.

The *consultative* register is used when strangers or slight acquaintances must converse about impersonal matters, usually business. Its lexicon is like that of the formal register with the addition of some colloquial terms. Sentences are spontaneous rather than carefully structured. Words are pronounced fully, but without the crispness of the formal register: /kæn/ rather than /kn/, but /bɛdər/ rather than bɛtər/.

The *casual* register is the one people use most often. It has many subtle variations expressing different degrees of friendliness and informality, but its two major qualities are *ellipsis* (omission) and *slang*. The speakers omit sounds and whole syllables for an easy pronunciation. Clipped words—"quote" for "quotation" (academic) "brekker" for "breakfast," (British) "con" for "reconnaissance" (military)—are common. The omission of words and phrases to form sentence fragments expresses the fact that the speakers understand each other so well that they do not need complete information. The use of slang signals that the speakers are friends, that they share the same nonstandard, nonpublic vocabulary. Even when the speakers don't know each other very well, they may choose to conduct their interaction as if they were friends. It's a sort of "social fiction."

The *intimate* register is used between lovers or within family groups, among people who know each other so well that language is hardly needed. It makes even greater use of ellipsis. Sometimes a grunt will express as much as a whole sentence in the casual register. Instead of normal slang, the speakers use special words of their own. People who are very close don't use the intimate register all the time, of course, but switch back and forth between intimate and casual expressions.

Here are some examples of different registers:

Formal: Ladies and gentlemen, may I present our distinguished guest, Professor Edward Smith.

Consultative: Professor Jean Jones, this is Professor Edward Smith.

Casual: Jean Jones, this is Ed Smith. (Or, to be even more casual: Hey, Jean, this is Ed.)

There are many degrees of formality and casualness shading subtly into one another, and these five registers merely represent the major types. It's important to notice, moreover, that all of these descriptions refer to spoken language. Written language has its own rules. If we look at primarily informative or communicative writing, we find degrees of formality and casualness being defined by the following characteristics:
1. length of paragraphs and sentences
2. degree to which misspellings and typographical errors are tolerated
3. use of contractions such as "isn't" and "we'll"
4. use of personal pronouns
5. use of passive verbs
6. use of sentence fragments
7. special vocabularies

On the basis of these items we define the following registers:

Superformal: Academic writing, scientific reports, legal documents. Paragraphs are long—at least 100 words and longer. Sentences average 25 words in length, and many are much longer than that. They have many subordinate clauses and phrases. Misspellings, typographical errors, contractions, personal pronouns, and sentence fragments are not acceptable. A high proportion of verbs are passive. The special vocabulary depends on the subject, of course.

Formal: Newspaper editorials, some business letters, some magazine articles. Same as superformal, except that the pronoun "we" is allowed. Sometimes it means "I the writer and the group I speak for" and sometimes it means "I the writer and you the reader."

Semiformal: Themes, most textbooks, letters to the editor, many newspaper columns and magazine articles. "We" meaning "I the writer and you the reader" is used most often, but "I" is used where avoiding it would lead to awkwardness and wordiness. "You" is allowed in some situations. Paragraphs may be shorter than those of the formal registers. Contractions are allowed. Some typographical errors may be tolerated, especially in newspapers and themes. The writer consciously tries to avoid passive verbs. Colloquialisms and some slang words are allowed.

Informal: Personal letters, interdepartmental memos, some special interest magazines. Characteristics include short sentences and paragraphs, free use of contractions and personal pronouns, avoidance of passive verbs. Typographical errors are tolerated, and sometimes misspellings. Some sentence fragments are used.

Casual: Lists, graffiti. Slang, personal pronouns, and sentence fragments are used.

Literature, as contrasted with informative writing, has its own rules. The novelist or poet imitates all the different speech registers, experiments with rigid verse forms and ambiguous syntactic structures, and sometimes uses uncommon punctuation and typography to create an artistic effect. A careful study of literature increases one's sensitivity to language, and this sensitivity can be transferred to the practice of informative writing. Thus, the study of literature benefits writing skills indirectly, but works of literature do not provide models for informative writing.

Learning to write acceptably is difficult. With all except the most casual writing, it's wise to expect to make a number of versions of the product. In the first one, concentrate on ideas; in the following ones concentrate first on revision of content and lastly on applying all of your conscious linguistic knowledge to achieve correctness and propriety of expression. The slogan for the first versions should be "Don't worry about getting it right—get it written." What is thus written can be criticized the next times around. Creation and criticism are opposite processes, and hardly anyone can do them simultaneously.

The solution to "the trouble with English" is even more complex and difficult. Part of it, surely, is to understand that many of the taboos on certain usages come from the opinions of amateur grammarians of the 18th and 19th centuries. Thus, we should ignore rules in the books which seem unnatural and farfetched. Another part of the solution is to realize that there is no one absolute standard, so that the demand for an authoritative dictionary or grammar handbook is unreasonable. Educated people must also develop an appreciation for the subtlety of language and the facility of its speakers in switching from one register to another. Paradoxically, the speaker is more apt to use acceptable forms and to choose the appropriate register when he is unself-conscious, when his attention is focused more on what he has to say than how he says it. Even in writing, people seem to make fewer spelling, punctuation, and grammar errors when they're truly interested in what they're saying. The final word on the subject, perhaps, is that we should all relax and let English teachers enjoy themselves at parties.

Exercises

1. Our Changing Handbooks

Every new edition of a handbook of correct English adds some new rules and drops some old ones. In order to see this for yourself, study the following examples of "poor English." The examples belong to the following three categories:
 1. expressions forbidden by the handbook of 1946 but not by the 1977 one;
 2. expressions forbidden by the 1977 handbook but not by the 1946 one;
 3. expressions forbidden by both.

Try to guess which category each sentence belongs to; then check your guesses against the answers on pp. 209–10. Your instructor may wish you to write a brief paper commenting on the changing standards of correctness. Note: Sometimes the error is in spelling rather than wording.
1. The guard checked the locks to see if they were alright.
2. We had an exam in math yesterday.
3. Augustine lived in the fourth century A.D.
4. He accidently found the arrowhead.
5. Mr. Jones has a horrid habit of clearing his throat.
6. Sometimes I think I will loose my mind.
7. I couldn't hardly see my own hand, it was so dark.
8. His statement inferred that he would resign.
9. Their are six team members who need new uniforms.
10. I wish I had of known about it.
11. She makes very unique jewelry.
12. Less than twenty people attended.
13. I was laying in my bed when the phone rang.
14. The gents were quite well dressed.
15. The union demanded shorter working hours, plus they wanted better health-care benefits.
16. They were real positive about it.
17. He was raised in the Midwest.
18. The professor told me to try and find more material for my term paper.
19. She is terribly worried about her mother.
20. Professor Seznec won't except late papers for any reason.

2. Commas

Oscar Wilde once explained his day's work as follows: "In the morning, I put a comma into one of my poems; in the afternoon, I took it out again." See if you can explain what difference, if any, the comma makes in the following pairs of sentences.
1. A. When Patio Parker eats dogs cluster around from all over the neighborhood.
   B. When Patio Parker eats, dogs cluster around from all over the neighborhood.
2. A. They keep a garden and fish.
   B. They keep a garden, and fish.
3. A. Bimbo the Clown has been hired for this rodeo.
   B. Bimbo, the clown, has been hired for this rodeo.
4. A. He went up the ladder, across the porch, and into his bride's room.
   B. He went up the ladder across the porch and into his bride's room.
5. A. Martha cooked and Mary listened to the Master.
   B. Martha cooked, and Mary listened to the Master.

Discussion Questions

1. The chapter suggests that people who belong to the lowest class and people who belong to the highest class have no need to be careful of their language. Are there any people in American society who fit this description?
2. Dialect researchers have found that women are more likely to use standard grammar than men. Comment.
3. Is spelling difficult or easy for you? How were you taught spelling? Do you see any relationship between the teaching and your present level of skill?
4. If you have met a new person recently, try to remember how you reacted to him or her. Were there any speech characteristics that affected your reaction either favorably or unfavorably?
5. Make a list of the last five writing assignments you've had. What register was required for each?
6. By observation of people in daily life, collect samples of each of the five spoken registers. Use these samples as the basis of either a written or an oral report.
7. What is the difference in what the linguist calls grammar and the way the ordinary person defines the term?
8. Some students of language have suggested that instead of teaching a standard language, the schools should teach everyone to be tolerant of individual differences. How do you feel about this issue?
9. Do you think people really feel embarrassed about their own language, or is this just something to say to the English teacher?

Writing for Insight and Review: Revising and Editing

It seems appropriate, after a chapter proving that correctness is not as important as many people think, to devote the writing lesson to the processes by which correctness is achieved. We've already suggested that the best writing results from several repeated attempts to achieve the best wording. Most people who fail to write acceptably have more than enough talent to do the job, but they suffer from the Pilate Syndrome. Pilate, you remember, responded to the request that he change the wording of Jesus's accusation with a firm "What I have written, I have written." Composition students usually feel the same way. Having wrestled their recalcitrant thought and pinned it to the mat once, they aren't about to risk letting it get away by changing anything. When asked to revise, they usually just make a fresh copy.

Nevertheless, learning to revise is one of the most powerful skills a writer can have. Instead of being a burden, it's a way of releasing the mind to do its best, its most creative work. Once we truly realize that it's ok for the first few versions to be asinine, boring, callow and on through the alphabet to trite, unfocused, vapid, and wordy, the blank page loses its terror. We can put down anything, knowing that it can always be changed. If the successful golfer had to shoot par every time, very few people would enjoy the sport or become good at it; yet we often expect ourselves as writers to produce a brilliant, rhythmic wording on a perfectly clean page, without second thoughts or strikeovers. Instead we should think of what Edith Wilson, wife of the President, learned from her black caddy. When she asked him whether she could make it to the green with her mashie (five iron), he replied, "Course you can, ma'am—provided you hits it often enough." One of the advantages of writing as opposed to speaking is that the writer can keep hitting the communicational ball until it goes where it is supposed to. And once the ball is in the hole, it's there forever, whether it took one stroke or twenty to get it there. In this writing lesson, then, we will look at some strategies for getting over the Pilate Syndrome.

1. Expect to change the first version. If you're writing by hand, skip lines. If you're composing on the typewriter, triple-space. Doing this not only gives you space to revise later, but it also provides great encouragement while doing the first draft. "There, I've gotten a page done already," you tell yourself. "This isn't going to be so bad." Write on one side of the page only, so that you can cut apart sentences and paragraphs and rearrange them later. (A few people find it impossible to use the cut-and-staple method. If you're lucky enough to have a word processor, you won't have to cut-and-staple; the machine will do it for you in its own way.)

2. After you've written the first version, try outlining it. If you find making an outline difficult, the paper may have organizational weaknesses. Some composition teachers recommend making an outline before writing the first version, and this method works for some people, especially if you don't feel bound to follow the outline perfectly. When students have difficulty following the outline and yet are required to hand one in with the paper, they often write the paper first and then write the outline to fit. This is a very good method, and not one to feel guilty about.

3. After checking the overall organization, check structures of individual paragraphs. Do most paragraphs have the movement from general to less general to specific examples recommended in Chapter 7? Is each paragraph related to the preceding paragraph and to the overall purpose in writing? If not, some rewording to make ideas clearer, some illustrative examples are called for.

4. Next check individual sentences. Can you recognize a lexical chaining by which each one refers back to the preceding sentence before moving on to new information? Can some of the coordinate clauses be reduced to verbal phrases or subordinate clauses? Do some of the sentences need free modifiers to add specific details? (See Chapter 5 for a fuller discussion of these matters.)

5. By this time, your copy, or one or two pages of it, may be so full of

rewordings that it's hard to read. It's time to write a second draft. For many people, it works best to put the first draft away and write the second one from scratch, but it's all right to look at the first one when you remember that the wording of a passage was particularly good.

6. If the second draft seems so bad that it's embarrassing, repeat Steps 2–5. If you're so tired of the project that you can't force yourself to do that, take a break and come back to it later. Maybe this second draft is not as bad as it seems.

7. As soon as you can do so without embarrassment, read your work aloud to yourself. Mark each thing that bothers you: sentences so long that there's no place to breathe, modifiers that don't seem to belong anywhere, awkward rhyming sounds, poor rhythm, words that don't look right and may be misspelled, words that you've used without being sure of the meaning. Don't interrupt the reading to work on these matters—just mark them for future attention.

8. The next step, of course, is to repair the weaknesses you located through the oral reading, and these two steps can be repeated until you're satisfied.

At this point you may wish to check your work by getting a close friend to read it. Don't ask for direct criticism, but talk to the person and notice carefully any misunderstandings or unfavorable reactions. Only a few people can point out weaknesses directly, and still fewer can tell you how to correct the problem. Don't expect your reader to do either.

9. If it's important that spelling and punctuation be entirely correct, take one reading to focus on each thing. Be sure that you have a reason for each mark of punctuation, especially comma, that you use. Not every pause in reading deserves a comma. Look up words whose spelling you doubt or, if you can, ask someone who is a good speller about them.

10. For the final copy, if the work is important enough, you may wish to hire a professional typist. Proofread carefully, once while reading normally, the second time reading backward word by word. Get someone else to read the paper also.

11. Submit it and hope for the best.

Answers to Exercise 1.

1. (3); 1946: "not recognized as correct"; 1977: "still a questionable spelling."

2. (1); The 1946 book considers all such clippings inappropriate for formal writing.

3. (1); Since A.D. means "in the year of our Lord," it is "absurd" to use it to refer to a century.

4. (2); An example of the increasing divergence between pronunciation and standard spelling.

5. (1); "Horrid" was apparently a trite, overused word in 1946.

6. (3); Another example of the great conservatism in spelling.

7. (3); This expression constitutes a double negative, considered illogical and incorrect since the 18th century.

8. (2); The confusion of "imply" and "infer" was not yet common enough to be included in the book. It would be interesting to determine just when it began to be included in handbooks. I remember correcting it on student papers in the mid-fifties.

9. (2); Because of the neutralization of pronunciation differences, "there," "their," and "they're" have become increasingly hard for people to keep separated in spelling.

10. (3); Both handbooks forbid this spelling of the contracted form of "have."

11. (1); The 1946 handbook insists that "unique" means *only* "one of a kind" and therefore should not be compared. The 1977 handbook seems to have given up on this particular purism.

12. (3); The distinction here is between count and non-count nouns, with "fewer" preferred for count nouns.

13. (3); The distinction between lie-lay-lain (intransitive) and lay-laid-laid (transitive) seems to me to have disappeared, but the 1977 handbook maintains it. It will be interesting to see what happens in the next edition.

14. (1); The clipping for "gentlemen" seems to have been replaced by "guy" in casual, and "men" in more formal contexts.

15. (2); This new use of "plus" to mean "and" had not come into being in 1946.

16. (3); Both books maintain the distinction between the adjective "real" and the adverb "really."

17. (1); The 1946 distinction was that animals and plants were raised, while people were reared.

18. (3); "Try to" is considered more grammatical by both books.

19. (1); Again, this was a trite, overused word in 1946. Earlier still, careful writers maintained its etymological meaning of "able to produce terror."

20. (3); Like other spelling errors, this one is not likely to be considered correct until almost everyone uses it.

Sources: John C. Hodges, *Harbrace College Handbook* (New York: Harcourt Brace, 1941, 1946) and John C. Hodges and Mary E. Whitten, *Harbrace College Handbook*, 8th ed. (New York: Harcourt Brace Jovanovich, 1977).

Index

Abercrombie, David, 39n.
Absolute phrase, 106
Acoustic phonetics, 38
Acronym, 23
Adjective, 65, 68–69, 71–72, 78; charts, 68, 73; comparison, 20
Adjunct, 97, 101–103, 116–117
Adverb, 65–69, 72–73; charts, 68, 73; comparison, 20
Affix, 15, 17–19, 21, 70–72
Agent, 129–132
Allen, Harold B., 171
Allomorph, 18
Allophone, 50
Ambiguity, 132; of conjunctions, 133
American Speech, 183–184
Anaphora, 159–160
Animal communication, 6–7
Anomalous sentence, 126
Antonym, 125–126
Articulation: organs of, 39–40; phonetic person, 42
Articulatory phonetics, defined, 38
Aspect, 83–84
Aspiration, 50–51
Auxiliary, 77, 82–85

Back-formation, 21–22
Black English Vernacular, 179–181
Bolinger, Dwight, 3n., 198
Borrowed words, 23–24
Bronowski, Jacob, 79

Case, 17–18, 72, 74, 131n.
Cassidy, Frederick N., 178
Casual register, 203–204
Caxton, William, 190, 199

Chaucer, Geoffrey, 191, 192, 195–196
Chimpanzees and language, 7–8
Chomsky, Noam, 103–105
Classifier, 66
Clause, 97, 103; slots, 98–99, 104; types, 109–112
Clause joining, 99–103, 117–118, 131–133
Clause reversal, 159–160, 163–165
Clipping, 22
Cohesion, 159–161
Coinage, 23
Collocation, 128–129
Color words, 123–124
Complement, 98, 101
Composition (see Rhetoric)
Compounding, 22
Conjunction, 68, 75–77, 133–134
Consonants, 40–45; chart, 43; natural classes, 40–41
Consultative register, 203
Conversion, 21
Coordinators, 68, 75–77

Dative movement, 111
DeCamp, David, 183
Deep structure, 103–105
Demonstratives, 68, 74, 77
Derivation, 17, 21
Determiner, 69–70, 77–79
Dialect: defined, 170; in literature, 182–183; map, 173; regional, 171, 197; social, 172
Dialects: American, 171–172, 176–178, 185–188; British, 192
Dialogue, 144–147
Dictionaries, 191–192, 196–198
Dictionary symbols, 57, 61

211

Diphthong, 48–49
Discourse: defined, 143; genre, 150; parts of, 152–156
Distribution, 69, 74
Double negative, 195–196
Dozens, playing the, 147

Edited English, 95–96
Eight-legged essay, 155–156
Emphasis, 157–159
Eponym, 23
Euphemism, 26
Etymology, 27–28
Explanatory discourse, 149–150
Extraposition, 107–108, 118

Focal area, 172
Focus, in discourse, 157–159
Folk etymology, 22–23
Foreign plurals, 19
Form class, 67
Formal register, 203
Fries, C. C., 67
Fry, Dennis, 2n., 37n., 39n.

Gender, 72, 74
General Semantics, 124–125
Gerund, 87; phrase, 106
Glottal stop, 39–41
Grapheme, 54–58, 61
Grimes, Joseph E., 154, 168

Headword, 70–71
Hierarchy, 5
Homonym, 127
Hortatory discourse, 150–151
Hyponym, 127

IPA, 45–46; charts, 43, 47
Idiolect, 172
Idiom, 128
Illocutionary act, 135
Incompatibility, semantic, 125–126
Indefinites, 68, 74
Infinitive, 86; phrase, 106–108, 110
-ing participle, 86–87, 105–106
Inflections, 17–20, 70–74
Intensifiers, 66, 69, 72, 77
Interjection, 68, 77
Intonation contour, 53
Intransitive verb, 110
Intrusive-r, 174
Isogloss, 171

Jargon, 200
Johnson, Samuel, 191–192
Joining words, chart, 76

Kurath, Hans, 171

Language community, 12–13
Leveling, 172–174
Lexical linkage, 156–157
Lexicon, 4–5
Linguistic atlases, 171
Linguistic chauvinism, 3
Linguistic competence, 9, 65, 125, 143–144
Linguistic exercises: Apinayé, 88; Guajajara, 92; Huichol, 88; Latin, 94; Vietnamese, 120–121
Linguistics: defined, 9–11, fields of, 11–12
Linking verb, 110
Literary criticism, 9
Longacre, Robert E., 149n., 151n.
Lowth, Robert, 194

Marking, semantic, 126
Miller, George A., 5n.
Milton, John, 191, 194
Minimal pair, 50
Modal auxiliary, 82–83
Monologue, 147–149
Morphemes, 15–17, 51
Mulcaster, Richard, 191
Murray, Lindley, 198

Narrative discourse, 148–150
New information, 157
Nominalization, 107
Noun, 17–19, 64–71, 97; charts, 68, 73
Noun clause, 101, 106
Noun phrase, 78–79, 97–98, 104
Number, 17–19, 72, 74

Obstruents, 40, 56
Old information, 157
Open classes, 67, 69; chart, 73
Oration, 155
Oxford English Dictionary, 29, 31–32, 78

Paragraph, 160–162
Parallel structure, 108–109
Participial phrase, 86–87, 105–108
Participle, 86–87, 105–106, 194
Particle, 85–86
Parts of speech, 64–67; chart, 68–69; Latin, 66

Index

Passive, 84, 86, 112–114, 120, 129, 131
Patient, 129–131
Pederson, Lee, 183
Philologist, 28–29
Phoneme, 49–51, 53–55, 61
Phonesthesia, 122
Phonetic transcription, 45–47, 51; dictionary symbols for, 57; Trager-Smith, 45, 47
Phonetics, 38–45; and poetry, 62
Phonology, 4, 37–38; and spelling, 54–59
Phrase, defined, 97
Pidgin, 180
Pike, Kenneth, 46
Pitch, 53
Plurals, 17–19
Polysemy, 127
Possessive, 18, 130
Post-modifier, 81, 86, 101–102, 117
Predicate, 97, 99
Prefix, 5, 15
Preposition, 65, 68, 74–75; ending sentence, 196; with verb, 75, 85–86
Prepositional phrase, 80–81
Presupposition, 134–135
Procedural discourse, 149–151
Pronoun, 66, 68, 72, 74
Pronunciation, 192–193, 197–198

Qualifiers, 72
Quest story, 153–155
Question words, 66, 68, 70, 74

Received Pronunciation, 192–193
Referent, 123
Regionalism, 200
Register, 202–204
Relative clause, 101–106
Relative pronoun, 74; charts, 68, 70
Relic area, 172
Restrictive clause, 101–102, 117
Rhetoric: defined, 8–9; lessons, 12–13, 35–36, 62–63, 92–94, 114–115, 142, 168–169, 187–188, 208–210

Saussure, Ferdinand de, 122
Sapir, Edward, 88
Sayers, Dorothy L., 199
Semantic change, 25–27
Semantics, 4–5; defined, 122; of conjunctions, 132–134; of roles, 129–132; words, 125–127; and syntax, 65–66, 81–82, 109–110
Sentence, 99, 103–109, 145–146

Shakespeare, William, 193–194
Shall-will rule, 198–199
Slang, 200, 203–204
Slots and fillers, 5–6, 51, 78–79, 80, 82–84, 97–99, 104, 115–117
Sound symbolism, 122
Speech acts, 135–137
Speech island, 172
Spelling, 54–59, 190–192, 196–197, 200–201
Split infinitive, 86, 196
Stress, 52–53
Structure class, 69–70
Sturtevant, Edgar H., 136
Subject, 98–99
Subordination, 100–101, 106, 117–118
Suffix, 5, 15
Surface structure, 103–105
Suzuki, Shinichi, 10–11
Syllable, 51–53
Synonym, 125–126
Syntax, defined, 5–6

Taxonomic sets, 126–127
Tense, 19, 82
Text linguistics, 143
Timing, 2, 52–53
Tone language, 53
Transformation, defined, 129
Transformation of clauses, 105–107, 109–112, 119–120
Transition area, 171
Transition words, 78
Transitive verb, 111–112

Universals, 4
Usage handbooks, 201, 205–207
Usage labels, 201
Utterance-response, 144–146

Veblen, Thorsten, 200–201
Verb, 19–20, 64, 66–69, 71, 81–86, 109–114; charts, 68, 73
Verb phrase, 81–86
Verbal duel, 146–147
Verbal phrase, 86–87
Vowels, 41, 46–49; chart, 47; spelling, 56–58
Vocabulary loss, 24–25

Webster, Noah, 196–197, 199
Webster's Third, 201–202
Whorf, Benjamin Lee, 123–124
Writing well (See Rhetoric, lessons)